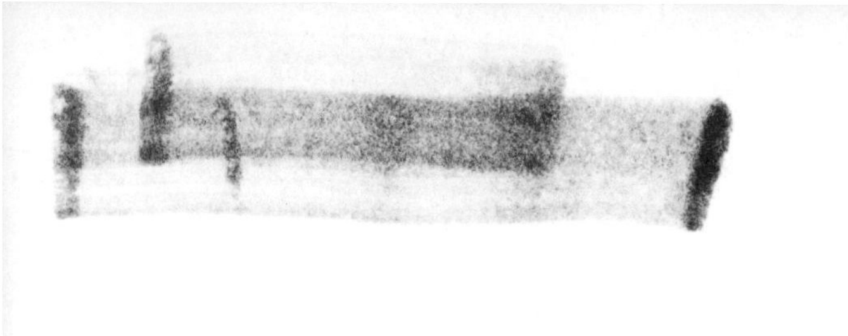

CAMBRIDGE STUDIES IN LINGUISTICS

A functional approach to child language

A study of determiners and reference

In this series

1 DAVID CRYSTAL: *Prosodic systems and intonation in English**
2 PIETER A. M. SEUREN: *Operators and nucleus*
3 RODNEY D. HUDDLESTON: *The sentence in written English*
4 JOHN M. ANDERSON: *The grammar of case**
5 M. L. SAMUELS: *Linguistic evolution**
6 P. H. MATTHEWS: *Inflectional morphology**
7 GILLIAN BROWN: *Phonological rules and dialect variation**
8 BRIAN NEWTON: *The generative interpretation of dialect**
9 R. M. W. DIXON: *The Dyirbal language of North Queensland**
10 BRUCE L. DERWING: *Transformational grammar as a theory of language acquistion**
11 MELISSA BOWERMAN: *Early syntactic development**
12 W. SIDNEY ALLEN: *Accent and rhythm*
13 PETER TRUDGILL: *The social differentiation of English in Norwich*
14 ROGER LASS and JOHN M. ANDERSON: *Old English phonology*
15 RUTH M. KEMPSON: *Presupposition and the delimitation of semantics**
16 JAMES R. HURFORD: *The linguistic theory of numerals*
17 ROGER LASS: *English phonology and phonological theory*
18 G. M. AWBERRY: *The syntax of Welsh*
19 R. M. W. DIXON: *The grammar of Yidiɲ*
20 JAMES FOLEY: *Foundations of theoretical phonology*
21 A. RADFORD: *Italian syntax: transformational and relational grammar*
22 DIETER WUNDERLICH: *Foundations of linguistics**
23 DAVID W. LIGHTFOOT: *Principles of diachronic syntax**
24 ANNETTE KARMILOFF-SMITH: *A functional approach to child language*
25 PER LINELL: *Psychological reality in phonology*

* *Issued in hard covers and as a paperback*

A FUNCTIONAL APPROACH TO CHILD LANGUAGE

A STUDY OF DETERMINERS AND REFERENCE

ANNETTE KARMILOFF-SMITH
Research Associate, Faculty of Psychology and Educational Sciences, Geneva University

CAMBRIDGE UNIVERSITY PRESS
CAMBRIDGE
LONDON · NEW YORK · MELBOURNE

Published by the Syndics of the Cambridge University Press
The Pitt Building, Trumpington Street, Cambridge CB2 1RP
Bentley House, 200 Euston Road, London NW1 2DB
32 East 57th Street, New York, NY 10022, USA
296 Beaconsfield Parade, Middle Park, Melbourne 3206, Australia

First published 1979

Printed in Great Britain
by W & J Mackay Limited, Chatham

Library of Congress Cataloguing in Publication Data

Karmiloff-Smith, Annette.

A functional approach to child language.
(Cambridge studies in linguistics; 24)

Bibliography: p.

Includes index.

1. Children – Language. 2. Grammar, Comparative
and general – Determiners. 3. Reference (Linguistics)
I. Title. II. Series.
P118.K3 401'.9 78-15450
ISBN 0 521 22416 0

Contents

To my daughters
Yara-Natasha and Kyrèna-Laure
whose sweet chattering was so often a delightful source of ideas

Acknowledgements

The intellectual debt I owe to my mentor, Jean Piaget, and to the experience gained in working with him at the International Centre for Genetic Epistemology, stretches well beyond the limits of the work reported on here. Discussions and arguments with various persons have greatly stimulated my thinking: on children's problem-solving behaviour with Alex Blanchet, Helga Kilcher, Madelon Robert and Edith Valladao; on language acquisition with Hermine Sinclair and her research team; on general issues of human growth with Guy Céllérier, Phil Johnson-Laird, Marvin Minsky and Seymour Papert. Bärbel Inhelder's kindness and encouragement will be warmly remembered. The perceptive criticisms of Jerome Bruner, John Lyons and Hermine Sinclair on the PhD dissertation upon which this book is based are gratefully acknowledged. None of the above persons necessarily agrees with its contents, of course! Special thanks are also due to the staff of the Cambridge University Press, and I should also like to thank the undergraduate psychology students who participated with me in the collection of experimental data. Especially, I wish to place on record my deep appreciation of the Geneva School Authorities and of the hundreds of children who so enthusiastically participated in our 'games' and jumped to their feet each time the classroom door opened, exclaiming 'c'est mon tour!' or, as one little five-year-old literally screamed: 'C'est mon mien de tour à moi!' (which is a clue to what the following chapters are about!). Finally, and above all, I affectionately thank Igor Karmiloff, without whose encouragement and constructive criticisms this work would never have been carried through. Living for a number of years with a curious mixture of 'doctoral student/teaching and research assistant/mother of two small girls/wife . . .' requires much good humour, patience and understanding...

> do you know, Carter, that I can actually
> write my name in the dust on the table?
>
> Faith, Mum, that's more than I can do. Sure there's
> nothing like education after all!
>
> (*Punch* 1902)

1 *The place of language in child development*

> it would be hard to overemphasize the importance of regarding Piaget as a genetic epistemologist rather than as a psychologist. (Elkind 1968)

Scientists have been concerned for decades with the polemical question of the role of language in human development. Philosophers, linguists, neurologists, anthropologists, ethologists, psychologists, psycholinguists and computer scientists have all sought, in one way or another, to reveal the secrets of *homo loquens*. As child development came to the foreground, the debate hinged on three main questions: Is the growth of thought entirely dependent on the language of the external environment? Is the structure of language innate and essentially independent of cognition? Is language part of broader cognitive developments?

When Piaget first focussed attention on the importance of cognitive development for language acquisition, many authors considered it a revolutionary position. Today, it sounds like a truism. Hardly a book or or article on child language appears without an explicit or implicit reference to Piagetian theory. This makes it necessary for the developmental psycholinguist to determine his own position with respect to Piaget's. In doing so, however, it is essential to recognize that Piaget is a psychologist only to the extent that Aristotle was a biologist or Leibniz a mathematician (Grize 1966). Despite the fact that he is widely regarded as *the* psychologist of the twentieth century, for Piaget psychology has always been simply a means for establishing a biologically based epistemology (Piaget 1950).

Child development data provided Piaget with the persuasive counterexamples he sought against nativism and empiricism. Piaget usually puts forward a somewhat caricatured, extreme version of these philosophical stands, making the contrast with his own all the more pronounced. Rejecting the sterile 'nature *or* nurture' debate, he was the first epistemologist to adopt an *explicit* interactionist–constructivist position. He set out to demonstrate theoretically and through empirical data drawn from child development, that thought structures are neither innate nor a static copy of the physical or linguistic environment. Convincing arguments were marshalled to claim that thought develops, not from language, but from the constructive interaction of the child and his environments. I purposely use the plural 'environments' for, whilst Piaget's theory is essentially built on the growing child's logico-mathematical interaction with an ever-extending physical environment, his epistemology could embrace equally constructive interaction of the child and his linguistic, social or emotional environments.

This book suggests a new focus on the child's constructive interaction with his linguistic environment. In discussing the role of language in child development, much can be gained in my view from separating the direct psychological content of Piaget's writings from their deep epistemological foundations. Thus, the argumentation in the next chapters will draw on Piaget's *epistemology* as the most adequate one for explaining my emphasis on the *psychological* importance of children's processing of their linguistic environment. Not, of course, with the intention of stressing language *per se*, as did the extreme Whorfians or logical positivists, but rather with the hope of developing a psychological theory which gives weight to the child's intensive activity on the linguistic input and to the child's progressive reorganization of his language processing procedures.

Deeply influenced as I am by Piagetian epistemology, a central argument of this book will be that in analysing psychological phenomena, Piaget has unjustifiably relegated language to a secondary role and thereby underestimated the importance of:

(a) language as a constructive factor in development;
(b) language as an object of the child's spontaneous cognitive attention (i.e. language as a problem-space *per se* irrespective of the specific content of children's utterances and of their semantic intentions);
(c) language as a relevant experimental variable in cognitive tasks.

These issues will be taken up fully in the experimental and theoretical sections.

The present chapter provides a description of the place of language in Piagetian theory; this is followed by a critical evaluation of a number of Genevan hypotheses. Finally a brief overview is given of the contents of the remaining chapters.

The Piagetian position

Piaget has never made a comprehensive study of the acquisition of language in a way similar to his rich studies of the child's acquisition of number, time, space and causality. However, many authors believe that Piaget's most substantial contribution to a theoretical interpretation of the origins of language resides in his profound study of the sensorimotor origins of knowledge. Piaget's description of the child's stages of cognitive development (sensorimotor, preoperational, concrete operational and formal operational) is so well known that it would be inappropriate to summarize them once again here (see Piaget & Inhelder 1969a).[1] His rich analyses are not restricted in application to a single, specific culture. Much Piagetian cross-cultural research (e.g. Bovet *et al.* 1972) has suggested the universality of cognitive structures. Despite enormous differences in culture, child-rearing practices, physical and linguistic environments, analogous behavioural patterns and structural coordinations appear to be operative in the formation of preverbal and postverbal intelligence. By pinpointing cognitive universals, not only in their highly structured final forms of thought but at every stage of the construction process, Piaget has greatly enhanced our understanding of child development, in which linguistic universals are taken to be part of broader cognitive universals.

Whilst Piaget has not himself studied language acquisition experimentally, he has discussed theoretically the place of language in cognitive development, and was a pioneer in demonstrating the important role of sensorimotor actions as a preparation for language and thought. He argued that 'it suffices to look at the sensorimotor intelligence which exists prior to the acquisition of language in order to find in the infant's elementary practical coordinations the functional equivalents of the operations of combination and dissociation . . . functionally comparable to the future operations of thought' (Piaget 1968a, p. 94).

Piaget does not only stress how the intricate organization of sensorimotor action schemes might pave the way for later thought structures, including those of language. In talking of language itself, he attaches great importance to the developmental interdependence of symbolic play, deferred imitation, mental imagery and the first verbal utterances, rather than merely singling out the specific characteristics of language:

[1] Dates are mainly from English translations. The dates of the original French editions are added in the bibliography.

'since de Saussure and many others, we know that verbal signs exhibit only one aspect of the semiotic function and that linguistics is really only a limited though especially important segment of that more inclusive discipline which Saussure wanted to establish under the name of "general semiology"' (Piaget 1970, p. 92). Thus not language alone, but all the aspects of the broader concept of the semiotic function are, for Piaget, symptoms of the gradual process of decentration from the immediate spatio-temporal restrictions of the sensorimotor action schemes. In essence, the semiotic function is the capacity to represent sensorimotor actions through signifiers which are differentiated from their significates. Piaget & Inhelder particularly stress this representative function: 'the ability to represent something (a signified something: object, event, conceptual scheme, etc.) by means of a "signifier" which is differentiated and which serves *only a representative purpose*: language, mental image, symbolic gesture and so on' (1969a, p. 51, my italics). Whilst emphasizing the common characteristics of the semiotic function, Piaget also stressed de Saussure's distinction between personal symbols (symbolic play, deferred imitation, mental imagery), on the one hand, and the conventional, communicable verbal sign, on the other.

Piaget argues that the representative capacity is not present at birth but develops gradually out of the evolution and progressive internalization of imitation throughout the prerepresentational period. 'Imitation constitutes both the sensorimotor prefiguration of representation and the transitional phase between the sensorimotor level and the level of behaviour that may properly be called representative . . . imitation constitutes during the sensorimotor period a kind of representation in physical acts but not yet in thought' (1969a, p. 55). In Piaget's writings the time factor is stressed to differentiate imitation from deferred imitation which takes place later and in the absence of the model. Another, and perhaps more crucial difference, lies in the child's *intention* in the case of deferred imitation to use imitation *for representation purposes*, either to communicate something to another person or to communicate it to oneself (i.e. to understand it).

In summary, it can be said that Piaget placed far more emphasis than did his predecessors on the *common* characteristics of the different manifestations of the semiotic function and above all on the *continuity* between sensorimotor action schemes and what he termed 'verbal schemes'. It was in stressing the common sensorimotor origins of language and thought that Piaget rejected Chomsky's innateness hypothesis. For

Chomsky, the human mind 'can itself be the exhaustive source of its linguistic competence, for which external stimuli serve only as occasions for activating what is already dispositionally in the mind's own structure' (Gewirth, cited in Chomsky 1975). Chomsky maintains that because the child's input is performance based, i.e. full of false starts, incomplete sentences, etc., it would be impossible to explain the young child's competence on the basis of any current learning theories. For Chomsky, the child's linguistic competence necessarily stems from innate, specifically linguistic structures (1967). Piaget suggests that whilst the innateness hypothesis cannot be disproved, it is sidestepping the problems to invoke it. For Piaget, only the *functional mechanisms* permitting the organization of the child's interaction with his environment are innate: 'cognitive functions are an extension of organic regulations and constitute a differentiated organ for regulating exchanges with the external world' (Piaget 1971, p. 369).

It should be pointed out in passing that Chomsky's assumptions about the child's early input are not based on empirical evidence. It has since been demonstrated that the child's linguistic input is far from being composed of the 'non-sentences', false starts, etc., often characteristic of adult dialogue. On the contrary, several investigators (e.g. Snow 1972; Snow & Ferguson 1977; Lieven 1978) have now shown that when the mother (or caretaker substitute) is talking to her small child, she uses *perfectly constructed* utterances of very gradually increasing complexity. These studies of 'motherese' indicate that the young child's input consists of a simplified, mini-grammar, increasing in complexity at a pace which is dictated by the child's needs. Indeed the mother is constantly updating her theory of her child's cognitive capacities and gradually changing her demands on the child with respect to his responses (Bruner 1975b). Thus the small child's linguistic input appears to be mainly comprised of those simple, well formed, often semantically and syntactically redundant utterances addressed directly to him. It remains to be demonstrated that this also holds true for children from non-privileged environments; the results of such as investigation would have crucial theoretical implications for language acquisition.

To return to Piaget's position on language, it should be recalled that it is not limited to discussing the sensorimotor roots. In a fairly lengthy discussion of the role of language at the three major stages of child development, Piaget reiterates his position regarding the early stage and then goes on to discuss the onset of concrete operations: 'logical operations are thus coordinations among actions before they are transposed into verbal form, so that language cannot account for their formation. Language indefinitely extends the power of these operations and confers on them a mobility and a universality which they would not have otherwise, but it is by no means the source of such coordinations' (Piaget 1968a, p. 93).

When the child later reaches the level of propositional logic (formal operational stage), Piaget again argues that 'it would be difficult to maintain that this system is a product of the evolution of language. On the contrary, the acquisition of combinatory operations permits the subject to complete his verbal classifications and to make these correspond to the abstract relationships inherent in the propositional operations' (p. 96). In the same article, Piaget concludes: 'It is also evident that the more the structures of thought are refined, the more language is necessary for the achievement of this elaboration' (p. 98). Indeed, this emphasis on language as a tool increasing in usefulness with development, is a recurrent theme in Piaget's discussions on the subject, including his more recent work on the relations between organic regulations and cognitive processes: 'language, although it is of course an essential instrument in cognitive constructions at the higher level, offers in itself no complete explanation' (Piaget 1971, p. 46).

Thus, for Piaget, there is nothing specific about the child's acquisition of language. It is governed by general regulatory mechanisms and is explained as part of the natural outcome of the child's need to go beyond the successive spatial and temporal restrictions of sensorimotor action schemes. Language and the other aspects of the semiotic function enable the child to free himself from the constraints of actions on real objects. Piaget draws on data from learning experiments (Sinclair 1969) to demonstrate that language is not 'sufficient' to explain development because possession of the correct linguistic expressions does not bring about immediate corresponding operatory changes. Moreover, he argues from certain data from the deaf (Furth 1966) that language is not even 'necessary' for the development of cognitive structures. These points will be taken up in the critical evaluation.

It is clear from this series of quotations that Piaget is stressing the representative function of language, 'the tool of intelligence' (Piaget 1968b), whose importance he considers increases with operational growth, but is dependent upon it.

The emphasis of the effects of cognitive growth on linguistic growth has been a central argument in Piagetian theoretical discussions. Language is seen to be particularly relevant only as the child reaches higher levels of structural development, but language is not considered to be dynamic in provoking changes in thought structures.

Whilst Piaget postulated the sensorimotor roots of language in very general terms, it was Sinclair, the major psycholinguistic interpreter of Piagetian theory, who made comprehensive studies of language acquisition and the sensorimotor heuristics used initially for this (Sinclair [-de Zwart] 1967, etc.; Sinclair & Ferreiro 1970; Inhelder *et al.* 1972; Sinclair & Bronckart 1972). In discussing in detail the group-like structure of sensorimotor action schemes, Sinclair frequently pursues the following argument:

we would like to suggest that this 'group' of action patterns also serves as a heuristic model for the acquisition of syntax and that it is precisely what the child (every child) has learned during his first 18 months or so that provides him with the necessary and sufficient assumptions to start this acquisition. The constraints on the form that human languages can take relate to characteristics of the human mind, to cognitive universals; and these constraints are what makes it possible for children to start talking during their second year and to go about language acquisition the way they do. (Sinclair 1975, p. 232)

From the very start, in the first Genevan psycholinguistic study, Sinclair placed emphasis on the relevance of cognitive structures for explaining language acquisition, an aspect ignored at the time by most other researchers in the field:

our experiments stem from our conviction that the profound nature of language is to be found in the syntactic structures and that the phonological, statistical and semantic aspects will ultimately have to be integrated into a general theory which will be based on a preliminary prior analysis of syntactic structures . . . to carry our hypotheses further, the syntactic structures will show isomorphisms with the logical structures described by Piaget. (Sinclair [-de Zwart] 1967, p. 149)

If the importance of cognitive structures is almost a truism today, very few investigators recognized this when Sinclair did her pioneer work. The special relevance of cognitive competence was emphasized in the work of Ferreiro (1971) on temporal relations in child language. In a discussion of other theories, it was argued: 'neither can such theories ignore the stages of cognitive development which, in our opinion, determine *the nature and the form* of the linguistic structures that children are able to produce and understand' (Ferreiro & Sinclair 1971, my italics).

It is above all in her comprehensive analysis of the links between sensorimotor intelligence and early language that Sinclair has furthered our understanding of the relevance that Piagetian theory might have to child language development. Sinclair argues, for instance, that:

The sensorimotor child can order, temporally and spatially: he can classify in action, that is to say, he can use a whole category of objects for the same action, or apply a whole category of action-schemes to one object; he can relate objects and action to actions. The linguistic equivalents of these structures are concatenation, categorization, i.e. the major categories (S, NP, VP, etc.) and functional grammatical relations (subject of, object of, etc.). (Sinclair 1971a, p. 126)

In the same article, Sinclair refers to the property of recursivity important in Chomsky's model: 'a psychological parallel to this so-called recursive property of the base can be found in the embedding of action-schemes one into the other, when the child can put one action pattern into another pattern. This can be traced back to the simple circular reactions of a much earlier stage' (p. 127). 'the principle . . . that transformations do not affect the meaning of relations of the base components, which are thus invariant, adds an important link with psychology, since it supposes an invariant for the system of transformational rules' (p. 129).

In a later article, Sinclair looks into the links between sensorimotor intelligence and the holophrase:

speaking in general terms, the very young baby does not differentiate between action, object and agent; an action or reflex pattern during the first months constitutes an unanalysable entity. It is only gradually . . . that action and object become differentiated. Similarly only gradually does the baby realize that not only he himself is an actor, but that other people, too, can perform the same action as he does. It would appear that at a different level, language patterns follow this development. Holophrases form unanalysable entities. They are followed by two and three word utterances . . . indicative of two differentiations: between action and object, and between the child himself as actor and another acting subject . . . (Sinclair 1973a, p. 411)

Sinclair has also given particular emphasis to Piaget's hypothesis that progress in language follows an evolution similar to sensorimotor intelligence, by reconstructing it at a higher level:

we might interpret the linguistic pattern as follows: at first the child expresses a (possible) action pattern related to himself, in which agent, action and eventual patient are inextricably entwined. Second, he either expresses the result of an action done by somebody else (but not the action–object link in that case), or an action he performs or is going to perform himself. In this way, the capacity for representing reality follows at a later stage the same evolution which took place when the child was still dealing directly with reality without representation. The first direction–action differentiations . . . give rise to the first grammatical functions of subject–predicate and object–action. (Sinclair 1973b, p. 23)

Similarly, referring to the links between operational structures and language, Sinclair stated that 'operational structuring and linguistic structuring or rather *linguistic restructuring* thus parallel each other . . . difficulties encountered by the child in the use of these expressions seem to be the same as those he encounters in the development of the operations themselves: lack of decentration and incapacity to coordinate' (Sinclair 1969, p. 325).

This outline of Sinclair's position clearly demonstrates her consistent emphasis on *cognitive* structures, in a scientific climate where *linguistic* structures were uppermost in the mind of the majority of psycholinguists. However, it would be wrong to conclude from this that Sinclair advocates a blind 'cognition hypothesis', as Cromer (1974) tends to imply. Sinclair argued against a reductionist attitude towards language: 'We certainly do not think that language acquisition can be explained by the laws of cognitive development alone; the structure of language itself is a necessary part of the acquisition model' (Sinclair 1971b, p. 205). However, her analyses have hitherto always placed main stress on how cognitive structures enable the child to come to grips with the structures of his language.

The fact that Piaget's theory is a structural one led to the structural aspects of language being emphasized rather than semantic or functional ones: 'some investigators analyze the early semantic relationships that can be inferred from early child speech; others are interested in the pre-language babbling period during which phonological categories are elaborated; Genevan psycholinguists are mainly interested in syntactic structures' (Sinclair 1973a, p. 408). This accent on structure explains why the Chomskyan model was initially adopted as the most appropriate language model to complement the Piagetian epistemology: 'It is Chomsky's work that is making possible the study of language acquisition within a Piagetian framework' (Sinclair 1971b, p. 204). Indeed, from the point of view of methodology and epistemology, both Piaget and Chomsky defined their positions in contrast to behaviorist trends (Chomsky 1964; Piaget &

Inhelder 1969b). Both sought to explain the structure of the organizational properties of cognition or language, and both sought to reveal universals: for Piaget this meant a set of general cognitive universals; for Chomsky it implied specifically linguistic universals. For both, the accent is on basic structures rather than on use or functions. As Hockett (1967) has pointed out: 'for Chomsky, phrase structure, transformations, etc. are *in the language* rather than merely useful descriptive devices'. Piaget, too, argues that cognitive structures are implicit *in the child's behaviour* rather than merely part of the observer's model. Both Piaget and Chomsky sought to construct an 'epistemic subject' or 'ideal speaker/hearer' and to attain their competence, i.e. the upper and lower limits within which behaviour takes place. Indeed, apart from the essential difference between Chomsky's innatism, versus Piaget's interactionism and stress on biological/cognitive continuity, the two epistemologists' goals are very similar. Chomsky's model was thus the most obvious candidate initially for Piagetian-oriented psycholinguistics. In the meantime, new studies in Geneva (e.g. Bronckart & Sinclair 1973; Cambon & Sinclair 1974; Bronckart 1976) shifted the accent from syntactic structures to the semantic functions of verb inflections and the semantic networks of certain verbs, whilst keeping in the foreground the cognitive difficulties involved. This led to the consideration of linguistic models other than the Chomskyan one (e.g. Culioli *et al.* 1970; Culioli 1976; Bronckart 1977).

Let us now take a brief look at recent use of Piagetian theory outside Geneva. It may even seem paradoxical that a theory like Piaget's which gained the reputation of rejecting language as a constructive factor in cognitive development, is now considered relevant by the majority of those involved in the study of child language. Brown, for instance, argues that 'the first sentences express the construction of reality which is the terminal achievement of sensorimotor intelligence . . . representation starts with just those meanings that are most available to it, propositions about action schemes, involving agents and objects, assertions of non-existence, recurrence, location and so on' (Brown 1973, p. 200).

Similar arguments are made with regard to the relations between the child's lexicon and his conceptual development. Nelson maintains that:

> Piaget's sensorimotor schemes provide an important principle of similarity for the young child to operate with. Those things are similar that can be acted upon in the same way. With some modification, this can serve as the foundation stone for a complete model of the child's early concepts and can help to illuminate both his word learning and sentence construction. (1974, p. 274)

Bloom also stresses the relevance of Piaget's theory for language acquisition: 'Piaget described objects as inextricably bound to context and to the action schemes in which they are perceived. It would follow that the substantive words that do occur are also a part of such action schemes' (1973, p. 79).

Edwards, in a very complete analysis of the correspondences between cognition and relational meanings in two word utterances, concluded that:

these semantic relations are compared to the concepts invoked in Piaget's descriptions of sensorimotor intelligence, in particular to the concepts of permanent objects and their spatial relations, to the dual concepts of persons as physical objects and as active beings, and to the role of persons as causers of changes in the locativity of objects. A close correspondence is found, and it is claimed that the nature of sensorimotor intelligence severely constrains the range of relational meanings expressed, including even the child's notions of possessive relations between persons and objects, of attributes of objects and his use of apparently experiential verbs. (1973, p. 395)

However, an important distinction must be drawn: it is one thing to seek in preverbal intelligence-in-action clues to explain the semantic *content* of early utterances, as some authors have done, but another, to seek in the heuristics provided by sensorimotor intelligence clues to explain the *structure* of early utterances (Sinclair 1969, etc.) or to explain linguistic *functions* (Bruner 1975a; Dore 1975).

Some unresolved problems

Despite the wealth of ideas that can be drawn from Piagetian theory on how cognitive growth structures and gives meaning to the child's language, there are issues which remain debatable both with regard to the role of non-linguistic cognition in language acquisition and vice versa.

The first concerns the sensorimotor heuristics which allow the child to cope with the linguistic input. This is an extremely rich hypothesis, which I endorse as a hypothesis, for it seems likely that linguistic development shares some common features with non-linguistic cognition and is part of broader mechanisms. However, little in the argument thus far suggests anything more than an analogy between sensorimotor behaviour and early verbal behaviour. It does not show that sensorimotor intelligence is in any way causal in language development. There remains the case of the paralytic child who acquires speech. Of course, Piaget's concept of sensorimotor action schemes does not imply the need for any *specific* modality to be activated. Thus, the paralytic child could learn to know the world through, say, visual coordinations alone. However, with so much accent on the intricate coordination of many *different* sensorimotor action schemes through the child's interaction with his physical environment (Piaget 1953, etc.), the very limited sensorimotor action potential of the paralytic child seems to weaken the argument. It may be necessary to invoke stronger innate predispositions for language than has hitherto been the case in Geneva. Another solution would be to shift the main emphasis for explaining the onset of language from the child's interaction with his physical environment to an equal or even greater emphasis on the child's interaction with his social environment. The question remains a very open one.

It seems clear that sensorimotor action schemes, however broadly defined, cannot alone explain the initial developments of language. Language is more than a symbolic system for representing knowledge. It is also a system for communicating and sharing knowledge, involving complex dialogic constraints between speaker and hearer. Prespeech development not only involves the child's structuring of his 'object world' but also of his 'people world'. Indeed, the past decade has witnessed many authors placing their research emphasis on prespeech communication, i.e. on the nature of early interaction between mother and infant (Bates 1976; Bruner 1975b, 1978a, 1978b), on the mother's output (Snow 1972; Snow & Ferguson 1977), on how the mother and infant slowly build up a dialogic structure prior to language, e.g. intonational and indexical devices for obtaining joint attention, turn-taking and so forth (Halliday 1975; Lieven 1978; Ninio & Bruner 1978; Ryan 1978).

It could thus be said that two complementary, and most probably interacting, processes are being developed during the first years of life: (i) prespeech cognition, i.e. the content, procedures and structures built up for the child's interaction with his 'object world'; and (ii) prespeech communication, i.e. the content, procedures and structures built up for the child's interaction with his 'people world' (Karmiloff-Smith 1977c). It remains to be seen whether emphasis should be placed on the fact that these processes are governed by even more general, common cognitive mechanisms (Piaget, preface to Ferreiro 1971), or whether it is the differences between them that are particularly relevant for understanding the acquisition of language. It may be that there are individual differences, i.e. that some children rely more heavily on prespeech cognition and others predominantly on prespeech communication. All children need a certain amount of both. Piagetians have always placed more emphasis on general cognitive mechanisms and on prespeech cognition. Whilst Piaget's theory does not negate the child's interaction with his social environment, it places no special emphasis on the 'people world', considering persons as an object of interaction amongst others. Other authors (e.g. Snow & Ferguson 1977; Bruner 1978b) argue that prespeech communication and mothers' output may in fact provide the matrix for the acquisition of language and give it its distinctive structure. Available evidence from both these positions strengthens the hypothesis that language does not have a *totally* specific status in overall cognition, but this does not of course exclude the possibility of many language-specific developments.

Another debatable issue of Piagetian theory with regard to the onset of language lies in Piaget's emphasis that language – and indeed the semiotic function as a whole – is the result of the child's need to go beyond the temporal and spatial constraints of immediate actions, i.e. to represent things absent, past and future events, and so forth. Whilst this is partially true, it should be recalled that small children's language is often incredibly redundant. Early utterances mainly seem to be about obvious features of the current situation. What other function, then, could these early utterances have for the small child? Outside their function as primitive speech acts in the communicative setting (Dore 1975), language could also be considered as a form of 'cognitive economy' from the very start. Piaget has always stressed that language becomes important at higher levels of cognitive development because it increases the rapidity and range of potential thought processes (Piaget & Inhelder 1969a). It could also be argued that language is crucial *from the outset*. For the small infant, objects are initially bound to actions; one object seems to have many different identities according to whether it is currently being sucked, banged, rolled, etc. And different objects seem to have a single, common identity if they are all currently being, say, rolled. But when the infant no longer needs to run through his repertoire, but 'knows' in some sense the various action schemes which could be potentially performed on a given object (suckable, bangable, not-rollable, etc.), then how can he render the object conceptually tangible, i.e. detach it from the series of current action schemes? Of course, this first requires object permanency (Piaget 1953). But beyond this, some other form of symbolic representation is required, and the mental image may require many costly details. It could be argued that it is through language that children can best detach their actions from objects. Words are handy building blocks and can be used positively before they are fully comprehended. Language does not merely serve *post factum* as a tool for representing what is already understood. Language is not only a symbolic representation of reality, but is a very essential part of that reality. It could be maintained, therefore, that language is not just the outcome of the need to detach objects from the child's sensorimotor action schemes: language can actually be considered as being constructive in the detachment process.

As stated above, language is far more than a tool for representing knowledge. Piaget's theory does not offer an explicit explanation as to why the child goes beyond the early phase and actually adds the grammatical morphemes specific to his mother tongue. Does it make for more effective representation or communication, or does it merely reflect the child's gradual adaptation to the adult model?

Amongst the earliest markers to appear in the small child's corpus are articles and certain verb inflections (Brown 1973). Do children add these markers because their productions are being corrected by their caretakers or because they are being misunderstood? Previous investigations (e.g. Cazden 1972) indicate that this is not the case; neither communicative pressure nor parental expansions of child speech are sufficient to explain why the child adds the specific markers of his mother tongue. It should be recalled that most of the child's early utterances *are* understood by the caretaker. Moreover, as argued elsewhere (Karmiloff-Smith 1978a), the early addition of certain morphological markers such as the articles and the progressive present tense add little or nothing semantically in the communicative setting; for instance, when the child points out a feature of the current context and states first: 'Look, Mummy, doll eat' and slightly later in development: 'Look, Mummy, *the* doll *is* eat*ing*', the message is substantially the same as far as the communicative setting is concerned. What encourages the child to add these markers so early in development, if they do not enhance his communicative effectiveness and if his semantic intentions are adequately conveyed without the additional markers? Previously, it was suggested that the initial distinctive marking of the noun and verb phrase may be 'metalinguistic' or 'metacommunicative' in nature, i.e. taking language as an 'object' of spontaneous cognitive attention, rather than solely as a means for clear communication (Karmiloff-Smith 1977c). It has been shown, for instance, that children make early use of word order to convey subtle differences in their semantic intentions (Braine 1976). Thus, one way of sorting out linguistic categories would be a function of their position in an utterance. However, word order alone cannot give a stable category identity to each constituent of an utterance, but only a relative one through their ordered relationship. By attaching determiners and verb inflections, categories are conserved irrespective of word order. When the child first introduces, say, articles consistently, it could be argued that he is doing so *for himself*. It is part of his attempt to sort linguistic objects into tangible categories, to render manipulable the linguistic system and to organize it meaningfully and tangibly for himself. Since 'things' and 'actions' are not necessarily clearly differentiated (e.g., is 'a noise' or 'a slap' a thing or an action for the child?), then marking a distinction linguistically before the child has fully understood subtle differences cognitively, may have repercussions on his non-linguistic cognitive understanding, thereby suggesting links different to those he has already made. In this respect, language-learning is like problem-solving with physical objects; language needs to be sorted, classified, compared, etc., and gradually organized into systems of relevant options. This will be taken up fully in the following chapters.

A simple explanation of the addition of initial markers could lie in the fact that the child is imitating the adult model. There are several arguments against this. First, it leaves unresolved the question as to why the child adapts to some markers much earlier than others. It also leaves unexplained why sometimes the child produces 'correct' forms initially and then overgeneralizes a new procedure, producing 'incorrect' forms subsequently (Ervin-Tripp 1973; Klima & Bellugi 1973). The central emphasis here will be on language as a problem-space *per se* for the child. Much of the new experimental evidence discussed in the following chapters will lead me to reiterate my contention that language has been unjustifiably relegated to a secondary position in Piagetian theory, particularly with respect to the first eight years of life. Why has Piaget consistently stressed the *un*importance of language for cognitive development? One reason is obviously historical. The epistemological scene in Piaget's young days was dominated by empiricism and logical positivism. Language was then considered an essential factor in development by many theorists. It was thus to be expected that when reacting against these positions and adopting his interactionist–constructivist epistemology, Piaget should underplay the role of language. But another and perhaps deeper reason for the minor role attributed by Piaget for many years to the child's interaction with language (in comparison to his emphasis on the child's interaction with the physical environment) may have stemmed from the stress Piaget placed on the fact that the laws of the physical world are 'necessary'. He sought to explain why the gradual construction of the necessary character of the child's logico-mathematical structures finally merged with the necessary character of physical laws (Piaget 1971).

Both Piaget and Sinclair have frequently stressed the distinction between the arbitrariness of language and the necessary characteristics of the physical world (e.g. Sinclair 1974, 1977). However, in my view, the stressing of this distinction may be less warranted if one places oneself in the position of the *child* interacting with his linguistic and physical environments.

Language is arbitrary from the point of view of the linguist who describes it or compares one language to another. From the point of view of the *child* plunged into a particular linguistic environment, the structures and lexemes of that language are as necessary for him, initially, as are the structures of the physical world for the adult. Whilst the laws of physics are necessary, this is something the child only discovers very gradually: the laws of gravity, for instance, may seem quite arbitrary to the child initially. Thus language and physics have *both* necessary *and* arbitrary features from the viewpoint of the child. In both cases, it is the child's constructive interaction with each particular environment which is important, and in both cases he can blithely ignore the information from the input; he can overgeneralize linguistic rules and ignore counterexamples, just as he can, and does, overgeneralize physical rules and ignore counterexamples (Karmiloff-Smith & Inhelder 1974/5).

Sinclair has frequently stressed that for language the child requires a specific model whereas for physical reality he does not (Sinclair 1977). However, one can argue that in both language and physics the child gets some sampling from which he must infer underlying structures. He needs a sampling of each linguistic structure (e.g. passive, question-formation, etc.) but no *specific* instantiation, just as he needs a sampling of each physical phenomenon (e.g. gravity, flat surfaces, liquids and solids, etc.) although no *specific* instantiation of it. The differences in the spatio-physical environments of different cultures may in fact be just as great, superficially, as those between different languages. In both cases, their common underlying structures must be discovered by the child, and he must make inferences about generality from particular examples.

There are of course differences between the physical and linguistic environments and it was important epistemologically to stress them as did Piaget and Sinclair. However, I believe that in placing emphasis on the *commonalities* between the two, it becomes acceptable to consider the child's interaction with his linguistic environment as an essential, rather than secondary, aspect of cognitive growth. Language learning is indeed a form of problem solving, a point made by Bruner (1978a) with regard to communication between individuals. It may well be that language is a *privileged* problem-space for children between 2 and 8 years, and only much later does it become perhaps *solely* the representational tool of intelligence (Karmiloff-Smith 1979).

The recurring argument of Piagetians against giving special weight to language in child development can be seen in the use of experimental evidence for maintaining that language is neither sufficient nor necessary for generating operational structures. Piaget cites Sinclair's often quoted argument that 'verbal training leads subjects without conservation to direct their attention to pertinent aspects of the problem (covariance of the dimensions), but it does not ipso facto bring about the acquisition of operations' (Sinclair 1969, p. 325). However, what does bring about the acquisition of operations 'ipso facto'? Is not the whole brunt of the theory that development takes place by very progressive interaction of various factors? Furthermore, in later work (Piaget *et al.* 1968a) on unidirectional functions, it was shown that covariance of dimensions is an *essential* step towards conservation. Is not language therefore extremely important if it can, in the space of an experimental session, bring about an essential step in the construction of conservation?

Piaget further argues that language is not necessary for cognitive development, because deaf children can attain certain operational structures without the aid of spoken language (Furth 1966). First, it should be stressed that sign language is not an impoverished communication system, but possesses a complex syntactico-semantic organization comparable to spoken languages (Bellugi & Fischer 1972; Bellugi & Klima 1975). Second, even if such children were totally deprived of any linguistic system (but not of social interaction) and yet *can* acquire some logical structures, it does not necessarily follow that hearing or signing children *do* construct their cognition without language. Furth (1970) pointed out that, epistemologically speaking, it requires only *one* child deprived of language to reach operational structures (if such unilateral deprivation does exist) for it is to be clear that language is not necessary in that construction. But is the example of the deaf child who has developed compensatory representative capacities through the visual mode typical of man's progress? If multiple representations are essential in discovery procedures (Karmiloff-Smith & Inhelder 1974/5; Blanchet *et al.* 1978), it could be that the deaf child using sign language is handicapped by not having access also to the auditory channel for representing a situation. On the other hand, it could be that the very abstract nature of sign language, albeit through a visual/manual mode, does not in any way interfere with internal, figural representations of a non-linguistic type. How important is spoken and sign language compared to the other manifestations of the semiotic function? Given the representational capacities of certain infra-human primates (Gardner & Gardner 1969; Premack & Premack 1972), is the grouping of these various manifestations under a single 'semiotic function' as heuristically valid as is taken for granted in the Genevan position? It is possible that language (spoken or sign) frees processing space to a far greater degree than any other manifestation of the semiotic function, and this from the very onset of language.

Piaget, it will be recalled, has always given psychological prominence to the child's interaction with his 'object world'. This does not of course mean that his theory excludes the child's interaction with his sociocultural environment. Piaget clearly considers this broader interpretation when he states:

> As far as the problem of the relations between cognitive operations or pre-operations and language is concerned, this therefore means that cognitive operations do not direct language in an external, unidirectional way, but that progress in language is due to a regulatory or organizational mechanism which is both internal and linked to other forms of the same process at work at the same level in other spheres. (My translation of Piaget, preface to Ferreiro 1971, p. 13)

However, the fact that for several decades Piagetian theoretical and experimental work has placed main emphasis on the child's constructive interaction with his physical environment does imply that herein lies for Piaget the privileged source of interaction for the child's cognitive development. Had Piaget hypothesized that the main or equivalent source of the child's cognitive growth stemmed from his constructive interaction with his socio-cultural, emotional or linguistic environments, then presumably his experimental and theoretical considerations would have explicitly conveyed this. A theory reflects its explicit statements and research emphases, even if its epistemological foundations do not preclude shifting the emphases. Other authors have, as was noted, placed their main research and theoretical emphasis on the child's complex interaction with his 'people world'. The work reported on in the following chapters is an endeavour to demonstrate that Piaget's interactive–constructivist epistemology should be *explicitly* extended to the child's constructive interaction with his 'language world'. Whilst very general, common cognitive mechanisms may underlie the child's interaction with all three 'worlds', linguistic developments are not simply the outcome of non-linguistic cognition. Emphasis must also be placed on language-specific developments.

About this book

Together with the general question of the role of language in the study of cognitive development, a specific hypothesis within language acquisition will also be examined theoretically and experimentally in the following chapters. Taking a functional approach to child language, it will be argued that language development involves passing gradually from a series of juxtaposed unifunctional markers and processing procedures, to the intralinguistic organization of plurifunctional systems of options for modulating meaning. Whilst much developmental research has concentrated on the structures of language and on the child's semantic intentions, the work reported on here seeks to understand the functions of certain linguistic categories in the adult input and the functions attributed to them by the growing child. In this respect, Searle's position seems particularly relevant. He argues that it is likely that 'many of the purely syntactic rules of language will have a deeper explanation in terms of the functions that the syntactic forms serve' (Searle 1976).

This is essentially also Winograd's argument when he states, as a criticism of the artificiality of isolated sentences in computer programming, that 'much of the structure of language comes from its being a process of communication between an intelligent speaker and hearer, occurring in a setting. The setting includes not only a physical situation and a topic of discourse, but also the knowledge each participant has about the world and the other's ideas' (1973, p. 153).

Chomsky (1975), in a lengthy, critical discussion of speech act theories, has objected that 'the communication theorists are not analyzing "meaning" but rather something else: perhaps "successful communication" . . . but communication is only one function of language, and by no means an essential one' (pp. 68–9). Many theorists, not only the speech act theorists, but also those working on systemic grammar, might argue just the contrary. Halliday (1975) stresses that language is a system for making meanings rather than a device for generating structures. Likewise, Searle (1976) emphasizes that 'many of the purely formal regularities of language are reflections of deeper functional principles . . . rules must do more than describe what happens, they must play a role in guiding behaviour'. It is a functional analysis of language which is felt to be most adequate here for analysing child development.

Given the rather broad aims of this book, it may seem surprising that children's acquisition of the rather narrow field of noun determiners was chosen as the experimental terrain. The reasons were threefold: first, determiners have a particularly rich plurifunctional status in adult language and yet they are little words which are rarely accentuated; second, surprisingly enough, determiners appear very early in child corpora (it was important to ascertain not *when* they appeared but rather how they gradually changed *function* from the child's point of view); and third, determiners appear to lie at the frontier between logic and language, i.e. between non-linguistic cognition and linguistic cognition. Contrary to a standard Piagetian position where the main emphasis has always been to seek how cognitive growth affects language growth, a central argument in the following pages will be that an explanation in terms of the child's ongoing development in logical concepts furnishes only a partial account of how the functions of determiners are acquired. Without denying the importance of cognitive development, emphasis should in my view also be placed on *intralinguistic* problems. A new analysis is required of the functions of determiners in the adult output, i.e. thereby examining the input available to the child. This leads to a critical review of experimental design based on previous linguistic analyses of determiners. Throughout the theoretical and experimental discussions, accent is placed on psychological *processes* and linguistic *functions*, rather than on specific cognitive or transformational *structures*. Although the child's use and understanding of the linguistic category of French determiners provides the data base, the psychological implications of the results and of the theoretical analyses reach well beyond the relatively narrow realm of the child's acquisition of a single grammatical category in one particular language.

The next chapter deals with some of the earlier linguistic, philosophical and experimental approaches to the specific problem of determiners and reference. As an introduction to the experimental data, chapter 3 briefly proposes a pyscholinguistic analysis of adult output. This suggests that one of the basic problems a small child has to face in his acquisition of language is to find processing procedures to cope with the fact that morphemes and lexemes are plurifunctional. Chapter 3 also deals with the 'experimental dilemma' where consideration is given to the thorny issue of distinguishing between *ad hoc*, experiment-generated behaviour versus normal language acquisition procedures. Following several chapters (4 to 8) analysing the results of comprehension and production tasks performed by some one thousand French-speaking children between the ages of 2 and 12, a synthesis is made in chapter 9 of the child's acquisition of the extralinguistic and intralinguistic functions of determiners. Chapter 10 puts forward some tentative suggestions regarding more general aspects of language acquisition and their possible extrapolation to other spheres of cognitive growth. Finally, the place of language in child development is rediscussed in the light of the new experimental and theoretical considerations.

2 *Determiners and reference*

Leaving one still with the intolerable wrestle
With words and meanings.
(T. S. Eliot, *East Coker*)

Previous theoretical approaches

It may at first sight seem rather strange that a study which aims at a general discussion of language acquisition should take as one of its main experimental terrains the study of articles which, far from being a universal feature of language, is a purely surface phenomenon. Articles do not even exist in certain languages, e.g. Russian, American Sign Language. With respect to the latter, Bellugi & Fischer have commented that 'there are no common signs for articles, inflections, copula and some prepositions . . . *non-essential elements* are almost invariably eliminated' (1972, p. 199. My italics). Why, then, study child acquisition of marginal surface markers which are non-essential elements in some languages?

The reason of course does not lie in the surface markers as such, but in the *functions* they fulfil. One of the essential functions of the articles, when they do exist in a language, is to mark specific/non-specific reference both extralinguistically and by intralinguistic cross-reference. Whilst articles are absent from certain languages, the means for making such referential distinctions are not. Indeed, most of the articles' functions seem to be universally expressed, but the surface forms by which the functions are realized are extremely varied from one language to another. This has been demonstrated by Fisher (1975) for a number of African languages and by Kramsky (1972) in a cross-linguistic typology of some 300 languages, classified according to the surface manifestations of the category of determinedness versus indeterminedness. Kramsky distinguishes seven main surface devices for expressing the category of determinedness versus indeterminedness, as follows:

(a) languages in which the category is expressed by independent words;
(b) languages expressing one member of the category by an independent word and the other by an enclitic or proclitic;
(c) languages where both members of the category are expressed by clitics;
(d) languages in which the category of determinedness versus indeterminedness is inherent in the noun itself;
(e) languages where the category is expressed by flexion on nouns, adjectives, etc.;
(f) languages expressing the distinction by prosodic means (stress or intonation);
(g) languages which use word order to express the category.
Kramsky's survey also shows that in some languages it is determinedness, whilst in others it is indeterminedness, which is the marked feature of the opposition. He concludes from his extensive analysis that there is 'no other linguistic category that is expressed by such diverse means as the category of determinedness versus indeterminedness' (p. 199).

Of course, many languages actually use a subtle interplay of more than one of the above devices for marking specific versus non-specific reference. Word order, for instance, frequently interacts with other devices and marks the distinction through structures such as the passive, the embedded relative, etc. Moreover, all the above-mentioned devices also have *other* functions than that of marking specific/non-specific reference. These issues, together with Kramsky's decision to exclude all deictic determiners, do somewhat restrict the scope of his interesting study. It would be useful, for instance, to have access to a cross-linguistic study of the interplay of various functions marked by the same surface device.

Whilst Kramsky's work pinpoints the variety of formal means that exist for marking specific/non-specific reference, other studies have shown that even where the same device is used, e.g. two independent articles, and even across closely related languages, article usage is surprisingly diverse. Biard, for instance, concludes from his study of the definite article in some of the principal European languages that 'la question de l'emploi de l'article reste une question d'une étrange subtilité, qu'aucune règle purement grammaticale ne saurait résoudre' (1908, p. 75).

Interestingly enough, foreigners with a near perfect command of, say, French or English, can often be detected as non-native speakers solely on the basis of their faulty article usage. It is thus almost to be expected that two very extensive surveys of article usage have been made by non-native speaking linguists (Matsubara 1932 for French, and Yotsukura 1970 for English). These two studies offer an extremely detailed analysis of the intricacies of article usage as it pertains to a wide variety of expressions, mainly typical of adult speech, and thus not always directly of concern to our study. It is interesting to note that Matsubara, whose study of course antedates transformational-generative grammar, concludes from her work that:

l'article change avec les différentes valeurs dont le nom est susceptible et qu'il n'y a point de règle mécanique de son emploi. C'est la pensée du sujet parlant qui atttribue au nom chacune de ces valeurs. Les noms eux-mêmes ainsi que les facteurs purement grammaticaux n'exercent qu'une influence secondaire ou supplémentaire sur l'article à employer. (p. 215)

Matsubara's early emphasis on the role of the speaker in article usage is an important facet of her study. However, whilst the speaker in a given context opts for one particular function, clearly the range of choices available is governed by conventional aspects of the linguistic code. Yotsukura's recent study represents almost the other extreme, for the author concludes her analysis with some forty formulae to account for the obligatory or permissive uses of articles, covering very intricate shades of meaning conveyed by noun phrases.

However, from the point of view of child language acquisition, it seems unlikely that the child's problems in article usage are due to the need to formulate a very large number of different rules. We should know more about how articles are functionally linked to other determiners, for, absent from much of the work in this field, is consideration of the relations which the articles have with other determiners, such as the demonstrative.

Are there any historical links between the determiners? All authors seem to agree that the definite article in French stems from the Latin demonstrative pronoun and that the indefinite article comes from the numeral 'one'. Moreover, Matsubara (1932) points out that the plural indefinite article in Old French usually conveyed the meaning 'a pair of X' (i.e. the numeral function) and less frequently the meaning of plural indefinite reference.

That the two articles had very different origins raises a question as to whether they are in fact contrastive terms, as is frequently presumed.

Related to this question is whether or not the articles appeared simultaneously. Gellrich (1881) in a study of the history of the French articles shows that neither form was present in texts available from the ninth century. The equivalent of the definite article first appeared in texts dating from the tenth century. The definite article was used particularly to substantify pronouns, adjectives and adverbs, but appears always to have retained the quality of a demonstrative. It was from the eleventh century onwards, according to Gellrich, that very subtle changes in meaning were introduced by the presence or absence of both the articles.

Similar developments seem to have taken place in Old English. Thorne (1972) points out that in Old English there were two definite determiners, both of which had separate masculine, feminine and neuter forms. They functioned as deictics, indicating familiarity. The definite determiner gradually split to form the modern definite article 'the' and the demonstrative pronoun 'that'. Warden (1973) refers to the importance of their non-simultaneity; it was not until considerably after the definite determiner was used that the numeral 'an' (one) was taken to convey unity but unfamiliarity. Previously a zero-form had conveyed various senses of indefiniteness.

Another historical fact attesting to the importance of the different origins comes from Frei (1940). He demonstrates that in some language families, e.g. the Semitic one, the old numeral form 'one' gave rise to both the indefinite article and to the interrogative pronoun. He goes on to argue that a somewhat similar evolution may be hypothesized for the Indo-European family, where the interrogative form '*k^{w}i' may have also been used to mark non-specific reference.

Other linguists, particularly in the first half of the twentieth century, endeavoured to describe the general psychological function of the addition of an article to a noun. Several works can be grouped under the general theory, already defended by the Port-Royal grammarians (Arnauld & Lancelot 1966), that the role of determiners when added to nouns is to 'actualize' or 'concretize' an abstract concept. Guillaume (1919) suggests that at first the noun moved away from the 'support of a particular concrete referent' and thus acquired several potential meanings. Then, he argues, articles were needed to move the noun back from its many potential meanings in language – 'le nom en puissance' – to one particular meaning in speech – 'le nom en effet'. Guillaumean theory postulates that the indefinite article is used to pick out a particular instance of a concept which then enables the speaker to proceed to make inductive generalization through use of the definite article (see Hewsen 1972, for discussion of Guillaumean theory as it pertains to articles).

Kramsky (1972) cites the theories of Hjelmslev and Deutschbein. The former refers to the articles as 'concretizing morphemes', the definite article indicating shared referential knowledge whereas the indefinite article points to the fact that the hearer has no prior knowledge of the speaker's intended referent. Deutschbein's theory postulates that the noun without an article is the name of a class of individuals; the function of the article is to render the noun 'topical and real'.

Christophersen (1939), in a revision of Buhler's theory of substantivization, argues that the main functions of the definite and indefinite articles are to denote 'familiarity' and 'unity' respectively. According to this author, the definite article makes explicit extralinguistic reference, whereas the indefinite article merely denotes unity, its use being neutral as far as familiarity is concerned (i.e. it does not preclude it). Familiarity, according to Christophersen, can be explained by three concepts: 'situational context' (e.g. 'the dean', 'the queen'), 'explicit context' (i.e. previous linguistic reference), and 'implicit context' (only one present when utterance is made). The definite article can be used for all these cases. According to Christophersen, the definite article thus modifies substantially the potential meaning of a noun, whereas the indefinite article leaves the noun close to its potential meanings.

Jespersen's theory of article usage (1949), which takes as its starting point classification of nouns into unit-words, mass-words and proper names, makes use of a concept of degrees of familiarity. He distinguishes three so-called stages: I. complete unfamiliarity (requiring plural and singular indefinite reference); II. nearly complete familiarity (definite article used anaphorically or to refer to extralinguistic context); III. complete familiarity (no article needed). Hill (1966), in a re-examination of Jespersen's theory, distinguishes between: I. nouns taking both articles; II. those taking both one article and a zero article; and III. fixed usage nouns taking only the definite article.

Many linguists, therefore, have been concerned to provide a description of the psychological functions of the articles and of the differences in meaning generated by the use of one article or the other in varying contexts. Articles are, however, also excellent candidates for formal analysis. This is a point stressed by Gleason when he states that 'the clearest examples in English are the articles, the, a, some. The greater number of nominal constructions contain one of these, almost always as the first member. They serve to signal the presence of a nominal and to mark one limit of the construction' (1961, p. 156). It is above all the transformational-generative linguists who were concerned with the formal analysis of the articles.

An interesting point raised by Spangler (1975) is the fact that whilst Chomsky broke with structuralist grammar on numerous basic issues, he nonetheless retained in his transformational-generative grammar the structuralists' concept that words like 'a', 'the', 'that', etc., *determine* that a noun construction will follow. The category created was initially called 'Noun Determiner' and later shortened to 'Determiner' or 'Det'. The latter is part of the rewrite rule for the noun phrase:

NP → Det + N

Thomas (1965) has distinguished three main subclasses of determiners: predeterminers, regular determiners and postdeterminers. In the regular category are grouped articles (including a zero-form), demonstratives and genitives. These determiners are mutually exclusive inside an NP, i.e. you cannot say 'a this boy' or 'John's that car'. This enables one to draw a clear distinction between regular determiners and modifiers. Post-determiners precede modifiers and, whilst they are not mutually exclusive, their order of juxtaposition is fixed (e.g. 'the third prettiest blonde girl'). This category covers ordinals, cardinals, superlatives and comparatives. Predeterminers precede both of the other two categories; their specificity lies in that they are separated from regular determiners by the predeterminer morpheme 'of' (e.g. 'many of the boys', 'a kilo of flour').

Dubois & Dubois-Charlier (1970) break down the determiner category in French in approximately the same way. They distinguish between 'préarticle' (e.g. 'tout, tous'), 'démonstratif' (e.g. 'ce, cette, ces'), 'article' (e.g. 'un, une, des, le, la, les') and 'postarticle' (e.g. 'même, autre, deux'). For these authors, all the constituents of the 'Det' category are optional in French except the category 'article'. The order of the subcategories is always 'préart–dém-art-postart'. This fixed order makes it possible for a distinction to be made, for instance, between the word 'même' when it is used as a postarticle meaning 'same' (e.g. 'le même homme') and the identical word when it precedes 'art' or 'dém' and conveys the meaning 'even' (e.g. 'même cet homme'). The Dubois refer to proper names as 'autodéterminatif' in that they require no determiner. Like many authors, they conclude their study by stating that determiners (and prepositions) 'sont les catégories qui semblent susceptibles de poser le plus de problèmes difficiles' (p. 287).

Chomsky himself raised the need to deal with the intricacies of the article transformation in 1958 when he stated: 'It is necessary to put in a transformation that tells you when you get "a" and when you get "the". Unfortunately the transformation is complicated and I do not know how to state it exactly' (cited in Yotsukura 1970, p. 27). As it stands, the 'Det' category contains many diverse morphemes which are multifunctional, the articles being one subfunction of no less than eight categories, listed by Spangler as follows:

(1) Articles, functioning to limit in number or make definite: *a/an, the.*
(2) Demonstratives, functioning to point out locatively: *this, that, these, those.*
(3) Cardinal numbers, naming counted quantities: *one, two, ninety-nine.*
(4) Ordinal numbers, naming the relation of items in a numerical sequence: *first, second, sixty-fifth.*
(5) Quantities, stating definite or indefinite measures, frequently joined to a cardinal number or article: *several, a few, three quarts.*
(6) Intensifiers, limiting or emphasizing a quantity or other word or phrase: *only* (*ten*), *just* (*a dozen*).
(7) Possessive pronouns, replacing a noun and showing possession: *my* (*book*), *somebody's* (*mother*).
(8) Possessive nouns, showing possession *John's* (*car*), (*the*) *boy's* (*money*). (1975, p. 67)

However, as pointed out previously, this broad category is partially a remnant of the structuralist or analytical approach. It camouflages the diversity of other functions which the same morphemes have. Moreover, it excludes certain morphemes, such as pronouns, solely because they are not followed by a noun, whereas their function can often be of a determinative nature (see Tanz 1977 on relations between determiners and the pronoun 'it'). Dubois & Dubois-Charlier have made a similar point when they note: 'il y a certes dans la terminologie adoptée pour "Det" une confusion entre la fonction et la catégorie, puisque la dénomination de "déterminant" renvoie à une fonction alors qu'elle désigne dans la formule une catégorie' (p. 33).

Spangler has argued that in retaining the original category of 'Det', transformational-generative grammar has overlooked two facts: (i) a fundamental type of noun modifier; and (ii) a fundamental principle about the structural relationship among groups of noun phrases. Spangler argues that the 'Det' category should not exist merely to identify nouns. First he suggests that the possessive forms of nouns and pronouns can be removed from the category and returned to subcategories of the Noun category. He then submits that the 'Det' category should in fact become a category of 'counting and quantity terms' which would give it *functional unity* within generative grammar, because of the fundamental importance of quantity in relation to the head noun. He considers ordinals to be the adjectival form of cardinals and thus suggests they be placed in a general Adjective category. After considering various other members of the previous 'Det' category, and making the important point about the different functions of the indefinite and definite articles, Spangler ends up with a new 'Det' category containing cardinal numbers and quantity terms (with which he places the indefinite article), plus the four demonstratives and the definite article. Whilst this is an interesting approach, Spangler's stress on 'quantity and counting terms' for the 'Det' category is not entirely satisfactory, for the indefinite article is frequently used for other functions than marking unity, this often being rather secondary. When I state: 'A woman has been elected president', I am not focussing on unity in the sense that this is a primary function, but focussing on 'womanhood', the quantity aspect being secondary. This will be developed later. In French, for instance, the definite article also can mark unity because of the number marks of the articles ('le/la/les').

Postal (1970), discussing the functional links between the so-called pronouns and the articles, suggests that articles should be represented as syntactic features of nouns, i.e. features which are similar to (± animate), (± countable), etc. Thus, instead of nouns occurring in deep structure with the article morpheme (ART), article differences in surface structure should be represented in deep structure by differences in features of nouns: e.g. (+ definite), (+ demonstrative), (+ speaker), (+ singular), etc. In French, of course, one would have to add gender features. Whilst a series of features of this nature would make it possible to choose the correct surface marker, such an analysis loses sight of the multifunctions each word has. Moreover, it fails to account for the differences inherent in nouns (e.g. mass, count, etc.) which was stressed in some of the theories discussed earlier.

Perlmutter (1970) has, on the contrary, argued that differences between definite and indefinite NPs are not mediated by a binary contrast of the type (± definite). This author stresses that the deep structure of the indefinite article is the numeral 'one', whereas the definite article is derived from a deictic relative clause. Whilst this reflects the historical origins of the articles, Perlmutter deals with only one of the functions of the indefinite article and neglects to distinguish between non-specific reference, numeral and generic functions.

It seems to be Smith (1964) who first discussed the selection restrictions which operate between determiners and relative clauses. She endeavoured to devise rules to explain why a determiner either took both appositive and restrictive relative clauses, or merely took one or the other. Typical of examples discussed by Smith are sentences like the following:

John is a linguist
*John is the linguist
John is the linguist who spoke at the meeting

However, Vendler (1967) demonstrated that Smith's arguments did not hold in view of the fact that a restrictive relative clause need not be stated *explicitly*. Use of the definite article implies a 'restrictive adjunct' but which may remain implicit (i.e. 'John is the linguist' may be quite acceptable in certain extralinguistic or discourse contexts). Vendler makes a distinction between 'identifying expressions' (e.g. 'I know a man who . . .') and definite descriptions (e.g. 'I know the man who . . .'). He accounts for anaphora by 'identification by contextual implication', a concept intended to cover both intralinguistic and extralinguistic reference.

Not only linguists in the Chomskyan school have been interested in the formal description of determiners, of course. Robbins (1968), a linguist working in the framework of Harris' theory, devoted an entire monograph to the problem of the definite article in English. She endeavours to demonstrate that anaphoric and determinative 'the' are entirely absent from kernel sentences and that they can be introduced as a 'transformational constant'. The brunt of Robbins' argument is based on Harris' principle that kernels are independent and combine freely. The definite article is the result of a combination of kernels and not present in the kernel itself (e.g. 'I know *the* man who came to town' is derived from: 'I know *a* man; *a* man came to town'). If one of the kernels were already to contain the definite article, then, Robbins argues, this would place undesirable restrictions on kernel combinations. However, this transformational constant theory requires the introduction of many exceptions to account for other functions of the definite article. Anaphoric 'the', for instance, is derived from an NP containing a restrictive relative clause which in turn is derived from kernels containing the indefinite article. Moreover, expressions referring to single entities, e.g. 'the moon', could hardly be argued to derive from a restrictive relative clause nor from two underlying indefinite kernels. It seems simpler to invoke shared world knowledge between speaker/hearer about the one-ness of the moon. Robbins also runs into problems accounting for the use of the definite article to substantivize modifiers (e.g. 'The rich prosper'), a device frequently used in French, or for comparative purposes (e.g. 'The longer he waits the worse it will be'). Robbins also had to make a special case of the generic use of the definite article (e.g. 'The whale is a mammal'). Clearly deriving the definite article by a transformational constant from kernels containing the indefinite article is not an entirely satisfactory solution.

Other linguists have also been concerned with accounting for the deep structure of the determiners in the noun phrase. Gough & Chiaraviglio (1970) work from the hypothesis that the indexical symbols (e.g. the demonstratives 'this' and 'that') co-occur with a common noun and form a compound symbol in which both multireference (i.e. the noun without a determiner) and reference (i.e. the adjunct of a determiner) can take place. They argue that 'this' and 'that' are the primitive 'referential symbols' underlying the noun phrase. An expression such as 'the red table' is thus spelled out as: (this, this plus N, this plus adj), i.e. 'this is this that is this table that is red'. According to Gough & Chiaraviglio, every noun phrase is closed at the level of its base structure by the demonstrative 'this', i.e. every NP is 'this'-based, which provides for extralinguistic ostension. The definite article, although considered to be an indexical symbol, cannot bring closure to the NP.

Thorne (1972), on the other hand, argues that the definite article 'the' in the nominative form is actually the surface manifestation of an underlying locative. To support the argument, he cites, for instance, French where the feminine definite article 'la' is similar to the locative 'là'. The underlying structure of a noun phrase such as 'the man' is seen by Thorne as:

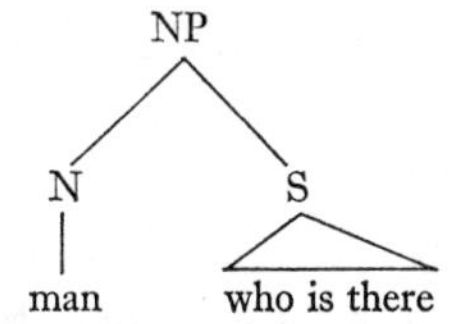

A rule produces the appropriate surface structure by moving 'there' to a position in front of N and deleting the relative and copula. This rule is rather general in nature, because of its analogy to the one required to move adjectives from the predicate of relative clauses. Whilst a deep structure locative might account for deictic uses of the definite article, there is some difficulty in applying the locative interpretation to the anaphoric function. Thorne suggests that in discourse the locative 'is there' is to be taken in the sense of a spatial relationship extended intralinguistically, i.e. as an expression of more abstract relationships forming the basis of the so-called 'localist theory of cases'. Thus, Thorne maintains that anaphoric definite article 're-identifies' an individual 'who is there' in discourse. All other senses of the definite article are considered to be residual meanings by which the basic locative is modified. For Thorne, 'is there' is a speaker-related explanation of the definite article usage.

Grannis (1974), in his criticism of Thorne's hypothesis, suggests that definite referring expressions cannot be explained by deep structure derivations from locatives. Grannis stresses the fact that when the speaker uses the definite article, he assumes that his hearer will be willing to accept, within the context of a particular situation, the uniqueness of his referent. He calls this the 'uniqueness conspiracy' in that both speaker and hearer enter into a sort of temporary conspiracy about the uniqueness of their referents, conveyed by the use of the definite article.

The speaker involvement in the choice of articles has also been discussed by Ducrot (1970, 1972), who (1970) argues against the overgeneralization of Benveniste's 'énonciation' to uses of the articles, particularly with respect to indefinite expressions. It is not always necessary to invoke speech acts to explain the use of indefinite terms, and in the majority of cases the logician's concept of existential description can account for these structures. Ducrot (1972) also discusses the use of articles in what he calls 'the speech act of presupposition'. For him, presupposition is not a condition for other speech acts, but a speech act within its own right and, he believes, the most important of all speech acts. The definite article makes it possible to presuppose a theme in discourse complicity between speakers. This is similar to the concept used by Grannis, but Ducrot places particular stress on extended discourse. In his analysis, he places on the definite article the *function of conserving the presuppositional structure of discourse*. Many authors have stressed the relationship, backed by historical evidence, between the definite article and the demonstrative adjective. For some, it has even been invoked to explain the deep structure of a definite referring expression. Ducrot, however, in an analysis of the substitutability in French of the demonstrative for the definite article, makes a strong case for separating the two. He shows that a demonstrative can always be replaced by a definite article (plus pointing, etc.), whereas the definite article cannot in all cases be replaced by the demonstrative.

The role of the articles, particularly that of the definite article in making unique reference, has been a question often of greater concern to philosophers and logicians than to linguists. However, it is beyond the scope of this book to attempt a comprehensive review of the philosophical discussions on articles, pronouns, demonstratives, etc., on the general issue of reference and meaning which dates back even to Plato. My intention is simply to outline a few of the recent issues raised on the relationship between a referring expression, usually definite, and its referent.

Russell's theory of definite descriptions (1919), for instance, holds that sentences containing a definite description are a form of proposition asserting the existence of an object which satisfies uniquely that description. Thus a proposition which contains a definite reference can be true only if the proposition asserting that the object exists is also true. Whilst Russell centred his discussion on the function of a definite expression to furnish a description of a uniquely specifiable object, Strawson (1950) emphasized the referring function of the definite expression. Strawson argues that a distinction must be made between a given expression or sentence and its use. For Strawson, it is the use of an expression or sentence which refers to a particular object and not the sentence itself.

It is interesting to note that much more discussion has been devoted to definite referring expressions than to indefinite referring expressions. This is particularly apparent in the debate on the relationship between the definite referring expression, and proper names which usually take no determiner. Mill (1949), for instance, has argued that proper names have 'denotation' but not 'connotation'. The definite description has 'connotation' in that it describes some aspect of the object referred to, whereas proper names, according to Mill, do not.

Searle, however, argues that proper names may also have some conceptual or descriptive content; he opts for a sort of compromise between Mill and Frege. Mill, he suggests, 'was right in thinking that proper names do not entail any particular description, that they do not have descriptions, but Frege was correct in assuming that any singular term must have a mode of representation and hence, in a way, a sense' (1969, p. 170). For Searle, an existential statement does not refer to an object and state that it exists, but rather it expresses a concept and states that that concept is 'instantiated'.

It is Searle, and previously Austin, who has most consistently developed the notion of reference as a speech act. Searle maintains that the definite article's function is not to imply uniqueness of an object. Rather the article has the function of indicating the speaker's intention to refer uniquely; it is the function of the descriptor (noun) to identify for the hearer the object to which the speaker intends to refer. Thus in its definite referring use, 'the' is a conventional device indicating the speaker's intention to refer to a single object. It is *not* an indication that the description which follows is true of only one object. Although the descriptor may actually be true of many objects, the speaker assumes that making the reference in a particular context will suffice for the speaker to be able to identify the particular object he means. Searle favours a concept of 'fully consummated definite reference'. This means that the speaker can, if requested, furnish necessary referential information. Thus, a prerequisite of a speaker's intention to refer to a particular object in the utterance of an expression is the speaker's ability to provide, if requested (i.e. if the hearer cannot make the same presuppositional assumptions), an identifying description of that object. Thus, the point of definite reference is to 'identify' rather than to 'describe'. However, Searle stresses that this is a limiting case and that most identifications rely on a mixture of demonstrative devices and descriptive predicates.

Although this brief review cannot do justice to the wealth of literature on the subject of reference and meaning, it can at least demonstrate how extremely varied are the functions of determiners, and anticipate how intricate must be the child's acquisition of the plurifunctionality of determiners.

Let us now look at some of the experimental approaches to understanding this phenomenon in child development.

Previous experimental approaches

We have seen that linguists and philosophers have stressed many varied aspects of determiners. In this section, a brief review will be made of child acquisition studies of determiners, as well as naturalistic data. A short summary will also be made of some of the issues faced by computer scientists writing procedures for determiner usage or understanding into their natural language programmes.

Those investigators who have studied child acquisition of determiners have concentrated mainly on the indefinite and definite article (e.g. Bresson *et al.* 1970; Maratsos 1976; Warden 1973, 1976), and have often designed their experiments to exclude the use of other determiners. Whilst other researchers have studied demonstratives (e.g. Clark & Sengul 1974; Garman 1977), the emphasis was on the deictic category of 'proximity to speaker/hearer' and not of course on the relationships between articles and demonstratives.

Let us first review briefly the work of the Bresson group (1970). The main emphasis in this research was the difference between using the indefinite articles for naming objects, anaphoric reference to the objects named, and then a second anaphoric reference to all or to part of the named collection. The experiment, which covered a narrow age span of 4 and 5 year olds, ran as follows: the experimenter showed the children a collection of toy animals which were placed on sheets of paper representing a meadow, a barn, etc. The animals formed either homogeneous groups (all came from the same species) or heterogeneous groups. There were two singletons. First the experimenter asked the child to describe the animals to a doll whose back was turned away from the table. The child was expected to use plural and singular indefinite articles: e.g. 'Il y a une girafe, des moutons, des cochons', etc. After this, the experimenter either moved an entire group or part of a group of animals and asked the child: 'Qui est parti?' In cases of singletons, the child should use the singular definite article. When the entire group of animals leaves, the child should use the plural definite article. When part of the group leaves, the child should use the singular or plural indefinite article to mark the subclass relationship. Typical items of the overall task are shown below:

Type	*Child*		*Experimenter*	*Child*
1:	Il y a une girafe	(it leaves)	Qui est parti?	La girafe
2a:	Il y a des moutons	(all leave)	Qui est parti?	Les moutons
2b:	Il y a des moutons	(some leave)	Qui est parti?	Des moutons
2c:	Il y a des moutons	(one leaves)	Qui est parti?	Un mouton

The results of the Bresson group's study show that neither 4 year olds nor 5 year olds had any difficulty using indefinite articles for naming. They were also very successful in using the definite article when all (i.e. the singleton or a whole group of animals) were involved in the experimenter's action (types 1 and 2a above). Significant difficulties arose, however, in the use of the indefinite articles in reference to a subclass of a group of already identified animals (types 2b and 2c above). Here children's overwhelming tendency was to use definite articles. Results were slightly better for the singular indefinite reference (type 2c) than was the case for the plural indefinite reference (type 2b). Thus whilst the surface forms of the singular and plural indefinite articles were used for naming, they were not used for reference to subclasses. In general, the results of the experiment show that as far as 4 and 5 year olds are concerned, their referring expressions are predominantly definite.

The Bresson group make use of two theoretical sources to interpret their results: one is Culioli's lexis theory (Culioli *et al.* 1970); the other is Inhelder & Piaget's (1959) comprehensive analysis of the child's class and relation concepts. Culioli's model, mentioned previously, is aimed at identifying linguistic universals and cannot easily be extrapolated onto child acquisition. In their adaptation of Culioli's model, the Bresson group have created two types of 'extraction': one entails the attribution of a predicate (i.e. 'There is an X such that . . .') and the other type of extraction is based on a previous pointer operation. However, this seems to alter the generality of the linguistic operator of 'extraction' in Culioli's system. Moreover, it is difficult to prove that children, even successfully using the indefinite articles in the second case, are necessarily using the complicated operations of extraction 1, pointer, extraction 2. Moreover, if the indefinite article really refers back to a previous pointer operation and in fact operates on that operation, then it would seem more appropriate to expect the child to use a partitive (e.g. 'one *of the*/some *of the*') rather than the neutral 'a' or 'some'. 'One of the' seems far closer to the idea of 'extraction'; and of course, such an extraction is quite different from naming. I would argue that very much depends on *what the speaker wishes to focus on*: if it is subclass extraction, then the partitive is designed to fulfil just that function. Perhaps children incorrectly using definite reference are in fact asserting something closer to the partitive than are those using the more neutral indefinite article, probably in its naming function. We shall return to this.

The arguments of the Bresson group based on Inhelder & Piaget's class and relation concepts seem to come closer to the child reality. Inhelder & Piaget (1959) made an important distinction between what they call 'partitive membership' and 'schematic membership'. The latter covers identification or naming an element(s) by recognitive assimilation to a perceptual or sensorimotor scheme. This seems rather different to 'extraction from a concept' as Culioli describes. Inhelder & Piaget are stressing the *intensional* aspects of the recognition process and not the *extensional* aspects of a class. Naming does not necessarily imply extraction but rather identification by recognition through successive assimilations over time and not the simultaneity of a class from which one can extract one or several members (p. 16). It is the concept of 'partitive membership', i.e. the relation of an individual or group of individuals to a class present in context or to a class present in world knowledge, to which the concept of 'extraction' could be applied. Aware of the difficulties of the Culioli/Inhelder–Piaget parallelism, the Bresson group created 'extraction 1'/'extraction 2', but this considerably changes Culioli's model and implies a stronger relation between 'schematic membership' and 'partitive membership' than Inhelder & Piaget's definitions would suggest. Nonetheless, whilst the parallel between the two models is not entirely satisfactory for the reasons discussed above, the results of the Bresson group's study are of course particularly relevant to my enquiry. However, the problem of what the experimenter induces the child to focus on seems to me to be an important consideration. In the Bresson research the experimenter always asked the child 'Qui est parti?', which implies a simple NP response focussing on the NP (inducing perhaps the definite reference). Had the experimenter asked the more neutral 'What happened?/What did I do?', then the focus would have been left up to the child and article usage might have been different. Also the fact that the Bresson study only covered 4 and 5 year olds and one production task, of course, renders impossible a more extensive discussion of their research. However, the authors do point out (Bresson *et al.* 1970) that this is part of a broader study yet to be reported on, but to my knowledge the only information currently available is a short note on the research of Cabrejo-Parra (1974).

Cabrejo-Parra is studying how French and Spanish children respond to the question 'What's that?' asked of a series of similar objects. The study covers children between the ages of 24 and 36 months. Cabrejo-Parra shows that small children first give the name of an object without a determiner and repeat this for each of the similar objects. The indefinite article seems to appear around 24 to 27 months. It is not until around 30 months that children respond 'a X' for the first object and 'other X' (without article) for a second similar object. (This is not correct in French but is the correct surface form in Spanish where the article is dropped: 'otro X'.) Around the age of 36 months children in French use 'une autre X' and at the same time begin to use the plural indefinite 'des

X'. Cabrejo-Parra draws from this data the hypothesis that plural operations are the result of iterating identification operations, but these results and the consequent hypothesis cannot be discussed until the research is more fully published.

The first major experimental study of child acquisition of the articles in English was made by Maratsos (1976). Like the work reported by the Bresson group, Maratsos concentrated on a narrow age span, i.e. on 3 and 4 year olds. Maratsos devised a series of ingenious tasks in both comprehension and production, e.g. story-telling tasks, acting out with dolls, imitation and expansion of the experimenter's story with a missing determiner, and so forth. The basic paradigm for the story-telling tasks was to tell the child a story about 'A X and a Y' or about 'Several Xs and several Ys'. At the end of the story the experimenter asks the child a question about one of the Xs or Ys. Questions for stories containing single entities should elicit a definite article from the child, whereas for the stories containing several Xs/Ys, the child's response about one of them should be indefinite.

Maratsos' aim was to narrow down the child's responses *solely* to the articles 'the' and 'a', that is to specific and non-specific referential devices. He was however faced with two methodological problems before he could proceed with the production experiments. First, in order to overcome the tendency in young children to point to objects when making reference, the subjects were asked to sit on their hands, or place their hands on their heads, throughout the experiment. Whilst it is a truism to point out that we do not normally speak with our hands on our heads, a more serious consideration stems from asking *why* it is in the first place that small children tend to point when making reference.

Some of Maratsos' other experiments were designed to elicit use of the indefinite article, but despite the fact that in certain situations the objects presented to the children were all ostensibly identical, the subjects tended to seek the slightest distinguishing feature and thus make definite reference. For example, instead of saying something like: 'The monkey jumped into *a* car' (because all the cars were identical), they tended to reply, e.g.: 'The monkey jumped into the red car with the little scratch on the side'. Whilst Maratsos ingeniously overcame this problem in his experimental design, it is again interesting to question why the young child has this tendency to seek at all costs to make definite, specific reference.

It can be argued that the methodological problems Maratsos encountered, rather than being extraneous to the experiment, in fact represent serious clues with respect to the *functions* children confer on each of the articles initially (Karmiloff-Smith, in press a). This will be taken up in the experimental sections and in the concluding discussion.

The interesting paradigm for the imitation with expansion tasks was that the experimenter told the child a story, which the child repeated sentence by sentence, and at a key point (reference to a singleton or one of several) the relevant definite or indefinite article was missing. In his repetition, the child is expected to fill in the appropriate article.

The paradigm for comprehension tasks was essentially as follows: 'X acted on one of the Ys . . . suddenly (the/a) Y performed another action'. 'The Y' entailed that the child act on the *same* Y as the one in the initial NP, 'a Y' entailing that he act on one of the *other* Ys present.

Maratsos had a series of other experimental tasks. He concludes from his extensive data on 3 and 4 year olds that competence is established very early in one of the abstract semantic distinctions encoded by the articles, i.e. specific and non-specific reference. Results showed statistically significant success rates for both 3 and 4 year olds. When it was necessary to take into account the referential knowledge of one's listener, however, only an advanced 4 year old group was free from error. In these far-reaching conclusions, Maratsos argues that 'as early as three years children obviously produce indefinite NPs to refer *generically* or to refer to *any member of a class* (my italics) in contrast to producing definite NP's in minimally contrastive situations where a particular referent had been established for them' (1976).

This is a different conclusion from Warden (1973, 1976) who also studied English-speaking children's ability to use the definite and indefinite articles in their referring expressions. Warden's study was developmentally more extensive than either of those mentioned previously. He covered a population of 3 to 9 year olds, as well as adults in some experiments, and concentrated on 4 year olds in others. In particular he looked at the use of the indefinite article to introduce a new referent to a context of discourse (identifying expression, not to be confused with naming) and the use of the definite article to refer to an already identified referent (anaphoric definite reference). Two of his experiments are particularly revealing: in the first, 4 year old children and adults described simple action events involving model animals to an ostensibly blindfold experimenter; in the second, children between 3 and 9 years, and adults, related cartoon stories to each other, the speaker and listener being selected from the same age group. The results of these studies indicated that, while adults identify new referents prior to using the definite article, children show a strong bias towards definite references, whether the referent of their expression has been identified or not. Only 9 year olds reliably identified their referents for their listener. Now, identifying expressions seem closer to 'extraction' in Culioli's sense, than does naming. Therefore, for Warden's results, 'extraction 1' (referred to by the Bresson group) gives rise to *definite* referring expressions just as did 'extraction 2'. It is 'naming', in my view quite a different quality of operation, which gives the correct indefinite reference.

An important fact mentioned by Warden is that although only 9 year olds reliably identify their referents, nearly every child did use *some* indefinite identifying expressions. Such inconsistency, Warden argues, indicates inadequate learning of an article rule usage. Whilst invoking egocentricity as a possible source of poor usage, Warden argues that a more potent source of children's difficulty may lie in the contexts in which they hear identifying expressions. To support this, he cites limited naturalistic data which seem to point to the fact that, although 2 year olds are exposed to all uses of the articles in their mothers' speech, the contexts in which mothers use identifying expressions are not easily discriminable from those in which they use definite references. Generally speaking, Warden's results indicate that under 5 year olds fail to take into account their audience's knowledge of a referent – their referring expressions are predominantly definite. Between 5 and 9 years, children inconsistently introduce referents with indefinite expressions.

Warden also looked at comprehension tasks (1973). He used a design within an extralinguistic context and presented children with pairs of pictures containing three identical Xs and one X odd-man-out (e.g. different colour, different hat, etc.). Instructions to the child were: 'Show me a, plus nonsense modifier, plus X', which should elicit pointing to any one of the identical Xs, or: 'Show me the, plus nonsense modifier, plus X', implying the one that was the only member of its subclass. Warden himself agrees that the results of the comprehension task were not entirely satisfactory due to the unusual setting and communicative burden placed on the articles.

Brown (1973), referring to Maratsos' comprehension tasks, likewise states that in many cases the use particularly of the indefinite article places 'a somewhat unusual communication burden' on the determiner.

(See chapter 3, under 'The experimental dilemma' for a critical review of such approaches.)

It is Brown who provides us with the most elaborate naturalistic data with regard to the acquisition of definite and indefinite reference (see Brown 1973, pp. 352, 354, for examples of correct and incorrect instances of reference). In his analysis of the order of acquisition of the first fourteen morphemes in child speech and of morpheme frequency in parental output, he shows that articles were ranked eighth as far as acquisition was concerned and were the most frequent morpheme used by the parents. However, in his calculations of acquisition, Brown grouped the two articles according to correct use in context, and did not take into account the difference between definite and indefinite article. Brown concludes from his analysis of the three children studied longitudinally that 'children somewhere between the ages of 32 and 41 months, roughly three years, do control the specific/non-specific distinction as coded by the articles' (1973, p. 355). Brown, like Maratsos, adds the proviso that this early productive control of the article contrast does not yet cover instances where the child is obliged to take into account his listener's knowledge.

Before turning to a brief description of some of the issues faced by the computer scientist when writing procedures for determiners into his programme, mention should be made of two recent studies on infants. The first is by Katz *et al.* (1974) on how very small children learn the difference between common and proper names. The subjects were eighty 17 month to 24 month old infants. The authors show that these very young children can distinguish between proper names, e.g. the nonsense word 'That's Dax' compared to common names, e.g. 'That's *a* dax', with the proviso that reference is made to animates (i.e. dolls). The distinction between proper names and common names is not made successfully in the case of inanimates (i.e. boxes). It is nonetheless particularly interesting that such young children can pick up the distinction in the case of animates solely on the presence or absence of the article. The authors' hypothesis, which the data seem to confirm, is that within certain classes of things (e.g. people) children first discriminate individuals and then learn the class names, whereas among other classes of things (e.g. physical objects) they do not discriminate individuals and learn names only for the class. These two processes are considered to be determinant in the way in which the children learn the syntactic distinction between common and proper nouns. This is drawn from the fact that the distinction as encoded by the presence or absence of article is successfully made at 17 months for dolls but not until later for inanimate objects. Thus the linguistic distinction would appear to be based on prior distinction among classes of objects. Whilst this study does not of course look at the distinction between the definite and indefinite articles, the results are particularly important regarding the presence or absence of an article-like word.

The other recent study on infants is that by Ninio & Bruner (1978) on the acquisition of labelling. The authors studied longitudinally one mother–infant dyad, making video recordings of free play between mother and child (8 to 18 months). The analysis of joint picture-book reading revealed that very early on such an activity had a dialogic structure. Ninio and Bruner hypothesize that the child's lexical labels might be regarded as more adult-like substitutes for earlier communicative forms of dialogue, such as smiling, reaching, pointing and babbling vocalizations, all of which were consistently interpreted by the mother as expressing the child's intention of requiring a label or providing one.

Whilst these early manifestations are not covered by the present study, they are clearly very important aspects of how the child gradually comes to grips with the plurifunctionality of determiners.

In a study of child language acquisition, it would be inappropriate to go into details of the work of computer scientists writing natural language comprehension and production programmes. However, it seems essential to refer to them briefly because I strongly believe that the fundamental need for the artificial intelligence scientist to be *entirely explicit* in formulating his procedures is of particular relevance to both the psycholinguist and the linguist, irrespective of whether the programme is completely successful as a whole. The computer scientist has to define all his conceptual tools operationally in the form of procedures which can be run to their last detail.

I shall merely illustrate from two examples how the problems of determiners have arisen. Indeed, for the construction of a natural language computer model, it is obviously not sufficient merely to distinguish between the fact that in some strings the definite article appears and in others the indefinite article. The programmer needs to render explicit *why* in some contexts one article is relevant and in others the other article. He thus has to make a very explicit analysis of the *functions* articles play, not abstractly, but in discourse. Of course, the scope of the discourse for any given programme must necessarily remain limited.

Both Winograd (1972) and Davey (1974) have opted for variants of generative systemic grammar, based on Halliday's work. Not only does systemic grammar use 'functions' as one of its basic conceptual units, but it accounts for important areas of language use, such as being sufficiently informative but not overly redundant. The grammar is used by these computer scientists to define a network of systems in which each system is a set of simultaneously exclusive alternatives, the structure of the network making explicit the relation of each system to the others. It also comprises sets of structure-building rules which state how the options open to any item may be constrained by that item's role in the grammatical environment. As far as the noun group is concerned, for instance, the grammar renders explicit not only how a given noun group is composed but also and primarily what the noun group *is doing*, i.e. what is its current function in the particular discourse context. The type of problems faced by Winograd and Davey with respect to determiners should therefore be briefly mentioned.

Winograd, when he constructed his block world programme, states, for example, that 'the different possibilities for the meaning of "the" are procedures which check various facts about the context, then prescribe actions such as "look for a unique object in the data base which fits this description"', or a procedure: 'assert that the object being described is unique as far as the speaker is concerned'. Winograd's programme is also capable of rejecting definite reference: if told: 'Pick up the block', the programme can return: 'Which block', which it does not do in response to 'Pick up *a* block' (1973, p. 175). As Winograd points out, knowing what 'the' refers to involves a detailed world model describing both the current state of the blocks world environment and its knowledge of procedures for changing that state and making deductions about it. 'The block' may not make sense in the current scene (extralinguistically) or in the current state of dialogue (intralinguistically). Moreover, 'the block' may mean the only one present or the one just referred to, and the same label 'the block' will have different referents according to the moment of discourse.

Davey's programme poses problems of production rather than comprehension. The programme describes in English a game of noughts and crosses which the programmer and computer have just played. Davey therefore had to include in his procedures decisions for calling a square 'a corner', 'the corner', 'the corner just taken', 'the edge', 'my edge' or 'the same edge', etc. Although it is not possible to enter into detail, it is important to point out that the Davey programme spouts a very *natural*-sounding dialogue – natural because words and structures are playing meaningful functions, as can be seen from the following example of the programme's description of a game just completed:

I started the game by taking *the* middle of *an* edge, and you took *an* end of *the* opposite one. I threatened you by taking *the* square opposite *the one* I had just taken, but you blocked *my* line . . . so I won by completing *my* edge. (Davey & Longuet-Higgins 1978, p. 127)

I have italicized the programme's decisions with respect to determiners. It is important to recall that none of the above sentences is taken from the programme's memory but is entirely constructed *de novo*. Each determiner reflects the current state of the discourse, as can be noted, for example, from the different determiners used with the term 'edge'. Intradiscourse coherence is a very important aspect of natural language.

The use of systemic grammar by Winograd (1972, 1973) and Davey (1974) for coping with these types of problem suggests that the implications of such a grammar for developmental psycholinguistics should be examined more closely. In the following chapters, however, I work from my own psycholinguistic intuitions (Karmiloff-Smith 1974) which form the basis of my experiments on children. When the experimental work was undertaken I was not aware of systemic grammar, and it therefore seems preferable to present, in the next chapter, the analysis of adult output upon which the experimental hypotheses were based, rather than attempting to translate this into any formal linguistic system.

3 *Introduction to the experimental data*

For words, like Nature, half reveal and half conceal.

(Tennyson)

Functional analysis of adult output and experimental hypotheses

Whatever the linguistic categories under study, it is essential to make an analysis of the input actually available to the child in daily discourse. Previous developmental studies, mentioned in chapter 2, have provided a fairly exhaustive list of the different situations (e.g. whether referent is specific/non-specific to speaker and/or addressee) in which either the definite article or the indefinite article should be used (e.g. Brown 1973; Warden 1973; Maratsos 1976). In the present analysis, an endeavour has been made to capture from a psycholinguistic point of view some of the dynamic intralinguistic functions involved in determiner usage. Thus, emphasis is placed here on the development of referential *functions*, on the *interrelations* between articles and other referential devices, and on the fact that determiners have *plurifunctional* status in the adult output. It is upon this psycholinguistic analysis that the experimental hypotheses were based.

Studies of the acquisition of referential devices have, as was pointed out, concentrated mainly on the definite and indefinite articles. However, language offers many other means for referring. Depending on the context in which an utterance is made, an adjective may for instance be an essential means for picking out a referent, whereas in a different context the same adjective may be superfluous as referential information. Thus, it is important to determine the *function* a word is playing within the present discursive and extralinguistic context. In doing so, one discovers that many words have more than one function and that a functional analysis cuts across category boundaries.

The study to be reported on in the following chapters covered the

French-speaking child's use and understanding of the functions of the singular and plural definite and indefinite articles ('le/la/les/un/une/des'), the possessive and demonstrative adjectives ('mon/ma/mes/ce/cette/ces'), colour modifiers ('rouge, vert/verte', etc.) and two postdeterminers ('même/autre'). It is suggested that these words have two general functions in adult language: the *descriptor function* and the *determinor function*.[1] The descriptor function is defined as follows: a word is used by the speaker to give additional information about a referent already implicitly or explicitly under focus of attention by speaker and addressee. The determinor function is defined as follows: a word is used by the speaker to enable the addressee to pick out a referent amongst other potential candidates. Thus the determinor function defines a *relationship* between the referent and its extralinguistic context (the concrete situation or world knowledge about the situation) or its intralinguistic context (created by the temporary universe of discourse set up between the speakers). The descriptor function is centred on the attributes of the referent and not on its relationship with other potential referents. Let us take a few examples:

(1a) My car has broken down so I came by bicycle
(1b) My car has broken down, this is my husband's
(2a) The red Foıd is the latest model but the green Volkswagen is more sturdy
(2b) The red Ford is the latest model, but the green Ford is more sturdy
(3a) Mary is wearing the same dress as Jane
(3b) Mary is wearing the same dress as yesterday

In example (1a) above, the possessive adjective 'my' could be replaced by a weaker determiner such as 'the' and thus in this case 'my' is used in its descriptor function. In example (1b), on the other hand, the possessive adjective is essential in its determinor function for identifying the referent. Examples (2a) and (2b), where in both contexts only two cars are present, make a similar distinction with respect to the modifier 'red'. In example (2a), the addressee is being informed about the 'redness' of the car under focus, whereas in example (2b) the addressee is called upon to pick out the referent which is red from another potential candidate of a different colour. In example (3a), the post-

[1] Henceforth, the term 'determin*or*' will be used to cover the function, and 'determin*er*' to cover the category (e.g. articles, demonstrative adjectives, etc.).

determiner 'same' is used by the speaker to convey the descriptive meaning 'same kind' whereas used in its determinor function in example (3b), it means 'same one'. Thus, in examples (1a), (2a) and (3a), the words 'my', 'red' and 'same' describe some aspect of the referent. These words are not used by the speaker to enable the addressee to pick out the referent. From the point of view of clearly establishing the referent, these words could be considered as redundant. Rather, they answer questions such as: 'What is X like/What attribute does X have?' In examples (1b), (2b) and (3b) on the other hand, the words 'my', 'red' and 'same' are used by the speaker to make it possible for the addressee to identify the referent. They answer a question such as: 'Which X is currently being referred to?' Of course, the extralinguistic context in which an utterance is made is an essential component for defining whether a word is currently being used in its descriptor or determinor function.

In situations where no indeterminacy of reference could occur, then words used by the speaker merely in their descriptor function actually suffice for the addressee to identify the referent. It is hypothesized that since daily discourse between child and caretaker is usually about very obvious referents, it will take small children some time before they discover the dual function of these words. It is suggested that children will initially expect words to function as descripters rather than as determiners, because the referent is already implicitly or explicitly clear from context and there is therefore no need to determine it linguistically. It is further hypothesized that young children's use of words in their determinor function may initially retain a strong descriptor content. For example, deictic reference, which for the adult defines a spatial *relation*, may initially for the child be partially descriptive in nature in that, cognitively speaking, an object's location may first be considered almost as if it were a permanent attribute of the object rather than a temporary location. The suggested descriptor content of early deixis is not dissimilar to Lyons' hypothesis that reference and predication are initially inseparable and correspond to a form of 'proto-reference' (Lyons 1977b).

Apart from the general distinction between the descriptor and determinor functions, the determinor function itself has been subdivided into five functions: deictic reference, exophoric reference, non-specific reference, anaphoric reference and generic reference. Deictic reference is considered to involve the speaker using an indexical definite referring expression together with paralinguistic markers such as eye gaze, head motion, finger pointing, etc. (e.g. 'Give me the/that pencil' in a context where several pencils are present, but an indexical gesture at the moment of uttering the determiner enables the addressee to identify the referent). Deictic reference is linguistically egocentric to the extent that the addressee must attend to paralinguistic markers emitted by the speaker if he is to pick out the correct referent. Whilst some excellent acquisition studies have been made on deictic contrasts *without* the use of paralinguistic markers (e.g. Clark & Sengul 1974; Webb & Abrahamson 1976; Garman 1977), it is argued here that in normal discourse available to the child, the use of deictic referential expressions almost always involves the use of additional paralinguistic markers. They are an essential feature of the deictic term. In other words, when uttering 'Give me this/that X', the speaker does not look directly at the addressee and rely solely on the lexical contrast between the demonstrative adjectives, but rather he looks at or points to the object to which he is referring. Thus, paralinguistic markers will be an essential component of the analysis one makes of the child's use of, say, the definite article or the demonstrative adjective.

Exophoric reference is taken to imply a distance between speaker and his utterance and is thus less egocentric in nature than deictic reference. It involves the choice by the speaker of a definite referring expression when a referent is the only member of its subclass in the current extralinguistic setting, and the choice of an indefinite referring expression when the referent is one of several identical ones (e.g. 'The boy pushed the red car' versus 'The boy pushed a car'). Exophoric reference thus means taking into account the *relationship* between objects in the extralinguistic setting, rather than the speaker's subjective involvement with an object upon which he is focussing all his attention. Unlike deictic reference, exophoric reference does not involve any implicit or explicit spatial markers.

In the above example, 'The boy pushed a car' in a context of several identical cars, the use of the indefinite article does not necessarily imply non-specific reference, since the indefinite article is chosen by the speaker because of the characteristics of the extralinguistic setting. It could have been expressed by a partitive together with a definite referring expression, e.g. 'The boy pushed one of the cars'. Non-specific reference, on the other hand, is considered to be closer to the generic function, and therefore acquired later in development. However, whereas the generic use of the articles involves a conceptualized reference with no concrete instantiation thereof (e.g. 'The lion/a lion is an animal'), non-specific reference retains the notion of potential instantiation implying 'any non-particular member of a class' (e.g. 'Give me a cigarette'). The generic use of articles has no possible materialization (e.g. 'The cigarette is a danger to health'). The different uses of the indefinite article for the determinor function are to be clearly differentiated from the naming function, or, more precisely from what Lyons suggests should be called the 'appellative or nominative function' (Lyons 1977a, vol. I, p. 217). Use of the indefinite article for nominating entities is very common in early discourse between child and caretaker, and it is suggested that small children will often decode a task which should call for the use of referential devices, rather as a task of nominating, i.e. giving a name to something.

Anaphoric reference is the only one which might be looked upon as involving purely intralinguistic procedures. Whilst linguists have mainly invoked for anaphora the notion of substitution and reference back to a previously mentioned antecedent, Lyons suggests that the anaphoric expression refers, not to the antecedent, but to the same referent that the antecedent refers to (1977a vol. II, p. 660). In this way Lyons highlights the deictic component of anaphoric reference. However, the fact that French language has grammatical gender, and not merely natural gender distinctions as in English, brings forth an important point. The word, for instance, for a victim in French is always of feminine gender. Thus, a newspaper report of a car accident will talk of '*la* victime' even when referring to a male victim. However, when continuing the report, writers will normally avoid pronominalization with 'elle' (which is the feminine pronoun which would follow a feminine word for an inanimate object: e.g. 'la table . . . elle'). However, they also avoid direct pronominalization with 'il' (which would refer to the extralinguistic male victim as 'he'), because the antecedent form is of feminine gender. Thus, before pronominalizing, the writer will usually interject expressions such as 'l'homme en question' [the man being referred to], or 'cet homme' [this man] and then continue with the pronoun 'il' [he]. A similar treatment can be seen for other terms where grammatical gender is inconsistent with natural gender, e.g. '*la* recrue' [the recruit], '*le* professeur' [female or male professor], etc. An analysis of limited spontaneous discourse using such terms tends to indicate that speakers will often introduce a new noun (synonym) for which grammatical and natural gender coincide, before they pronominalize. The frequent avoidance of following a feminine noun by a masculine anaphoric pronoun, or a masculine noun by a feminine anaphoric pronoun, indicates that anaphoric reference contains both a deictic and a textual component. In other words, whilst I endorse Lyons' analysis (1977a) that the anaphoric expression refers not to the antecedent but to the same referent that the antecedent refers to, I should like to argue that the anaphoric expression is *filtered intralinguistically* through the antecedent form and out to the same extralinguistic referent.

It is suggested that intralinguistic reference is of a more abstract, and thus cognitively more complex, nature than deictic reference. Thus, whilst following Lyons' hypothesis of the deictic roots and component of anaphora, I should like to distinguish between the juxtaposition of two deictic coreferential expressions, and the use of anaphoric reference where the coreferring terms are also *intralinguistically* linked. Because of the lack of grammatical gender markers in English, it is suggested that camouflaged in most instances of true anaphoric reference is *both* a deictic and a textual component. Some aspects of the experiments on the gender-indicating function of French determiners (chapter 6) were devised to separate the two components and to analyse the developmental implications of this. My general hypothesis is that reference is initially extralinguistic in nature, and that only gradually does the child acquire the capacity for the intralinguistic filter implied by true anaphoric reference. In most cases, it is difficult to distinguish between deictic and anaphoric reference, particularly if we take Lyons' analysis of the deictic component of anaphora. However, the functions of deictic and anaphoric reference may be different. It is suggested that deictic reference is used by the speaker to clarify a referent or a coreferent, whereas anaphoric reference is used by the speaker to hold discourse together and implicitly to inform the addressee that he is keeping to the same theme of discourse.

It was stressed at the beginning of this chapter that the words under study here have plurifunctional status in adult output. This statement can imply two things. First, that a word may take on any one of its several functions. We have already discussed this with respect to the descriptor and determinor functions. A further example can be gleaned from the French indefinite article 'un/une' which can be used either to mean 'a' or to mean 'one' – there is no surface distinction in French between the numeral and non-specific reference functions of the indefinite article. Second, and it is with this aspect that we shall deal now, plurifunctionality can imply the *simultaneous* expression of several different functions. This is perhaps more prominent in the use of French determiners than in English because of number and gender markers on the determiners. Let us take a few examples. The plural definite article 'les' in French indicates simultaneously pluralization (as opposed to the singular definite article 'le/la'), and totalization (as opposed to the partitive 'des' meaning 'some' or the zero form of the plural English indefinite article). Thus, in a spoken utterance such as:

'Les garçons jouent au football'
[The boys are playing football]

the definite article alone conveys the fact that there are several boys and that all the boys in the present discourse context are playing football. Apart from a few exceptions (e.g. 'cheval/chevaux'), the singular and plural forms of most French nouns have the same pronunciation in spoken utterances although they are kept distinct in written French (e.g. 'garçon/garçons'). The same applies quite frequently to singular and plural verb forms (e.g. 'arrive/arrivent', 'joue/jouent') which are kept distinct in the written system but not in speech. Thus, the vowel of the definite article can carry a particularly heavy communicative burden in spoken French. Likewise, the plural possessive adjective 'mes' in French indicates simultaneously possession to speaker (as opposed to 'tes/vos'), pluralization (as opposed to the singular 'mon/ma'), totalization of a subclass of possessed objects (as opposed to 'certains de mes . . .') and the partitive (as opposed to 'les'). Thus, in a spoken utterance such as:

'Mes élèves jouent au football'
[My pupils are playing football]

the plural possessive adjective alone conveys the fact that several pupils are playing, that it involves the totality of the speaker's pupils, that this is a subclass of all the pupils in the school.

The simultaneous expression of several functions is an essential component of language. The speaker is dynamic in his choice of expressions and will therefore, according to the context, wish to bring into focus one or other of these functions. It is therefore suggested that a distinction should be made between the 'primary focussing function' of an expression and its 'secondary focussing function(s)'. In a spoken utterance such as 'Les garçons jouent au football', the primary function of the definite article here would seem to be to indicate plurality. Whilst it simultaneously indicates totality (as opposed to 'Des garçons . . .'), it is argued that if the speaker wished to focus on the fact that *all* the boys were playing and not just some of them, he would normally add the relevant linguistic emphasizer (e.g. 'Tous les garçons . . .' [All the boys . . .]). A similar argument can be made for the French plural indefinite article 'des'. An utterance such as 'Elle a cueilli des fleurs' [She picked (some) flowers] is not primarily a statement about the fact that not all the flowers were picked, but rather non-specific plural reference. A secondary, or weaker, function is that of implying 'some, but not all'. If the speaker wished to express primarily the latter, then again there exist linguistic devices for doing so, e.g. 'quelques fleurs' [some flowers], 'pas toutes les fleurs' [not all the flowers], etc. Moreover, it should be recalled that 'des', although implying 'some', does not have the dual construction as in English, e.g. 'some boys left' versus 'some of the boys left.' Thus, whilst 'les' and 'des' in principle mark the class inclusion distinction, it is argued that if the speaker wishes to focus on the fact that sometimes a total class and sometimes part thereof is being referred to, he would not do so by using the weak article contrast but rather add linguistic emphasizers. In other words, it can be argued that 'les' and 'des' never have as their primary function that of indicating class inclusion, an important point taken up in the section on 'The experimental dilemma' below.

With respect to the singular indefinite article, it is suggested that its primary function is rarely, if ever, to indicate unity (although it always has this as a secondary function). Rather, its primary functions are to name or nominate entities or to make non-specific reference to them. When the speaker wishes to stress the numeral function, it is again suggested that he will add linguistic emphasizers or paralinguistic markers, e.g. 'N'a qu'une X', 'A une seule X', or by adding prosodic features such as intonation and stress, e.g. 'A *une* X'. Thus, whilst the singular indefinite article indicates simultaneously non-specificity and unity, or both names and indicates unity, unity is secondary and not the function primarily focussed upon by the speaker. This would constitute an argument against Spangler's (1975) stress on quantity and counting terms as the definition for the 'Det' category, discussed in chapter 2 above. Thus, whilst the indefinite article may have developed diachronically from the numeral, and whilst the results will show that it also develops ontogenetically from a temporary concentration on the numeral function, it does not necessarily follow that the indefinite article's primary function in adult output is the numeral one, as some authors have presumed.

Important in the notion of primary and secondary focussing function, is that a word does not necessarily have one primary function at all times. Amongst the various possible functions, the speaker may use one function as primary in one situation (e.g. plurality of 'les') and in a different situation one of the other functions may become primary (e.g. 'les' used anaphorically meaning the total subclass just referred to). Thus, the plurifunctionality of a word is a heterarchical, and not necessarily hierarchical notion. Moreover, it is up to the speaker to make a choice within a system of options of different determiners (e.g. when a colour modifier must be used, when the possessive adjective must be used or when it can be replaced by the definite article, etc.). The choices available to the speaker involve, in my view, a dynamic concept of language use rather than a static description of intralinguistic functions. Depending on what the speaker currently wishes to focus, he has a variety of linguistic means from which to choose. This general characteristic of language in its normal use may constitute one of the difficulties of acquisition.

Thus, the general hypothesis underlying my experimental approach is that children not only have to cope with the problems of passing from descriptor to the dual descriptor–determinor functions of a large number of interrelated words, as well as from extralinguistic to intralinguistic referential devices, but they also have to learn to consider a word not as a series of unifunctional homonyms but as one simultaneously plurifunctional word.

Dividing words into categories such as articles, adjectives, nouns, verbs etc., loses sight of category interface that becomes apparent when a functional analysis of language is taken into account. For instance, 'red' has functional links with 'the' through their determinor function, just as 'red' has functional links with 'finished' through their descriptor function. It is hypothesized that children approach language initially from a functional point of view, i.e. the intralinguistic groupings they gradually make are based on analogous *functions* rather than merely on syntactic categories. Indeed, one might go as far as suggesting that spontaneous linguistic processing is based on functions, and that categorization is more of a metalinguistic capacity.

Having considered a series of psycholinguistic hypotheses and their implications for language acquistion, it is now appropriate to see how these hypotheses can be translated into experiments on children. Whilst in the next section a critical discussion is made of certain approaches to language acquisition studies, this should certainly not imply that I believe my own work has surmounted all the problems. On the contrary, there are no ready-made recipes for psycholinguistic studies, for we are indeed faced with an 'experimental dilemma'.

The experimental dilemma

A striking aspect of some of the discussions on language over the past two decades is the unusualness of the examples taken, either to prove that linguistic structures are innate, or to show that if a model can handle the complicated example, it must necessarily cover simpler cases. Such unusualness becomes even more questionable when the linguist's reflections are then extrapolated to child language acquisition. Chomsky's work exemplifies this approach. He sets out to demonstrate (1975) how children must necessarily be basing themselves on innate structure-dependent rules, because, for example, one never encounters *errors* in children's use of the intricate rule for embedding a relative clause into an interrogative sentence. But are such complex structures ever encountered in natural child language?

Another striking aspect of language discussions is the problem of ascertaining what is 'grammatical'. Unusual examples are again taken to confirm the theoretical stand. Levelt (1974) has shown how, depending on the linguist's training, identical strings may be judged as 'grammatical' by one linguist and 'deviant' by another, and the judgement in both cases will necessarily confirm the theory.

Both 'unusualness' and 'grammaticality' are real problems in experimental design for language acquisition studies. If one places the structure to be studied in its usual setting, with normal extralinguistic and discourse clues, then the child's decoding may simply be due to the accumulation of clues and not to his understanding of the structure itself. Many investigators have raised this problem. Those who adopted the Chomskyan model and studied the acquisition of syntactic competence, explicitly removed from their experimental design extralinguistic, paralinguistic and discourse clues.

However, it may well be that normal usage, rather than abstract structure, is more important than is sometimes assumed. Indeed, the very notion of 'grammaticality' might be usefully extended to the functional aspects of language usage. Thus, an isolated sentence, whilst both syntactically and semantically well-formed, may be 'ungrammatical' because it is afunctional, i.e. it is not functioning the way it normally does in discourse. Such a notion would also make room for certain strings normally judged 'ungrammatical' syntactically.

It can be argued that one of the major functions of a whole group of linguistic structures which violate canonical order (e.g. questions, passives, embedded structures, reversed temporal relations, etc.) is to place special stress or to distinguish between the 'given' and the 'new' (in Halliday's terms, 1975), i.e. to perform the 'speech act of presupposition' (in Ducrot's terms, 1972). If this were to prove one of the major functions of those structures which violate canonical order, then their use in the *absence* of such presuppositional constraints could be judged 'ungrammatical', functionally speaking. To take the argument further, it might be contended that psycholinguistic investigators using sentences which seem perfectly normal semantically and syntactically, but which do not observe functional constraints, have in fact been testing children with 'ungrammatical' strings.

It is argued that the necessity for an utterance to be functionally meaningful is as important as semantic and syntactic well-formedness. We might therefore ask whether children are implicitly aware of the need for 'functional grammaticality'. Ferreiro (1971), in an interesting study of temporal relations in child language, has results which suggest that children may indeed be implicitly aware of the need for sentences to be functionally grammatical. Ferreiro demonstrated that young children have difficulty in understanding and producing the reversed temporal order, e.g. 'Before the boy went upstairs, the girl washed the boy'. However, small children find it much easier to use and to understand a much longer but redundant string, e.g. 'The boy went upstairs, and before the boy went upstairs, the girl washed the boy'. The redundancy in fact makes the isolated sentence 'grammatical' functionally speaking, because it introduces a distinction between 'given' and 'new' information. One good reason for reversing in an utterance the temporal order of events may be due to the fact that new information is frequently placed last. Moreover, as Ducrot (1972) has suggested, language may be generally redundant with respect to presupposed information and economical about new information.

The analysis of function has important implications for child language acquisition. From a taxonomic point of view, sentences such as 'The boy pushed the fat girl' and 'The elephant carries heavy loads' are considered to be structurally related. However, Chomsky's transformational-generative model brought to the fore the formal links between 'The boy pushed the fat girl' and 'The fat girl was pushed by the boy', and rendered explicit the differences between 'John is easy to see' and 'John is eager to see'. An analysis of function, however, should be able to render explicit the links between, say, the embedded relative, the reversed temporal, the passive, and other structures violating canonical order. This is why it might have important implications for child development, because it may be possible to give a more powerful explanation of the acquisitions of a given level due to the *functional* links between structures, rather than to their semantic or syntactic links.

Now if the competence/performance distinction is valid, then unusual examples and afunctional uses are very important spheres of study. But if, as Searle (1969) has argued, an adequate study of speech acts *is* a study of competence, then special attention should be given to the functional aspects of language when one studies child acquisition.

Having raised a series of problems with regard to the functional aspects of language, it is no simple matter to find an experimental solution. On the one hand, we are all aware that if we make sentences functional by setting them in normal extralinguistic and discourse contexts, then the child has a variety of clues to draw on. Yet if we remove all these clues, we can never be sure that we are not dealing with *ad hoc* 'experiment-generated' procedures. One cannot necessarily extrapolate from the latter onto normal language usage. I have argued elsewhere (Karmiloff-Smith 1978a) that there may be special '*ad hoc* procedures' generated for unusual examples or unusual uses, 'basic procedures' to take care of the most consistent fashion in which a particular category is used, and 'standby procedures' for regular exceptions.

This brings me to the case of the articles. Experiments could be set up which would demonstrate that children *can* use the indefinite and definite articles as contrastive terms, but the question would remain whether they actually function contrastively in their language. Do children let the articles convey such a heavy communicative burden in cases of potential ambiguity, or do they use a series of other linguistic means for this? If we have removed all other possible responses apart from the articles, and we show that children can use them contrastively, how can we be sure that in normal language usage children *do* use them in this way?

Suppose an experimenter decides to study children's comprehension of the 'article contrast'. The very use of the word 'contrast' carries strong theoretical assumptions which are built into the experiment but which need not necessarily be true of the child's way of organizing the articles. How do we know that they function as contrastive terms for the child (or for the adult)? In order to set up as clean an experiment as possible, the task is narrowed down to one linguistic contrast (e.g. 'the/a') and the situational context to one cognitive contrast (e.g. singleton/group of identical objects). However, the child's problem in a comprehension task of this nature need not be specifically linguistic at all. Rather he may seek to discover what are the salient distinctions in the task, both linguistically and situationally, and then map one pair onto the other. A very small amount of knowledge of the functions of one of the terms (e.g. definites refer to singletons) might suffice to elicit, by exclusion because the experiment is narrowed to two contrasts only, correct responses for the other term. From work on general cognitive procedures, it seems clear that children do build up a series of good, standby heuristics for coping with new situations: classifying, spreading objects out spatially, counting, picking out oppositions, and so forth. These are applicable to physical, spatial, logical or linguistic tasks. Thus, it could be argued that children often display *ad hoc*, experiment-generated behaviour, which is very consistent in the two-way mapping, and therefore statistically significant, but which is not necessarily symptomatic of how the child normally uses the particular linguistic category. In other words, it may be possible to show experimentally that the small child *can* use the articles as contrastive terms, but it does not necessarily follow that he *does* use the articles contrastively as part of a common system in his everyday language.

When speakers do use the articles contrastively, they add stress (e.g. '*A* source of reference, not *the* source of reference'), or linguistic emphasizers (e.g. 'The only source'). This does not imply that the singular or plural definite and indefinite articles never appear alone without linguistic emphasizers in normal discourse. Of course they do. The essential point is that it is not the function of the articles to encode alone such strong contrasts, whereas this is exactly how they are used in experimental design. In the first part of this chapter it was argued that a distinction should be made between the 'primary focussing function' and the 'secondary focussing function(s)' of a word. It is suggested that in many psycholinguistic experiments, distinctions are encoded by markers used in their secondary focussing functions to avoid specific clues, whereas in normal discourse those markers are chosen whose primary focussing function it is to convey specific semantic contrasts. In other words, to a certain extent it could be maintained that many psycholinguistic experiments do not study 'language' as it is normally used, but rather the way in which subjects cope with *unusual* uses of linguistic contrasts (Karmiloff-Smith, in press b). This is of course part of the subjects' competence, and it is important to ascertain this fact, but it would be unwise to draw conclusions about child language acquisition solely from this type of data.

Another problem every investigator has to face is that of the child's attitude to the experimental setting. Often one finds that the first few responses to a task seem 'spontaneous', and then there is a subtle change. It is as if the child started to seek to understand what the *experimenter* is trying to analyse. Older children rapidly adopt a sort of 'meta-experimental' attitude, in an endeavour to discover the regularities in task items and so forth. This fact can get completely lost when data are merely quantified.

How does one, in a production task, keep the child's responses 'spontaneous', narrow down his responses to those relating to the area of study and yet leave the setting and functions as close to normal use as possible? Is the Piagetian exploratory method the answer to the problem? In part, yes. However, we are faced with the real danger of the fact that what Piagetians have always called 'vérification sur le vif' is extremely tricky in the field of psycholinguistics: we are using language to study language. Thus we are faced with the choice between standardizing the items in advance and having the same, but rigid experimental setting for all subjects, or taking a more exploratory approach and running the risk of collecting rich, but incomparable intersubject data. There is no doubt that the hypotheses of even the most able of clinical investigators influence to some extent the subjects' responses. Thus, neither approach alone is in my view satisfactory.

I should like to give a brief example of what happens when a 'Genevan' sets up a standardized experiment. In experiment 2, for example, I made a particularly careful plan of objects, situation types, order of presentation and manipulation of parameters I wished to study. When running the experiment, however, I was constantly faced with a dilemma. I would hear a child's response (together with false starts, hesitations and other meaningful clues), form a hypothesis about the reason for that response, and yet know that this hypothesis was the parameter manipulated in, say, item 14 later in the order. However, I would feel very strongly that the hypothesis should be tested immediately, i.e. that information gathered would not have the same value if tested when hypothesized, as when tested randomly during the experiment. Any experienced clinical investigator feels strongly that Piaget was essentially correct in his view that the experimenter should guide the child whilst simultaneously being guided by the child (see Inhelder *et al.* 1974, pp. 18–24, for concise description of the method of critical exploration). These authors reaffirm that 'the fundamental feature of the critical exploration method requires that the experimenter constantly formulate hypotheses about the children's reactions from the cognitive point of view, and then devise ways of immediately checking these suppositions in the experimental situation'. However, the dangers of influencing the child do not lie merely in the experimenter's approach but can also be revealed in what observers 'hear' or 'see'. (I have informally confirmed this by telling two recorders opposite hypotheses about what I was seeking, and then having them take a protocol of the same child.) Perhaps the use of the audio-videotape can partially overcome these problems though it raises others (see Blanchet 1977, for comparitive discussion of various methods). It is clear that one can neither experiment nor record behaviour without explicit or implicit hypotheses. The 'clean', statistically valid experiment can leave one just as uneasy about having tapped real psychological processes as the supple, 'empathetic' Geneva approach. As will be seen, I have endeavoured to combine some aspects of both, but have had to face all the problems discussed in this section.

The experimental dilemma – not only in psycholinguistics – is by no means a settled issue.

Experimental approach

Despite many presumptions on the subject, it is still not clear whether comprehension simply precedes production, production simply precedes comprehension, or whether there is an intricate interplay between the two. Nor is it yet clear, in my view, whether the two involve analogous acquisition and processing procedures, although it is often implicitly taken for granted that they do.

Many authors have assumed that comprehension does precede production. The weaker version of the assumption is that comprehension initially precedes the onset of any verbal productions (e.g. Lenneberg 1967). The stronger version is that comprehension precedes production on a feature by feature basis (Fraser *et al.* 1963; McNeill 1966). Both versions have been seriously challenged, particularly in a rich study by Benedict (1978) on the subtle aspects of the *nature* of comprehension and production in 9 to 15 month old infants, and in Halliday's (1975) functional analysis of one infant's production system.

It is also commonly assumed that comprehension is in some sense easier and more passive than production, because of the presumed smaller number of potential choices in comprehension. Minsky, however, has convincingly argued that although this is a tempting hypothesis, just the contrary may actually hold true. After discussing what he calls the 'folk phenomenology' about active and passive processes in vision, he carries the argument over to language:

> In language, a similar contrast is tempting: In listening (which includes parsing) one has little choice because of the need to resolve the objective word string into a structure consistent with grammar, context, and the (assumed) intention. In speaking, we have much more choice, because there are so many ways to assemble sentence-making frames for our chosen purpose, be it to inform, convince, or mislead. However, these are dangerous oversimplifications; things are often quite the other way around! Speaking is often a straightforward encoding from a semantic structure into a word sequence, whilst listening often involves extensive and difficult constructions – which involve the totality of complexities we call understanding. (1975, p. 238)

Nonetheless, Levelt has pointed out that one of the reasons why Yngve's depth hypothesis is only relevant to speaker procedures is that 'the hearer often need not perform any syntactic analysis in order to understand the sentence, whereas the speaker must cast the sentence in the proper syntactic form' (1974, p. 81). Both Schank (1972) and Charniak (1972) have also argued that much of comprehension of discourse is not based on explicit syntactic or semantic information in the text, but stems from extralinguistic world knowledge. Comprehension involves complex anticipatory and implicatory processes and not simple decoding of words.

Many psycholinguistic researchers tend to think that comprehension tasks are easier to design than production tasks, due to the fact that in production one cannot be sure of narrowing the subject's utterances to those structures or morphemes one wishes to study. As pointed out, this 'narrowing' device may be misleading because it may not give us access to the subject's real procedures compared to when the number of choices is wider. Some of the difficulties in devising production experiments may be due to the fact that investigators have opted for studying syntactic competence rather than functional usage, as discussed earlier.

Production/comprehension clearly is by no means a settled issue theoretically or experimentally. One point seems essential in psycholinguistics. In any endeavour to analyse children's acquisition of a given category, be it syntactic, semantic or functional, and at any given age of acquisition, we should look into *both* production and comprehension. Looking at only one side of the coin could lead to extrapolations which are only narrowly valid.

The decision to carry out both production and comprehension experiments does not *ipso facto* overcome the 'experimental dilemma'. Of course, many of the problems raised in that discussion apply to my own experiments. For both production and comprehension tasks, it obviously feels 'safer' to standardize items and run them identically for all subjects. However, having used the Piagetian exploratory method for a number of years, one is overwhelmed by the intuition that strict standardization misses out on just those aspects of child behaviour one wishes to study. The dangers of the purely exploratory approach loom high too. My approach has been a compromise between the two, in that I have devised a series of semistandardized items (which did not exclude repetition where necessary, etc.), followed by a clinical exploration. However, as with all compromises, rather than the problems of both approaches being overcome, the number of problems may be doubled! In an endeavour to compensate for this, I have preferred to take a very large number of experiments focussing on different aspects of the plurifunctionality of determiners, thus avoiding the danger of drawing general conclusions from one or two uses only. A wide age span has also been covered. Stress has been placed as far as possible on the different functions involved in normal language usage when making the experimental designs. Some production and comprehension experiments were purposely 'afunctional' (i.e. based on contrasts expressed differently in normal language use) in order to demonstrate the differences in results.

All of the experiments contain a quantified analysis in the form of percentage comparisons, followed by a more qualitative approach. The comparison of percentages has been made to indicate trends and to show that the qualitative analysis is indeed confirmed by the quantitative trend. Though the percentages are not of course intended as firm statements about the *age* at which a given function becomes operative, they are not misleading in view of the fact that the number of responses on which percentages are calculated is high. My aim has been to pinpoint the problems that are involved for children in coping with the plurifunctionality of determiners, and plurifunctional surface markers in general, as well as to bring forth the procedures children use in the face of potential indeterminacy of reference. Furthermore, the type of experimental approach where the exploratory method was used, together with a series of semistandardized items, where the quality of the information gathered was stressed more than the equivalence of quantities, makes a statistical analysis of much of the data extremely arduous and often impossible. Since my approach has not been 'strictly experimental', it seems inappropriate to make a 'strictly experimental' analysis of the results. In some previous studies, small subjects often refuse to respond to certain items. Investigators use in their analysis of such non-responses the average score of the other children in the same age group which makes possible strict numerical comparisons and statistical analyses. Such an approach may be open to as much criticism as a 'non-statistical' approach. My data and my analysis thereof are offered as illustrations of the *general trends* of the child's acquisition of the plurifunctionality of determiners.

All of the experimentation was carried out in French, by individual interview, with monolingual children from French and Swiss families living in two residential suburbs of Geneva. A total of 1,012 protocols were taken, from subjects between the ages of 2,10 and 11,7 years. Some case study data were also collected from two children of 2,0 and 2,3 years. Some of the experiments used subjects that had previously been interviewed in my other experiments, in order to gather some intrasubject data. An intrasubject analysis will not, however, be attempted here. Several subjects were also seen in two non-linguistic tasks involving problem-solving procedures (Karmiloff-Smith & Inhelder, 1974/5). The latter are not of course reported on here, but are mentioned in passing because their results bore witness to the representability of children within age groups, with respect to both linguistic and non-linguistic tasks.

At the end of each experiment, the child was questioned about his awareness of the rules that he had been using implicitly in his spontaneous responses. A distinction has been made between 'metalinguistic' data (e.g. 'What is a word?', 'Is "the" a word?', 'How many words are in this sentence?', 'Is it funny to say X?', etc.) and what may be termed 'epilinguistic' data (e.g. tapping the child's awareness of the implicit grammatical rules he is using, such as gender concord, use of one article in preference to the other, anaphoric reference, etc.). Whilst there is obviously some overlapping between metalinguistic and epilinguistic approaches, the distinction is felt to be heuristically valid in that it may cover different cognitive demands on the child.

In describing experimental items and children's utterances, I shall give the original French and add an English gloss. It should be noted that children's utterances were not always entirely grammatical but corresponded to colloquial French (e.g. 'Y en a pas' instead of 'Il n'y en a pas'). In each case the French utterance is given in the child's form, whereas the gloss is provided in grammatical English.

Whilst it will be seen that some experiments are obviously broader in scope than others and are thus given a more detailed analysis, all of the experiments reported on in the following chapters were designed to answer questions about one or other of the plurifunctional aspects of determiners.

4 *Production experiments: deictic, exophoric and quantifier functions of determiners*

Singular and plural definite articles as well as indefinite articles, possessive adjectives, common colour and size adjectives are known to appear very early spontaneously (Guillaume 1927; Brown 1973). However, what their actual function is when they appear in these early corpora remains to be clearly determined, and it is to this problem that the first four experiments were addressed.

Experiment 1: the playrooms

This experiment concerns the exophoric and deictic functions of determiners as well as the question of 'overdetermination'. When children add redundant modifiers or use possessive adjectives, for instance, are they overdetermining or are they in fact using the expression in its descriptor function rather than its determinor function?

Experimental context. Fig 1 illustrates the layout of the experiment. A girl-doll and a boy-doll (clearly differentiated) were each given a playroom. For half the subjects the girl's playroom was on the left; for the other half it was on the right. The child was told that the little girl and the little boy would receive some toys in their playrooms. The girl-doll was given:

one X	or	three X
three Y		one Y
one Z		one Z

The boy-doll was given:

three X	or	one X
one Y		three Y
one W		one W

Fig. 1. Layout for experiments 1 and 12

The Xs could be distinguished by colours. The Ys were all identical and therefore mention of colour was redundant information. Z and W were singletons. The following gives an example of a situation:

girl-doll	*boy-doll*
one blue book	three books (one green, one red, one yellow)
three multicoloured balls	one multicoloured ball
one baby-bottle	one car

In the vast majority of cases, the objects chosen were those whose names take feminine gender in French. For protocolling, it is much easier to distinguish between the vowels in 'une/la' as compared to 'un/le'.

The playrooms were at a distance from the child so that he could not reach the objects: pointing or demonstrative pronouns would therefore be indeterminate.

Experimental procedure. The child was told that he had no toys himself and that he must therefore pretend to go into the girl-doll's playroom or the boy-doll's playroom and ask the doll to lend him a toy. Some practice items were carried out with Z and W type toys. The experimenter told the child: 'Demande à la petite fille de te prêter ça' [Ask the girl-doll to lend you that], and the experimenter touched a toy within the girl-doll's playroom; similarly with the boy-doll. Children using demonstrative pronouns or pointing were told twice that the doll did not know what they wanted to borrow. If after being told twice the child continued to use demonstratives or to point, then this was noted as part of the protocol proper. In all cases the experimenter avoided saying 'Quelle voiture?' [Which car?] or 'Laquelle' [Which one] and used the more neutral 'Quoi' [What]. The experimental items were as follows:

Context	*E.'s utterance and action*	*Child's expected response*
Type 1		
Reference to singleton	Demande au garçon/à la petite fille de te prêter ça [Ask the boy/girl to lend you that (E. touches boy's only Y or girl's only X)]	Prête-moi *la/ta* Y (X) [Lend me *the/your* Y (X)]
Type 2		
Reference to one of several different coloured	Demande au garçon/à la fille de te prêter ça [Ask the boy/girl to lend you that (E. touches the boy's/girl's coloured X)]	Prête-moi *la/ta* X (*bleue/verte*) [Lend me *the/your* (*blue/green*) X]
Type 3		
Reference to one of several identical	Demande au garçon/à la fille de te prêter ça [Ask the boy/girl to lend you that (E. touches one of the boy's/girl's identical Ys)]	Prête-moi *une/une des/une de tes Y* [Lend me *a/one of the/one of* your Ys]

Each child received at least two examples of each item type. Depending on the consistency of their responses, some children received more than six trials. The objects were renewed after every pair of trials.

Population. Forty-seven children between the ages of 3,0 and 9,11 years participated in the experiment:

Age	*Subjects*	*Average age*
3,0–3,11	7	3,7
4,0–4,11	8	4,5
5,0–5,11	8	5,6
6,0–6,11	6	6,5
7,0–7,11	6	7,4
8,0–8,11	7	8,5
9,0–9,11	5	9,5

Two 3 years olds refused to give any verbal response and left their seats each time to pick up the object the experimenter had touched. Their results were therefore not included in the analysis.

Results. Table 1 gives a breakdown per age group of the types of referring expressions used by children according to item type. Under 'demonstratives' both demonstrative adjectives and pronouns have been grouped together in view of the fact that apart from the 3 year olds, this type of deictic referring expression hardly ever appeared. The definite article and the possessive adjective are grouped under 'definite referring expressions'. The purpose of this experiment was not to distinguish between the possessive in its descriptor function and in its determinor function (as will be the case in experiment 3). It should be recalled that, unlike English, gender of the possessive adjective in French tallies with the gender of the noun and not with the sex of the person to whom the object belongs. 'Definite referring expressions plus modifier' covers again both the definite article and the possessive to which is added a colour adjective or a localizer (e.g. 'The book on the right hand side', 'The blue book'). 'Indefinite referring expressions' covers the use of the indefinite article and, in a few rare cases for older children, use of the indefinite article plus partitive (i.e. 'une des X' [one of the Xs]). The final line for each age group in the table covers the indefinite article to which is added a modifier. In the vertical columns, I have separated item types. Under 'Singleton' are included those situations where the object was the only one of its kind present in a given room. The most appropriate answer here would be a definite referring expression, although an indefinite referring expression would not be incorrect. Addition of a modifier is redundant information. The following column, 'One of several different-coloured objects', covers situations where the playroom contained several similar but different-coloured toys. The definite referring expression alone would be incorrect here; either the definite referring expression plus appropriate modifier or an indefinite referring expression would be correct, the former being the more appropriate response. In the last vertical column, 'One of several identical objects', the appropriate response would be an indefinite referring expression. Addition of a modifier would be redundant, and all definite referring expressions incorrect. In all cases, demonstratives are indeterminate.

The use of bold type in the table indicates in each case the most appropriate response. As will be seen in the discussion, it is important to note not only the percentage figure for the most appropriate response, but above all whether this is a discriminating response, e.g., whether there is a difference between the use of the definite article, say, when it is obligatory as compared to when it is incorrect. Figures have been translated into percentages for comparison purposes because of the different number of total trials per age group. In view of the latter and because order of presentation was not identical for all subjects, these figures are intended to show overall trends and will not, of course, be subjected to statistical analyses.

TABLE 1. *Type of referring expressions used expressed as a percentage of total trials per item type*

Age group	Type of referring expression (RE) (%)	Singleton (%)	One of several different-coloured objects (%)	One of several identical objects (%)
3,0–3,11	of demonstratives	38	41	49
Total number of	of definite RE	**46**	45	39
trials = 51	of definite RE + modifier	16	**13**	9
	of indefinite RE	0	1	**3**
	of indefinite RE + modifier	0	0	0
4,0–4,11	of demonstratives	8	10	12
Total number of	of definite RE	**81**	61	63
trials = 72	of definite RE + modifier	11	**10**	11
	of indefinite RE	0	19	**14**
	of indefinite RE + modifier	0	0	0
5,0–5,11	of demonstratives	8	10	9
Total number of	of definite RE	**72**	38	17
trials = 67	of definite RE + modifier	12	**36**	17
	of indefinite RE	8	13	**49**
	of indefinite RE + modifier	0	3	8

Age group	Type of referring expression (RE) (%)	Singleton (%)	One of several different-coloured objects (%)	One of several identical objects (%)
6,0–6,11	of demonstratives	0	18	0
Total number of	of definite RE	**84**	37	41
trials = 45	of definite RE + modifier	8	**33**	15
	of indefinite RE	8	12	**44**
	of indefinite RE + modifier	0	0	0
7,0–7,11	of demonstratives	0	15	18
Total number of	of definite RE	**75**	32	45
trials = 49	of definite RE + modifier	6	**37**	9
	of indefinite RE	19	16	**19**
	of indefinite RE + modifier	0	0	9
8,0–8,11	of demonstratives	0	0	9
Total number of	of definite RE	**72**	16	9
trials = 68	of definite RE + modifier	16	**52**	0
	of indefinite RE	12	24	**82**
	of indefinite RE + modifier	0	8	0
9,0–9,11	of demonstratives	0	0	0
Total number of	of definite RE	**100**	0	0
trials = 34	of definite RE + modifier	0	**57**	0
	of indefinite RE	0	43	**100**
	of indefinite RE + modifier	0	0	0

The results of this small experiment seem clear from table 1. Let us first look at the 3 year olds' responses. It is only amongst these small children that the use of demonstratives is high. Whilst 3 year olds use definite referring expressions for singletons in 46% of their trials, this is clearly not a discriminating response since the definite referring expressions are incorrectly used to refer both to one of several different coloured objects (45% of the trials) and one of several identical objects (39% of trials). Indefinite referring responses are very low. Figures for the addition of modifiers are low; they are clearly not being used in their determinor function.

Whilst there is a clear-cut increase (81%) as of 4 years for the definite referring expressions for singletons, due to the quasi-disappearance of demonstratives, it should be noted that there is also a marked increase in definite referring expressions for the other two context types (61% and 63%) where such use is inappropriate. Thus the definite article is still not a discriminating response. Addition of modifiers is still not determinitive in function, as can be seen from the similar figures in the three columns. The increase in indefinite referring expressions is, however, slightly discriminating (19% and 14%), in that there are no indefinites used for singletons.

From 5 years and systematically from 8, the definite referring response becomes separated from the others. Although the erroneous use remains fairly high, there is at all ages from 5 years and above a marked difference between correct use of definite referring expression (ranging from 72% to 100%) as compared to inappropriate use for the other two contexts (ranging from 45% to 0%). The addition of modifiers, whilst remaining fairly low where it is essential between the ages of 5 and 8 years, is nonetheless a discriminating response in that figures for the centre column are markedly higher than those in the other two contexts where the modifier is redundant. It is not until 8 years that indefinite referring expressions reach over 50% where they are essential in contexts with identical objects. The few demonstratives occurring for older children were different from those of 3 year olds. The small children would merely say 'Lend me that duck' and at best point at the same time, whereas older children got up and touched the object whilst saying 'That X', aware that a demonstrative alone did not determine adequately.

The epilinguistic data for this type of experiment were collected in comprehension experiment 12 (see p. 170 below). Two older children did, however, provide interesting comments during the present production task:

9,10 years
Elle, elle a plusieurs voitures, donc il faut dire prête-moi la voiture *rouge*. Lui, il en a qu'une, alors on peut dire prête-moi *la* voiture
[She has several cars so you have to say lend me the *red* car. He's only got one so you can say lend me *the* car (stressed)]
9,8 years
Si je savais pas combien de montes elle a, elle, alors je dirais donne-moi une montre. Mais j'avais vu qu'elle en avait qu'une seule, alors je peux lui dire donne-moi *ta* montre
[If I didn't know how many watches she has, then I'd say give me a watch. But I saw she only has one, so I can say to her give me *your* watch (stressed)]

With respect to the indefinite referring expressions, the vast majority of responses cover the indefinite article. Only in a very small number of responses did the child use the more appropriate partitive 'one of the', as can be seen from table 2. This table also shows that when it was used, the partitive was preferred for the context with identical objects, the definite article plus modifier being more appropriate for the other context. As will be seen in some of the other experiments, the appropriate use of 'one of the', which marks both non-particularity and the class extension, as contrasted to 'a' which only marks the former, rarely appears and then usually only from 8 to 9 years of age. This raises a question regarding the function of the indefinite article for under 8 year olds, which will be discussed in the synthesis.

TABLE 2. *Use of the partitive 'one of the Xs'*

Age group (years)	Context: One of the different-coloured Xs (%)	Context: One of the identical Xs (%)
3	0	0
4	0	0
5	0	0
6	0	15
7	0	10
8	0	9
9	14	27

The overall results of this experiment show that 3 year olds mainly used demonstratives or definite referring expressions in a situation which called for distinctive use of indefinite and definite exophoric reference. It should be recalled that in this experiment, there was no need to take into account the listener's knowledge. Whilst 4 year olds did not make use of the demonstrative (which is always potentially indeterminate), they still used predominantly definite referring expressions, even in contexts which necessarily called for indefinite reference. It is around 6 years of age that the singular definite article marks exophoric reference successfully and is no longer purely deictic in nature. It was not until 9 years in this experiment that children could explain the determinor function of modifiers in the epilinguistic part of the session.

Why is it not until 6 years, and consistently only at 8 years, that children use discriminatingly definite referential expressions for singletons and indefinite referential expressions for one of several identical objects, in this situation? It is suggested that whilst the use of the demonstrative as such disappears from 4 years, the use of definite referential expression is in fact *deictic*. Like the demonstrative, the definite article *points to* an object under focus of attention and is not yet an exophoric reference to the singleton characteristic of the referent in relation to its current context. Small children often actually pointed when uttering the definite article. This was even clearer in experiment 2 when under 6 year olds pointed a finger when using the definite article, which they never did when using the indefinite article. This is a clue to the deictic nature of early definite reference.

The fact that the experimenter *touched* the object may have sparked off the large quantity of inappropriate definite referring expressions, since both speaker and hearer shared the same information about the referent. However, it will be seen from the results of other experiments that they also showed a large amount of early deictic reference. The fact that in the present experiment over 8 year olds could use the indefinite article where appropriate, even when the experimenter had touched the object and no possible ambiguity existed, indicates that the older child relies less on the addition of extralinguistic and paralinguistic support for identifying referents.

Experiment 2: hide and seek

This experiment was designed to analyse the use of the singular definite and indefinite articles and the redundant versus obligatory use of adjectives. It contrasts with the playroom experiment in that use of the possessive was removed, and that the object to which the child must refer was not visible. As mentioned, the fact that the experimenter actually touched the object in the previous experiment could have provoked a definite referring expression on the part of small children in cases where objects were identical or similar, in view of the fact that both the child and the experimenter (and the doll) knew which of the several objects was concerned. As will be seen, this possibility was eliminated from experiment 2.

Experimental context. Sixteen opaque bags contained groups of four objects. Four of the bags contained four totally different objects (e.g. doll, book, brush, cup). Four other bags contained two different objects and two totally identical objects (e.g. watch, pencil, two identical blue cars). Four bags contained two different objects and two similar objects of different colours (e.g. cow, plate, one blue fish, one yellow fish). The vast majority of the objects chosen were, for the same reasons as in experiment 1, those whose names take feminine gender.

Experimental procedure. The child was shown the contents of one of the opaque bags containing four objects (three objects for very small children to avoid memory problems), and was asked to look at the objects very carefully. The experimenter then asked the child to close his eyes or turn his back while she removed an object from the bag. Then the child was asked: 'Qu'est-ce que j'ai fait?' [What did I do?] or 'Qu'est-ce que j'ai caché?' [What did I hide?], depending on the item.

Four variables were introduced as follows:

(a) whether or not the child named the objects aloud before hiding took place;
(b) whether it was the child or the experimenter who did the hiding (in the latter case the experimenter pretended not to remember and asked the child what he had done);
(c) whether, as mentioned above, the experimenter asked: 'What did I hide?' involving a simple NP response, or 'What did I do?' involving a response including also a verb;
(d) the groupings of objects as explained under experimental context.

Sixteen items were presented: for the first eight items the child did not name the objects before hiding took place; for the second series, the experimenter asked the child 'Qu'est-ce qu'il y a dans le sac?' [What is in the bag?] and the child named the objects before each hiding. The majority of the 3 and 4 year olds were only presented with the second series of eight items due to concentration problems. Many items were repeated, but in such cases reserve opaque bags were used with collections of new objects.

Test items were as follows:

	Expected response
1. No naming, E. hides 1 of 4 different objects. Do?	Tu as caché *la* X [You hid *the* X]
2. No naming, E. hides 1 of 4 different objects. Hide?	*Une* X [An X]

	Expected response
3. No naming, S. hides 1 of 4 different objects. Do?	J'ai caché *la* X [I hid *the* X]
4. No naming, S. hides 1 of 4 different objects. Hide?	*Une* X [*An* X]
5. No naming, E. hides 1 of 2 identical objects. Do?	Tu as caché *une* X [You hid *an* X]
6. No naming, S. hides 1 of 2 identical objects. Do?	J'ai caché *une* X [I hid *an* X]
7. No naming, E. hides 1 of 2 similar objects. Do?	Tu as caché *la* X (*bleue*) [You hid *the* (*blue*) X]
8. No naming, S. hides 1 of 2 similar objects. Do?	J'ai caché *la* X (*verte*) [I hid *the* (*green*) X]

Order of presentation for all subjects for the first series was: 1, 2, 6, 5, 7, 8, 4, 3.

9. Named first, E. hides 1 of 4 different objects. Do?	Tu as caché *la* X [You hid *the* X]
10. Named first, E. hides 1 of 4 different objects. Hide?	*La* X [*The* X]
11. Named first, S. hides 1 of 4 different objects. Do?	J'ai caché *la* X [I hid *the* X]
12. Named first, S. hides 1 of 4 different objects. Hide?	*La* X [*The* X]
13. Named first, E. hides 1 of 2 identical objects. Do?	Tu as caché *une* X [You hid *an* X]
14. Named first, S. hides 1 of 2 identical objects. Do?	J'ai caché *une* X [I hid *an* X]
15. Named first, E. hides 1 of 2 similar objects. Do?	Tu as caché *la* X (*rouge*) [You hid *the* (*red*) X]
16. Named first, S. hides 1 of 2 similar objects. Do?	J'ai caché *la* X (*jaune*) [I hid *the* (*yellow*) X]

Order of presentation for all subjects for the second series was: 10, 9, 16, 15, 13, 14, 11, 12.

Population. Sixty-five children between the ages of 3,3 and 11,7 were interviewed, as follows:

Age	*Subjects*	*Average age*
3,3–3,11	4	3,6
4,0–4,11	12	4,6
5,0–5,11	6	5,6
6,0–6,11	8	6,7
7,0–7,11	11	7,6
8,0–8,11	6	8,6
9,0–9,11	9	9,5
10,0–11,7	9	10,8

Results. Table 3 shows the number of naming trials, i.e. responses to the experimenter's question 'What's in the bag?' before each of the test items 9–16 was administered. It also contains any spontaneous naming on the part of the child during items 1 to 8.

The results show clearly that use of the indefinite article for naming, i.e. in its 'nominative function', is no problem at any age. The definite article is practically never used in such circumstances. A very few responses are to be found with no article (some 20% up to 5 years only). The slightly lower figures for zero article at 3 years may of course be due to the unfortunately small number of subjects in that age group. The results show that the nominative function of the indefinite article is fully acquired very early.

TABLE 3. *Naming task, expressed as a percentage of total naming trials per age group*

Age group	Total number of naming trials	Indefinite article (%)	Definite article (%)	Zero article (%)
3,4–3,11	43	93	0	7
4,0–4,11	245	82	1	17
5,0–5,11	151	80	0	20
6,0–6,11	195	100	0	0
7,0–7,11	279	99	0	1
8,0–8,11	114	100	0	0
9,0–9,11	190	97	3	0
10,0–11,7	166	98	0	2

Table 4 gives full details of the types of referring expressions used for items 1–16 according to the different contexts. Only responses to task items were counted, and not any responses to the experimenter's question 'Which X?', etc. Tables 5, 6 and 7 break down the results of table 4 according to the variables manipulated. For the context 'singletons', the appropriate response would seem to be the definite article, and the results indeed show this to be the case. Contrary to the results of experiment 1, it can be seen from table 5 that in this experiment the definite article becomes very early (from 4 years) a discriminating response, e.g. 72% for singletons as against only 24% and 15% for the other two contexts. Although the percentage of definite articles drops between 7 and 8 years, it is nonetheless at all ages a discriminating response. By discriminating response, I mean that a given determiner is used when relevant and the same one is used far less frequently when not relevant.

TABLE 4. *Referring expressions used for items 1–16, expressed as a percentage of total trials per age group*

		Singletons					Similar but different coloured objects					Identical objects				
Age group	Total number of trials	Indefinite article (%)	Definite article (%)	Indefinite + superfluous modifier (%)	Definite + superfluous modifier (%)	Ø (%)	Indefinite article (%)	Definite article (%)	Indefinite + relevant modifier (%)	Definite + relevant modifier (%)	Ø (%)	Indefinite article (%)	Definite article (%)	Indefinite + superfluous modifier (%)	Definite + superfluous modifier (%)	Definite article + relevant modifier (%)
3,4–3,11	108	32	56	0	10	2	22	45	18	11	4	46	50	0	0	4
4,0–4,11	249	24	72	1	2	1	53	24	4	18	1	59	15	2	15	9
5,0–5,11	132	16	70	0	14	0	9	35	6	50	0	14	39	4	18	25
6,0–6,11	199	22	70	3	5	0	20	7	20	53	0	48	12	21	0	19
7,0–7,11	296	36	49	5	10	0	25	10	25	40	0	52	9	26	9	4
8,0–8,11	134	38	49	6	7	0	32	4	28	36	0	71	14	4	0	11
9,0–9,11	223	6	77	3	14	0	2	0	12	86	0	53	11	18	2	16
10,0–11,7	206	15	70	2	13	0	11	0	14	75	0	69	1	14	0	16

TABLE 5. *Differential use of definite article expressed as a percentage of total trials per item type*

Age group	Definite article *correct* (% of total trials for singletons)	Definite article alone incorrect (% of total trials for similar but different-coloured objects)	Definite article incorrect (% of total trials for identical objects)
3,4–3,11	56	45	50
4,0–4,11	72	24	15
5,0–5,11	70	35	39
6,0–6,11	70	7	12
7,0–7,11	49	10	9
8,0–8,11	49	4	14
9,0–9,11	77	0	11
10,0–11,7	70	0	1

TABLE 6. *Differential use of indefinite article expressed as a percentage of total trials per item type*

Age group	Indefinite not incorrect (% of total trials for singletons)	Indefinite not incorrect (% of total trials for similar but different-coloured objects	Indefinite *essential* (% of total trials for identical objects (figure in brackets includes 'another X' 'the other X'))
3,4–3,11	32	22	46 (50)
4,0–4,11	24	53	59 (68)
5,0–5,11	16	9	14 (39)
6,0–6,11	22	20	48 (67)
7,0–7,11	36	25	52 (56)
8,0–8,11	38	32	71 (82)
9,0–9,11	6	2	53 (69)
10,0–11,7	15	11	69 (85)

What is striking is the large number of indefinite articles used at all ages, as compared to the previous experiment. Whilst the indefinite article is not incorrect for any context, it is essential when referring to one of the identical objects. It is only for 5 year olds that it does not seem to be a discriminating response. The 5 year olds' low figure for using the indefinite article in the identical context is surprising compared to all other age groups. This may be due to the 5 year olds' tendency to use the indefinite article in its numeral function (see below p. 170). Apart from 5 year olds, the use of the indefinite article increases with age, particularly if one also takes into account the two other possible procedures for that context, i.e. 'another X' or 'the other X'. It is from

9 years that the indefinite article clearly becomes reserved for the identical context, due of course to the appropriate responses to the other two contexts. Only from 9 did children use the indefinite partitive 'one of the Xs'.

Table 7 gives details of the use of modifiers. In certain contexts they are superfluous, i.e. in the case of identical objects or singletons. For the context containing similar but different-coloured objects, the modifier acts as a determiner. As the table shows, whilst 3 year olds only add modifiers in 29% of their responses for similar contexts, this is nonetheless a discriminating response since they never add modifiers for the identical context. As of 5 years, the addition of modifiers increases and is clearly a discriminating response. In other words, these children use the modifier in its determinor function.

TABLE 7. *Differential use of modifiers (descriptor or determinor) expressed as a percentage of total trials per item type*

	Descriptor		*Determinor*
Age group	Addition of modifier superfluous (% for singletons)	Addition of modifier superfluous (% for identical objects)	Addition of modifier essential (% for similar but different-coloured objects)
3,4–3,11	10	0	29
4,0–4,11	3	17	22
5,0–5,11	14	22	56
6,0–6,11	8	21	73
7,0–7,11	15	35	65
8,0–8,11	13	4	64
9,0–9,11	17	20	98
10,0–11,7	15	14	89

Finally, table 8 shows the effect of either the child or the experimenter performing the action. Figures have been calculated only for the context with singletons in view of the fact that only in this context are both the definite and indefinite article (without modifiers) correct. It is of course not the absolute percentages that are important in this table but the differences between the two columns 'Child hides' and 'Experimenter hides'. My hypothesis was that if the object was in the child's hand, he would be more likely to *name* it, i.e. give the indefinite article, whereas if the experimenter did the hiding, the child would furnish a definite referring expression because he would relate it to the other objects in the bag in his search for the one which was missing. Whilst the differences are not striking in table 8, the hypothesis is to some extent borne out. At all ages, when the experimenter did the hiding the children's responses were predominantly definite, ranging from 67% to 97%, whereas when the child did the hiding definite article responses ranged from 47% to 67% up to 6 years, dropped to 44% and 28% between 7 and 8 years, and only after 9 seemed to be similar to the situation when the experimenter did the hiding. If nothing else, this table illustrates how many factors may interact in article usage, and why a large number of different experimental contexts and techniques are necessary. In general the differences between the results of experiments 1 and 2 are not to be overlooked.

TABLE 8. *Differential use of definite and indefinite articles as a function of experimenter performs action versus child performs action (as percentage of total trials for singleton only)*

		Child hides		*Experimenter hides*	
Age group	Total number of trials for singletons	(%) of definite article	(%) of indefinite article	(%) of definite article	(%) of indefinite article
3,4–3,11	65	47	53	74	26
4,0–4,11	130	67	33	78	22
5,0–5,11	50	53	47	97	3
6,0–6,11	117	57	43	86	14
7,0–7,11	194	44	56	70	30
8,0–8,11	78	28	72	67	33
9,0–9,11	139	81	19	96	4
10,0–11,7	112	62	38	93	7

It should be pointed out that the variable 'no prior naming/prior naming', i.e. items 1–8 as compared to 9–16, could not be calculated in view of the fact that many subjects spontaneously named the objects as they were taken from the bags during the first eight items. As will be seen, it was to overcome this problem that experiment 3 was designed.

The difference between asking 'What did I do?' and 'What did I hide?' was also difficult to calculate because many children when asked 'What did I hide?' picked up the latter part of the experimenter's utterance and responded 'You hid. . .', rather than furnishing a mere NP as I had hoped. However, for those subjects who did respond just with article plus noun for 'hide?', and verb plus article plus noun for 'do?', differences in article usage could be noted. For 'What did I do?' the children tended to furnish definite referring expressions, whereas for 'What did I hide?' they tended to give the name of the object, i.e. an indefinite article plus noun.

Taking a more qualitative look at the results, one finds first, with regard to the addition of modifiers, no child forgot the colour of the hidden object. When in the exploratory part of the session the child furnished a definite article without modifier, in the context where the modifier was essential referential information, it was not due, not to the child having forgotten that there were two objects of different colour, but to his not understanding that the modifier can function as a determiner. The exploratory part of the session also led me not to count the word 'petit' [small] as a modifier in the same sense that colours were counted, because it seemed clear that 'petit' referred to extra world knowledge outside the experimental setting. The elephant was always referred to as 'petit éléphant' (for obvious reasons), as was a little doll's shoe. Pencils, etc., were never referred to as 'petit' although some were small compared to others in the experimental setting. It is interesting to note in passing that when naming a singleton, one 4 year old said 'Un des souliers' [One of the shoes], i.e. referring to extra world knowledge that shoes come in pairs; in the context there was only one shoe, and this should therefore have been referred to as 'un soulier' or 'le soulier'.

One very interesting pattern occurred in the use of the demonstrative and definite article amongst the youngest subjects. There were actually only two demonstratives used, for one 4 year old and one 5 year old, so these were not plotted on the tables. In both cases they concerned the hiding of one of two identical objects and the child responded 'You hid that' and pointed to the other one present although clearly meaning the one which had been removed. One other 4 year old for a singleton said 'You hid that one' and pointed to the empty space where it had been. Pointing was also used by children making definite reference. Several of the youngest children said 'You hid the X' and pointed when uttering 'the', showing clearly that for them it was a sort of demonstrative, i.e. that they were making deictic reference. This they never did when using the indefinite article. As discussed in chapter 2, in many languages the definite article can be traced back historically to the demonstrative.

Some of the children's spontaneous corrections and intonations, as well as responses to the epilinguistic part at the end of the session, are interesting clues to article usage, as can be seen from the following set of examples:

Singleton context

4,6 years
Tu as caché le camion
[You hid the lorry (points at same time as uttering the definite article)]
4,10 years
Tu as caché le camion ↗ . . . le camion ↘
[You hid the lorry (rising intonation) . . . the lorry (falling intonation) (clearly the child decided the modifier 'bleu', which is postposed in French, was unnecessary)]
6,9 years
Tu as caché le petit ours ou une autre chose bleue
[You hid the little bear or another blue thing]
6,9 years
Tu as pris le . . . un animal
[You took the . . . an animal]
6,10 years
Tu as pris la chaussure ↗ . . . j'allais dire la chaussure rouge mais y en a pas deux de chaussures
[You took the shoe (rising intonation) . . . I was going to say the red shoe but there aren't two shoes]
8,1 years
C.: Un porte . . . le porte-monnaie
E.: Pourquoi changer?
C.: Parce que si y en avait plusieurs on dirait *un* porte-monnaie
[C.: A pur . . . the purse
E.: Why change?
C.: Because if there were several of them, you'd say *a* purse (stressed)]
9,0 years
. . . pris un chameau, le chameau qui était dans le sac.
[. . . took a camel, the camel which was in the bag]
. . . pris un chien . . . le Dalmatien
[. . . took a dog . . . the Dalmatian]
9,2 years
C.: J'ai ôté une poupée . . . la poupée
E.: Pourquoi changer?
C.: *La* poupée parce qu'il y en a qu'une dans le sac
[C.: I took a doll . . . the doll
E.: Why did you change?
C.: *The* doll because there is only one in the bag (stressed)]

J'ai caché l'assiette jaune pleine de fleurs . . . ou bien l'assiette, y en a pas d'autres

[I hid the yellow plate with the flowers . . . well, the plate, there aren't any others]

10,1 years

E.: Pourquoi as-tu dit *le* cheval?

C.: Parce que je l'avais déjà vu, alors je savais très bien de quoi on parlait, de quel cheval quoi

E.: Mais pourquoi dire alors: vous faites rouler *une* bouteille?

C.: Parce que j'avais pas vu la bouteille avant, maintenant c'est *la* bouteille

[E.: Why did you say *the* horse?

C.: Because I had already seen it, so I knew which horse it was

E.: But why say: you're rolling *a* bottle?

C.: Because I hadn't seen the bottle before. Now it's *the* bottle]

Difference responses were evident particularly amongst 4 year olds according to whether the experimenter merely hid an object or whether the object was involved in an action and the child referred to it in the subject position of his utterance:

4,4 years

T'as pris *une* poupée

[You took *a* doll]

Le cheval, i est tombé

[*The* horse, it fell over]

T'as caché *un* ours

[You hid *a* bear]

La voiture, i est allée faire un tour

[*The* car, it went for a ride]

In one case the child appears to be naming and in the other referring. Another plausible explanation is that when the child uses the indefinite article he is introducing new information in a series of hiding events. The definite article is clearly deictic.

Identical objects context

4,5 years

Encore un peigne comme ça

[Another comb like that (points to other one)]

4,9 years

Ça

[That (and points to the other one)]

4,11 years

Là, mais l'autre

[There, but the other one (points)]

5,2 years
J'ai enlevé le plot que j'ai enlevé
[I took the cube which I took (this is an interesting attempt to determine)]
5,7 years
La petite, la même que ça
[The small one, the same as that]
6,3 years
L'autre, celle qui est aussi rouge
[The other one, the one that is also red]
7,8 years
(upon seeing the objects) Mais comment je vais pouvoir vous dire lequel que je veux, si y a les mêmes . . . euh je sais, je dirai *un* avion
[But how shall I tell you which one if they're the same . . . oh I know, I'll say *an* aeroplane (stressed)]
8,1 years
J'ai caché la voi . . . *une* voiture
[I hid the c . . . *a* car (stressed)]
8,9 years
Vous avez enlevé l'avi . . . l'autre avion, l'avion mais y en avait deux
[You took the aero . . . the other aeroplane, the aeroplane but there were two of them]
9,0 years
Tu as caché l'avion . . . un avion vert
[You hid the aeroplane . . . a green aeroplane]
9,4 years
Vous avez ôté la bro . . . une brosse
[You took out the br . . . a brush]
11,0 years
E.: Pourquoi as-tu dit l'un des deux peignes mais pas l'une des deux voitures?
C.: Parce que les deux peignes ils étaient rouges, et les voitures il y avait une bleue et une rouge, alors on pouvait préciser
[E.: Why did you say one of the two combs (identical) but not one of the two cars (different-coloured)?
C.: Because for the combs the two combs were red, but the cars, well there was one blue and one red, so one could give details]

The final example for the identical context is of an older child's explicit search to determine linguistically which of two identical objects had been hidden:

11,5 years
J'ai enlevé la voiture rouge qui a pas de volant . . . enfin qui a un volant mais pas tout à fait au milieu . . . on voit pas très bien d'autres différences

[I took the red car which has no steering wheel, well which has a steering wheel not quite in the middle . . . I can't really see any other differences]

Vous avez enlevé un . . . le deuxième avion. Ben, je cherchais une différence entre les deux avions . . . pour donner un renseignement plus précis
[You took a . . . the second aeroplane . . . I looked for some differences between the two aeroplanes . . . to give more precise information]

Different-coloured objects context

4,9 years
Tu as pris la voiture . . . une . . . bleue
[You took the car . . . a . . . blue one]
4,11 years
Ça, mais l'autre rouge de mouchoir (note here the partitive construction with 'de' which gives the modifier a determinor function for the child)
[That, but the other red handkerchief]
5,2 years
Une autre qui était là
[Another one which was there]
6,4 years
Tu as caché le . . . un poiss . . . le poisson bleu
[You hid the . . . a fi . . . the blue fish]
8,6 years
J'ai ôté le mouchoir . . . là
[I took the handkerchief . . . there (shows it; this child otherwise used modifiers and it thus would appear that he showed the handkerchief because of the inadequate definite article)]

Finally I would like to quote the very explicit explanation of an 11 year old from the epilinguistic part of the session:

11,7 years
C.: Sur la table, il y a une télé, quand tu la prends alors c'est *la* télé, on sait de quoi il s'agit. Ça c'est une bague . . . tu as laissé tomber la bague
E.: Pourquoi changer de une bague à la bague?
C.: Parce que si on continue à dire une, ben, ça pourrait être une petite, une grande . . . mais ici c'est pas n'importe laquelle. *Une* bague, ben ça appartient à n'importe qui, alors tu dois dire *ta* bague. Je dois dire *ma* bague si la tienne elle est là, mais *la* bague si je la compare à tout ça (points to a pile of objects containing no rings)
E.: Puis-je dire pour ça (singleton): tu as ôté un chien?
C.: Non, parce qu'on aurait pu croire qu'y en a plusieurs

[C.: On the table there is a television, when you take it, well then it's *the* television, you know which one it is
That's a ring, you dropped the ring
E.: Why change from 'a' to 'the'?
C.: Because if you continue to say 'a' then it could be any old ring, a small one, a big one . . . but here it's not just any ring. *A* ring, well, that belongs to anyone, so you must say *your* ring. I have to say *my* ring if yours is here, but *the* ring if I compare it to all that (pile of non-rings)
E.: Can I say: you took a dog (singleton) for that?
C.: No, because one could have thought that there were several]

Clearly the presuppositions implied by the use of one article or the other are understood explicitly by this child, but such explicit statements were rarely encountered.

The overall results of this experiment show that at no age do children have difficulty in using the indefinite article in its nominative function, a fact which is supported also by the results of other investigators (e.g. Bresson *et al.* 1970; Warden 1973). In my view, the nominative function is the earliest function acquired for the indefinite article.

It should be recalled that in experiment 2, the child is called upon to make reference to a hidden object, i.e. one he can no longer point to. Whilst this would seem to render deictic reference impossible, some of the youngest children did use the demonstrative and point to the empty space where the object had been. However, because the setting did render mere pointing difficult, the use of modifiers in their determinor function appeared much earlier than in previous experimental settings. The determinor function first appeared with slightly agrammatical constructions around 5 years, e.g. 'Tu as caché le rouge de mouchoir'. From 6 years particularly, the grammatical addition of modifiers was rather consistent where relevant, i.e. for the items where objects were similar but different-coloured. Whilst percentages were fairly low for under 6 year olds, it should be mentioned that both 3 and 5 year olds nonetheless made a distinction between items where modifiers were relevant and those where they gave redundant information. Those small children who did not use modifiers where relevant, could nonetheless always recall the colours of the hidden objects if required to do so. This again confirms that the small child does not consistently understand the determinor function of modifiers, but rather their descriptor function.

It was also in experiment 2 that younger children made appropriate use of the indefinite article far more frequently than in other experiments. This may be explained by the fact that one of the duplicate objects remains visible whereas the other is hidden. The fact that the child has to refer to one of *two* objects, by indirect reference to the missing one, may elicit the numeral function. Thus, the young child's use of the indefinite article may not be the same as older children's use of it for non-specific reference. This is further borne out by the general tendency of the same young children to make very specific reference, e.g. 'The X which was there' (pointing to the empty space), etc. Moreover, the results of experiment 3 show that the plural definite article 'les' is used by young children to convey pluralization only, so that it may be that number indicators are important at this age. Thus when a situation calls for reference to one of two missing objects, the small child uses the numeral function of the indefinite article.

In comprehension (see discussion of experiment 12, p. 170 below), 5 to 7 year olds preferentially interpret the indefinite article in its numeral function, whereas older children look upon it as a non-specific reference. It is also noteworthy that when the child did the hiding in experiment 2, he tended to name the object, i.e. use the indefinite article in its descriptor function, whereas when the experimenter did the hiding he used the definite article deictically. It is not until after 9 years that hiding had no effect and children consistently tended to refer. Use of the verbs 'hide/do', whilst not reliable data, does point to the trend that one of the question forms elicits naming and the other referring. Finally, the epilinguistic part of the experiment indicates that both the use of modifiers in their determinor function and the implications of the *absence* of one determiner are explicitly understood and mentioned earlier than in previous experiments (6 years and 8 years respectively).

Thus, experiment 2 is particularly relevant in that it shows that indirect reference elicits earlier attempts to determine than direct reference, and earlier epilinguistic awareness of the functions used. The indirect/direct reference distinction does not make a difference to the over 8 year old. This again confirms the hypothesis that the younger child relies more heavily on extralinguistic support for reference and that the older child will tend to do this intralinguistically.

Experiment 3: the parking lots

Previous experiments mainly concerned the singular forms of determiners. As pointed out in chapter 3, in spoken French it is frequently the determiner which alone indicates number. It therefore seemed important to include in my study an experiment concerning children's production of plural definite articles and plural possessive adjectives. This experiment was thus designed to cover the use of plural determiners and their relationship with the addition of modifiers. Another essential question was raised in this experiment: is there a sort of hierarchical order or force amongst the different determiners, and do children develop a tendency to be economical by avoiding what might be termed 'overdetermination'? In other words, do children gradually construct a 'system' of relevant options which are organized in such a way as to give neither too much nor too little referential information?

Experimental context. Fig 2 illustrates the context of this experiment. Two parking lots, containing vehicles and other objects, were separated by a wall (a long piece of wood) in front of which is placed a toy petrol station. The cars and lorries were match-box size; some cars were sports models with no roof (called 'open cars' in the experiment), some were closed saloons (called 'closed cars') and all the lorries were open. Some vehicles were blue, others red, yellow, white or green (see fig. 2 for details). Different colours, shapes, etc., were chosen, rather than size variations, to avoid any discrimination difficulties. The parking lot *not* belonging to the child contained the following objects:

four red cars, of which two open and two closed
four blue cars, of which two open and two closed
two blue lorries.

The child's lot had identical objects, with the following additional ones:

one red lorry
two yellow closed cars
one white closed car
one white balloon
one green aeroplane
several objects belonging to the child.

The layout of the objects (see fig. 2) was identical for all subjects. Half of the population had their parking lot on their right, the other half on their

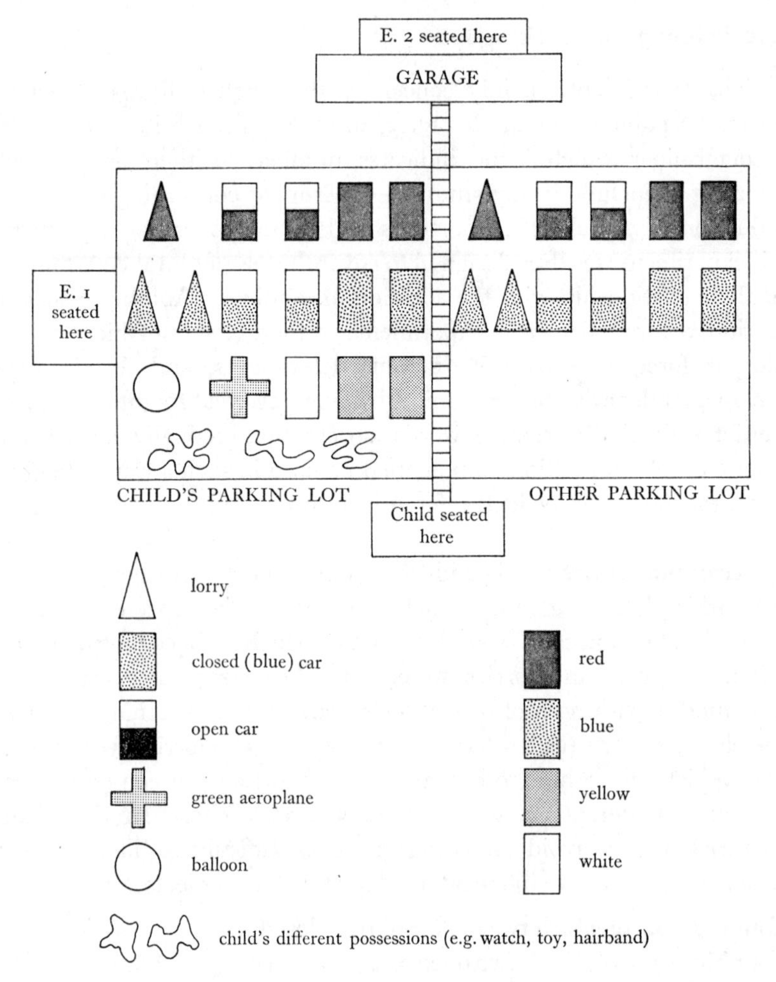

Fig. 2. Layout for experiments 2 and 14 (E.2 did not participate in experiment 14)

left. There was in fact no difference in the results, but we wished to ensure that right-handedness would not affect the children's responses.

Experimental procedure. The child was familiarized with the material. Experimenter 1 (E.1) made sure that the child understood the difference between 'closed' and 'open' cars as well as between lorries, cars, and the various colours. The child was informed that one of the parking lots belonged to him during the game and that all that was on that lot was his. The experimenter asked the child to give him some of his own belongings (e.g. handkerchief, pen, toy, watch, hair-band, etc.). These were placed on the child's parking lot to clearly mark which was his. The child was told that these objects were also part of the game. The vehicles in the other parking lot did not belong to the child, but he was assured that they were part of the game and that he could touch them whenever he wanted to. He was not told that the other parking lot was E.1's although some children did assume that this was the case. In fact none of the experimental items concerned this other parking lot alone; items either concerned both lots or just the child's.

In order to explain to the child what was expected of him in the task, E.1 added temporarily to the parking lots some groups of coloured cardboard shapes. He reminded the child that objects could be taken from both or from either one of the parking lots. E.1 then told the child: 'Mets les ronds rouges au garage' [Put the red circles in the garage]. The child was expected to remove all the red circles from both lots and put them in front of the garage. He was then asked: 'Mets tes carrés bleus au garage' [Put your blue squares in the garage]; this time the child was expected to take all the blue squares from his lot but not those from the other lot. Determiners were not stressed. If the child failed to understand the possessive adjective or the plural definite article, experimenter 1 corrected his responses and continued these easy introductory tasks until the child appeared to understand what was required of him.

Then E.1 asked experimenter 2 (E.2) to turn his back and close his eyes. E.1 placed in the garage a group of shapes, say all the squares, and told the child that when E.2 turned back to the game and reopened his eyes, the shapes would all have been put back on the parking lots. E.2 would have to put in the garage exactly what had been there before, and E.1 asked the child to tell E.2 what to do to achieve this. If the child gave an erroneous message with a second utterance, several demonstrations were continued with the shapes until the child had understood. Care was always taken to say: 'Dis-lui ce qu'il doit faire' [Tell him what he must *do*] rather than: 'Dis-lui ce qu'il y a au garage' [Tell him what *is in* the garage], because the child needed to relate what was in the garage with what was left in the parking lots and not merely describe the former.

After the introductory part of the session, the shapes were removed and the real test with the vehicles began. E.1 placed in the garage groups of experimental objects which involved the following type of expected responses:

	E.1's action	*Child's expected message to E.2*
1.	all the lorries from both lots	Il faut mettre les camions dans le garage [You must put the lorries into the garage]
2.	all the cars from child's lot	Il faut mettre mes voitures ... [You must put my cars ...]
3.	the red cars from both lots	Il faut mettre les voitures rouges ... [You must put the red cars ...]
4.	the blue lorries from child's lot	Il faut mettre mes camions bleus ... [You must put my blue lorries ...]
5.	the open cars from both lots	Il faut mettre les voitures ouvertes ... [You must put the open cars ...]
6.	the closed cars from child's lot	Il faut mettre mes voitures fermées ... [You must put my closed cars ...]
7.	the blue closed cars from both lots	Il faut mettre les voitures bleues fermées ... [You must put the blue closed cars ...]
8.	the red open cars from child's lot	Il faut mettre mes voitures rouges ouvertes ... [You must put my red open cars ...]
9.	the aeroplane from child's lot	Il faut mettre l'avion/mon avion ... [You must put the/my aeroplane ...]
10.	the yellow cars from child's lot	Il faut mettre les/mes voitures jaunes ... [You must put the/my yellow cars ...]

The order of presentation of items for all subjects was as follows: 1, 4, 8, 5, 9, 3, 7, 6, 10 and 2. Clearly the above 'expected responses' are the most economical ones; if a child for item 5, say, responded 'Il faut mettre toutes mes voitures rouges et bleues ouvertes et toutes les autres voitures rouges et bleues ouvertes au garage' [You must put all my red and blue open cars and all the other red and blue open cars into the garage], E.2 of course gave the correct action response. For each item, E.2 placed vehicles in the garage exactly in accordance with the message received from the child. If the child's response was inadequate for selection, it was hoped that the child would react to the difference between his utterance and the consequent action by E.2. The child, upon seeing that E.2 placed in the garage a different group of vehicles to those placed by E.1, could correct his utterance and give more or different information in the two subsequent trials for that item. After three trials, the next item was taken. For the second and third trials, E.2 again closed his eyes and the child gave his message whilst the vehicles were in the garage again. This of course was to avoid any memory problems. For some small children, concentration difficulties made it impossible to have three trials for each inadequate response. If the child was correct on the first trial, then the next item was taken immediately. If the child gave a message that enabled E.2 to select correctly, but his utterance was not economical, the child was then asked if he could give a 'shorter/better/clearer' message. For example, if the child could have merely said 'Put the red cars into the garage', but actually said 'Put eight cars in all, my red open and my red closed plus all the red cars on the other parking ...', he was asked whether he could find a shorter way of telling E.2 who 'had a poor memory', etc.

The ten experimental items were followed by a more exploratory approach, where the same technique was used but including the child's possessions and various new groups of vehicles. This was to test the experimenter's hypotheses about what was underlying the child's responses during the task. Children were also asked at the end of the session to explain why they had used 'my/all/the' or certain adjectives at one time and not at another. Although the exploratory and epilinguistic parts depended on the age of the child and his responses, the following list gives a general idea of the type of questions raised:

(a) Comparison of 'the lorries' versus 'the blue lorries'. Why does one need to use more words when there are less vehicles?
(b) Comparison of 'the red and blue cars' versus 'the lorries'. Why is 'the lorries' enough although they are also red and blue? Why does one not say 'green aeroplane'. What would be needed in the experimental context so that one would be obliged to say 'green', etc.?
(c) Comparison of 'my yellow cars' versus 'the yellow cars'. Why can one say 'the' despite the fact the cars come from the child's lot? Which is better: 'the' or 'my'? Why?
(d) Does one need to say 'the five lorries'. Why/why not?
(e) Is there a difference between 'the cars' and 'all the cars'?
(f) Why is it not wrong to describe what *is in* the garage, i.e. 'There are some red cars', but why is this nonetheless insufficient for E.2 to make the correct choice amongst all the cars?

Two experimenters, E.1 and E.2, interviewed the child, whilst a third, E.3, recorded the child's responses, hesitations, spontaneous corrections, gross eye movements, marked intonational patterns, etc. E.2 also noted the child's responses in the exploratory part of the session.

As can be seen from the ten task items, the experiment was designed to analyse the determinor function of the possessive (subclass of 'my' extracted from the total class of 'the') versus its descriptor function ('my' watch, because it's mine, and not because of extraction from a class of watches). Items 9 and 10 were particularly interesting in this respect because they could be referred to by the definite article, despite coming from the child's lot, due to the fact that they referred to non-duplicated items. It was also important to ascertain whether 'aeroplane' (item 9), being a singleton, would be more easily referred to by the definite article, whereas 'yellow cars' (item 10), being a subclass of 'my cars', might give rise to more difficulties.

Population. Experiment 3 covered fifty-five children between the ages of 4,7 and 11,5 years, distributed as follows:

Age	*Subjects*	*Average age*
4,7–5,11	13	5,3
6,0–6,11	11	6,4
7,0–7,11	9	7,5
8,0–8,11	7	8,4
9,0–9,11	7	9,4
10,0–11,5	8	10,7

One 5 year old refused to cooperate; one 7 year old persisted in considering the task as a difficult guessing game for E.2 and therefore purposely gave the *least* information possible, i.e. 'Some vehicles, not of the same colour nor the same size . . .' These two children are not included in the results. A pilot study was also made on twenty-four English speaking children between 5,0 and 11,4 years. However, these children all live in a French speaking community. Despite the encouraging similarity in results, they will not be reported on here due to the non-monolingual status of the subjects.

Results. In view of the fact that the plural definite article ('les'), the plural possessive adjective ('mes') and the adjectives all have more than one function of a descriptive or determinative type, it would seem inappropriate to analyse our results quantitatively. Indeed, calculating the number of correct uses of, say, the plural definite article would fail to take into account the fact that for some children this is used merely as a plural operator whereas for others it plays the role of a determiner contrasted to the possessive and the partitive. Likewise when adding modifiers, some children correctly add these *only* when relevant for determining, whereas for others they are again descripters used redundantly. Thus children may give certain 'correct' responses, the function of which is quite different to identical responses in other children. This fact not only justifies but renders essential a qualitative analysis. Adequacy of message and redundancy can, however, be analysed from a more quantitative point of view. The results of experiment 3 are therefore presented first by a qualitative analysis of the *functions* of the definite article and the possessive adjective, and then with respect to general quantitative trends for adequacy and redundancy of message.

The plural definite article 'les'. If one were to calculate the number of items where 'les' should be used (i.e. items 1, 3, 5, 7), small children would appear to be just as correct at using 'les' as older children. Such a quantitative analysis would camouflage the fact that the functions of the plural definite article change with age. Therefore, a semantico-functional analysis will be made.

In spoken French the singular and plural forms of most nouns have the same pronunciation, although they are kept distinct in the written language (e.g. 'voiture/voitures'). There are a few exceptions (e.g. 'cheval/chevaux') and cases of liaison (e.g. 'grand enfant/grands enfants'). All the nouns covering the experimental items did not differentiate in pronunciation between plural and singular. Thus, the definite article carried the communicative burden of differentiating between singularity and plurality.

The plural definite article can be said to have a dual function: it indicates plurality, and the class extension. In other words, 'les voitures' tells us that more than one car is involved and that those referred to comprise the entire extension of the cars present in the context. 'Les' has a common function with the partitive 'des' [some] in that both operate as pluralizers. However, the two words contrast in respect of class extension functions: 'les' indicates the whole extension whereas 'des' indicates subclass inclusion, as in the following two examples:

Les paquets sont arrivés
[(All) the parcels have arrived]
Des paquets sont arrivés
[Some parcels have arrived]

The results show the following: first, no child at any age ever gave the singular article to cover more than one object. However, it would appear that when the small child uses 'les', he is in fact focussing on pluralization; he is not using the definite article to indicate class extension. Moreover, when using 'les' small children added other information, clearly indicating that the plural 'les' acted as a pluralizer and not yet as a totalizer, e.g.:

4,7 years (item 1 – the lorries)
Mettez au garage les camions . . . les camions bleus, le camion rouge et les camions bleus
[Put into the garage the lorries . . . the blue lorries, the red lorry and the blue lorries]

This example clearly shows that the child uses 'les' really to mean 'some'; he is describing the little groups of lorries he perceives.

In accordance with the linguistic hypotheses developed in chapter 3, it is argued that the plural operator has a descriptor function. It is not used as a referring expression and does not tell us about the relationship of the vehicles described by the plural indicator to the other vehicles left in the parking lots. This tallies with the fact that when the youngest children concentrate on describing what is 'in the garage', their global eye movements are only amongst the objects in the garage area and at E.2, whereas older children's eyes move to and fro between the garage and the two parking lots in the course of giving their message.

But this does not mean that the young child cannot express totalization, as the results concerning the use of the plural definite article would suggest. Since 'les' is functioning as a pluralizer, and since the small child seems at first to endow each surface marker with one function at a time, he first expresses totalization by adding the word 'all'. However, even the word 'all' seems initially to have another function for the small child; before becoming a totalizer, it has the meaning 'a lot', contrasted to 'les' which conveys: 'more than one but not necessarily many'. 'All' was added by many subjects in their responses to items when four or eight cars were placed in the garage, but only one child (aged 5,10 years) added 'all' when only two cars were in the garage, although this also represented a total subclass. 'All' seems to be an intensifier but not yet a totalizer, for when adding 'all', children at first did not seem to be sure of its scope, as can be seen from the following examples:

5,2 years (item 3 – the red cars)
Toutes les voitures rouges, les miennes et les vôtres . . .
[All the red cars, mine and yours . . .]

5,2 years (item 1 – the lorries)
Tous mes camions, un camion rouge à moi, deux camions bleus à moi et tous vos camions, deux camions bleus à vous . . .
[All my lorries, one red lorry of mine, two blue lorries of mine and all your lorries, two blue lorries of yours . . .]
5,5 years (item 1 – the lorries)
Tous les camions, de ce côté et de l'autre côté . . .
[All the lorries, on this side and on that side . . .]
5,8 years (item 3 – the red cars)
Toutes les voitures rouges, aussi ceux qui sont pas couverts . . .
[All the red cars, even the ones with no roof . . .]
6,7 years (item 1 – the lorries)
Tous les camions, les camions bleus et le camion rouge . . .
[All the lorries, the blue lorries and the red lorry . . .]

Gradually 'all' also becomes a totalizer. This can particularly be seen from spontaneous corrections, which also point to the fact that the acquisition of the totalizer function of 'tout' precedes the acquisition of the totalizer function of 'les':

6,9 years (item 3 – the red cars)
Les . . . toutes les voitures rouges
[The . . . all the red cars]
7,11 years (item 7 – the blue closed cars)
Les . . . toutes les voitures bleues fermées
[The . . . all the blue closed cars]

It is also evident from responses of 7 to 8 year olds that they either use 'all', e.g. 'All the red cars', or they spell out the same item, e.g. 'The red open cars and the red closed cars'.

Intonation was another clear indication of transition, e.g. 'Les voitures rouges ↗ . . . rouges ↘'. The rising tone after the first 'rouges' shows how the child was about to give more details and *post factum* realized that the message was sufficient. Such examples bear witness to the transition between the use of a totalizer and the careful description of all relevant criteria. What is important is that such variations in responses can be found in the same child during the transition. Furthermore, as 'all' gradually becomes a clear totalizer, the child seems to become explicitly aware of its function, e.g.:

7,10 years
On doit dire *toutes* les voitures rouges, si on dit simplement *les* voitures rouges, on ne saura pas combien prendre

[You must say *all* the red cars, if you just say *the* red cars, you don't know how many to take]

Finally, 'all' is differentiated from the totalizer function of 'les' which now covers class extension, freeing 'all' as an intensifier for particular emphases. Indeed, once 'les' is used as a totalizer, 'all' is only added to item 2 ('all my cars') because of the very large number of vehicles involved compared to the other items; in these cases, 'all' plays its dual function of 'intensifier' and 'totalizer'.

It was stressed earlier that young children not using 'les' as a totalizer nonetheless attempt to express the latter. Apart from the gradual development of 'all' as described above, another procedure young children use is to cover class extension aspects by using a numeral. However, this procedure only by chance enables E.2 to choose accurately in some contexts, as can be seen from the following examples:

4,7 years (item 1 – the lorries; second trial, requested by E. for shorter/clearer message)
Tu mets un rouge et deux bleus, des camions, cinq camions, non quatre camions bleus et un camion rouge
[Put one red and two blue ones, some lorries, five lorries, no four blue lorries and one red lorry]
4,11 years (item 7 – the blue closed cars)
Mettez les voitures fermées, juste les quatre
[Put the closed cars, just the four]
5,2 years (items 6 – my closed cars)
Il faut mettre une voiture blanche au garage, puis deux voitures jaunes au garage, puis deux voitures rouges et deux voitures bleues
[Put one white car in the garage, then two yellow cars in the garage, then 2 red cars and two blue cars]
6,7 years (item 5 – the open cars)
Les deux voitures rouges ouvertes et les deux voitures bleues ouvertes à moi vont au garage et les deux voitures rouges ouvertes qui ne sont pas à moi vont au garage avec les deux voitures bleues ouvertes qui ne sont pas à moi. (E.: Dire plus court?) Je sais, toutes les voitures rouges ouvertes vont au garage et toutes les voitures bleues ouvertes vont aussi au garage
[The two red open cars and the two blue open cars of mine go to the garage, and the two red open cars which are not mine go to the garage with the two blue open cars which are not mine. (E.: Shorter?) I know, all the red open cars go to the garage and all the blue open cars also go to the garage]

In the first example above, E.2 can in fact give an adequate response because all the lorries are in the garage and therefore 'five' covers them all. E.2 can make an adequate choice for the final example also. With respect to the middle two examples, however, the addition of the numeral does not enable E.2 to make her choice unambiguously. Quantification by numeral operators alone does not determine. Addition of the article to the numeral does determine, as can be seen in the final example, but in such cases the numeral is in fact redundant. Paradoxically numerals only seem to have a descriptor function. Adding a numeral e.g. '*two* cars' makes a statement about the cars under focus of attention, but this does not necessarily relate them to the context from which they are extracted. Thus the numeral does not necessarily help the addressee to pick out the appropriate referent(s). If there are only two cars in the current context, a definite article without the numeral is sufficient information, e.g. 'the cars' refers uniquely in that setting, and the 'two' in 'the two cars' for the same context is redundant. If there are more than two cars in the current context and one wishes to refer to two of them, then the addition of a numeral does not enable the addressee to identify the referents. In other words, 'two' would be playing a descriptor function; objects may be 'big', 'red', or 'two'.

Finally, 'les' seems to be clearly used as a totalizer. This can best be seen from children's corrections when asked in a second trial to give a shorter message. When, for instance, they have given 'all the' in the first trial, they give just 'the' in the second trial. Spontaneous corrections during the first trial were revealing in this direction, as can be seen from the following examples:

8,11 years (item 3 – the red cars)
Les voitures rouges ouvertes et fermées . . . non, les voitures *rouges*
[The red open and closed cars . . . no, the *red* cars]
8,11 years (item 1 – the lorries)
Des camions . . . non *les* camions
[Some lorries . . . (as E.2 places three of the lorries) no, *the* lorries (stressed)]
9,2 years (item 5 – the open cars)
Toutes les voitures ouvertes . . . les voitures ouvertes
[All the open cars . . . the open cars]
9,3 years (item 3 – the red cars)
Toutes les . . . les voitures rouges
[All the . . . the red cars]
10,11 years (item 1 – the lorries)
Tous les camions . . . ou bien on peut dire *les* camions
[All the lorries or you can just say *the* lorries (stressed)]

Possessive adjective. It should be stressed that no child had any difficulty remembering that one parking lot belonged to him nor any problem using the possessive adjective when referring to his own belongings. I shall argue from the data that the difficulties encountered by children in their use of the possessive lie in the diverse functions of the possessive adjective.

As with the definite article, the plural possessive adjective marks both plurality and aspects of class extension. In other words, 'mes' tells us that more than one object is involved and that it covers the whole of the particular subclass of objects possessed by the speaker. In this particular context, 'mes' covers the subclass relationship to the whole, i.e. the child's lot versus both parking lots. 'Mes' and 'les' are here contrastive in a similar way to 'des' and 'les', except that 'mes' also quantifies the extension of the possessed subclass. Furthermore, 'mes' can have either a descriptor function or a determinor function.

Although children take some time before they can correctly use 'mes' to distinguish it from 'les', this does not imply that they are unaware of the need to differentiate between the two contexts. Thus again, a quantitative analysis of the number of correct 'mes' responses would tell us relatively little about how the cognitive distinction is gradually encoded linguistically by the child.

Seven different procedures were used for the possessive. These reflect either developmental changes or children's subsequent trials on the same items within one session. A zero level, covering very few responses, concerned children who used 'les' indiscriminately for both possessed and non-possessed objects, i.e. no distinction was made for the possessive. Again merely the plural operator is functioning. Children were fully aware that only part of a given subclass had been put into the garage, since they strongly objected when E.2's reaction was to put all of the cars, based on the child's definite article.

Procedure 1 for indicating the possessive subclass was to use an ostensive gesture (pointing) or to use a demonstrative and locative: e.g. 'Les camions bleus, *ceux-là* seulement' plus pointing, 'Les voitures fermées *de ce côté*. Procedure 2 still involved a locative but the possessive was also added: e.g. 'Les voitures *de mon côté*', 'Les voitures *au garage de moi*'. Procedure 3 covered the disappearance of the use of locatives in favour of the possessive alone, but in such cases the child repeated the possessive for each small subclass: e.g. 'Les voitures rouges *à moi*', 'Les voitures bleues *à moi*', 'Les voitures jaunes *à moi*' (or similar constructions with 'de moi' added). It would thus seem that the previous locative represented a sort of spatial envelope covering the class extension, since the child was not sure of the scope of the possessive alone. With procedure 4, the child merely added a possessive operator once, in postposition, e.g. 'Les voitures rouges, jaunes, et bleues *à moi*', 'Les voitures rouges, jaunes et bleues, *c'est les miennes*'. Up to procedure 4 inclusive, all attempts to include the possessive operator were made in postposition, whereas in normal French the possessive adjective is usually preposed. In colloquial French conversation, the postposing of the possessive is used for emphatic purposes. Thus, this would be part of children's input. However, the very same children using the postposition procedures did prepose the possessive adjective when talking of their own objects. In such contexts, therefore, the preposed possessive is not playing a determinor role. Indeed such children refused the use of the definite article for their own objects, whereas older children understood that weaker determination was possible in these cases, because there were no duplicates in the other lot.

The first appearance of the possessive in anteposition is clearly determinative; procedure 5 involved adding the possessive to the definite article and making a slightly ungrammatical form with a partitive, e.g. '*Les miennes de* voitures rouges ouvertes'. As we shall see from certain of the other experiments, this type of ungrammatical construction is frequently used by children for determinative purposes (e.g. '*La même de* voiture', '*La rouge de* voiture', '*Une de* voiture', etc., see below p. 206). Finally, the possessive was anteposed alone, first in procedure 6 where the child was still a little unsure of its scope and added a closing bracket, e.g. '*Mes* camions bleus *à moi*', 'Toutes *mes* voitures *à moi* vont au garage', 'Mes voitures . . . (hesitates) les rouges, bleues et jaunes *qui sont à moi* vont au garage', 'Elle a mis *mes* camions bleus . . . *juste les deux*'.

Procedure 7 showed finally the possessive adjective anteposed and covering the whole subclass extension, e.g. '*Mes* voitures vont au garage'.

The seven procedures are shown diagrammatically below. In some respects, they are a function of age, but several can also be found in any given child's protocol as he attempts to improve his message. P represents various forms of the possessive, L the locative, D the plural definite article and a, b, c, the various criteria (colour/open/closed):

Procedure

1 D(a, b, c) L (or + demonstrative)
2 D(a, b, c) P + L

3 DaP, DbP, DcP
4 D(a, b, c) P
5 D + P (a, b, c)
6 P(a, b, c) P
7 P(a, b, c)

Whilst a large number of older subjects (from 8,2 years) used procedure 7, i.e. anteposing the possessive adjective alone in its determinor function, a distinction can be made between those children who, for singletons or non-duplicated subclasses coming from their parking lot (e.g. the aeroplane and the yellow cars), preferred the definite article, and those who insisted on using the possessive. Amongst subjects who clearly distinguished between 'les' and 'mes' for duplicate classes, only the oldest subjects (i.e. 8,10; 9,0; 9,11; 10,11; 10,11; and 11,1) preferred the definite article for non-duplicated classes. However, some very young subjects also used the definite article for these items and again a quantitative analysis would camouflage the different meanings underlying similar behaviour.

It should be noted, first, that the possessive was used far more frequently for item 10, the yellow cars than for the aeroplane. It would seem that, since the possessive adjective was needed as a determiner in many situations for cars, it was more difficult for children to see the subclass yellow cars as not necessarily requiring a possessive determiner. The fact that the aeroplane was a singleton, i.e. required a singular determiner, may have been a factor in the choice of the definite article. It would have been interesting to have had a plurality of 'non-cars' to see whether belonging to a superordinate class or singularity was the factor which determined the differences between possessive for the yellow cars and definite article for the aeroplane.

Several young children used the singular *indefinite* article for the aeroplane, whereas since it was the only aeroplane present, the definite article would have been more appropriate. It can be hypothesized that they were using the numeral function of the indefinite article ('one aeroplane' rather than 'an aeroplane') to contrast with the plural operator they were using for the definite article ('many') in all other cases. Of course many of these children did not just say indefinite article plus 'aeroplane', for it will be recalled that messages were rarely economical. Since the translation of the indefinite article is not clear, I have put 'a' and 'one' in the English gloss.

6,8 years
Un avion vert avec des ailes
[A/one green aeroplane with wings]
6,9 years
Un avion qui est à moi vert
[A/one aeroplane which is mine and green]
7,1 years
Un avion vert clair et vert foncé
[A/one light green and dark green aeroplane]

Several children between 4,11 and 6,8 years used the definite article to refer to the aeroplane. However, these children were not using the possessive correctly elsewhere where it was *essential*, and thus their use of the definite article for aeroplane was due to the singularity of the aeroplane in the context, rather than to their understanding the cases where possessive was essential versus non-essential. Between 5,11 and 8,7 many subjects used 'my aeroplane' and in fact refused to accept that it could be referred to as 'the aeroplane'. The anteposition of the possessive with such subjects ('mon avion') should also be noted, since this reinforces the hypothesis that the scope of the anteposed *plural* possessive is a real problem for the child when he uses it in its determinor function. It is again in children's spontaneous corrections that the difference between using the definite article merely to indicate singularity, and using it consciously as a weaker determiner than the possessive, may be noticed.

8,2 years
Les . . . mes voitures jaunes . . . les voitures jaunes . . . les miennes
[The . . . my yellow cars . . . the yellow cars . . . mine]
9,1 years
Mes voitures jaunes . . . les voitures jaunes
[My yellow cars . . . the yellow cars]

The first example illustrates a real conflict, whereas the second shows the child's tendency not to 'overdetermine'. The use of the definite article for such items, whilst retaining the possessive adjective where essential, was encountered only in the responses of the oldest subjects.

It seems clear from the foregoing that many different problems are simultaneously involved for the child. An explanation merely in terms of the logic of classes would seem to be only a partial explanation of the child's activity. It seems clear that intralinguistic problems are also affecting the child's behaviour. The youngest children mainly used determiners in their descriptor function and not in their determinor function:

4,11 years (item 6 – my closed cars)
Les voitures bleues et les voitures rouges qui sont fermées et aussi les voitures jaunes qui sont fermées et aussi une vévé blanche qui est fermée . . .
[The blue cars and the red cars which are closed and also the yellow cars which are closed and also a white VW which is closed . . .]
4,11 years (item 10 – my/the yellow cars)
Seulement les voitures jaunes, qui sont fermées
[Only the yellow cars, which are closed]

The second example is even more strikingly descriptive (i.e. a non-restrictive relative clause) since there are no yellow cars which are open. Such young children also gave a lot of extra information because they were describing rather than determining. The following exchange occurred in the epilinguistic part of the session with the child quoted above.

4,11 years (item 6 – my closed cars]
E.: Est-ce que je peux dire seulement mes voitures fermées ?
C.: Non, parce qu'elle saurait pas quelles couleurs qu'il faut prendre
[E.: Can I just say my closed cars?
C.: No, she wouldn't know which colours to take]

Other responses to the epilinguistic part were also characteristic of the descriptor function:

5,2 years
E.: Pourquoi puis-je dire les camions ici, mais mes camions *bleus*, pourquoi ajouter bleu?
C.: Parce qu'ils sont bleus
E.: Pourquoi avais-tu besoin de dire voitures *ouvertes*?
C.: Parce qu'elles n'ont pas de toit
[E.: Why can I say the lorries but my blue lorries, why add blue?
C.: Because they are blue
E.: Why do you need to say open cars?
C.: Because they have no roof]

Younger children, who were able to give adequate messages which were fairly economical, were nonetheless unable to explain the implicit rules they were using, as the following examples demonstrate:

5,11 years
E.: Pourquoi as-tu dit mes camions et pas mes camions bleus et rouges?
C.: Parce que c'est tous [tus] des camions

[E.: Why did you say my lorries and not my blue and red lorries?
C.: Because they're all lorries (not: It's all the lorries)]
6,1 years
E.: Pourquoi as-tu dit seulement mon avion et pas mon avion vert?
C.: Parce que c'est un avion
[E.: Why did you just say my aeroplane and not my green aeroplane?
C.: Because it's an aeroplane]
6,9 years
E.: Pourquoi dire fermées?
C.: Parce qu'elles sont pas ouvertes
[E.: Why say closed?
C.: Because they're not open]

From roughly 6,5 years, but more systematically from 7 years, the epilinguistic responses seem to be closer to an explanation of determinor functions as the following responses attest:

6,5 years
E.: Est-ce qu'on peut dire l'avion, au lieu de mon avion?
C.: Oui, parce qu'y en a pas là
[E.: Can one say the aeroplane instead of my aeroplane?
C.: Yes, because there are none there (other parking lot)]
7,3 years
E.: L'avion?
C.: L'avion, oui ça va, parce qu'ily y en a qu'un seul, alors on sait tout de suite lequel c'est
E.: Pourquoi pas vert?
C.: Parce que c'est un avion et puis c'est tout seul
[E.: The aeroplane?
C.: The aeroplane, that's okay, because there's only one, so one knows straight away which one it is
E.: Why not green?
C.: Because it's an aeroplane and it's all alone]

It is also around 6,5 years that problems of presupposition seem to be taken into account in this context, as can be seen from the following examples:

6,5 years
E.: Est-ce que je peux dire *les* voitures jaunes?
C.: Non, parce que si vous dites les, alors ça veut dire qu'il y en a des deux côtés
[E.: Can I also say *the* yellow cars? (stressed)
C.: No, because if you say the, it means there are some on both parking lots]

6,7 years
E.: Aussi l'avion?
C.: Oui, parce qu'on sait déjà qu'il y a qu'un seul avion dans le jeu
[E.: Also the aeroplane?
C.: Yes, because we already know there's only one plane in the game]
6,9 years
E.: Mes voitures jaunes ou les voitures jaunes?
C.: Il faut dire mes voitures jaunes, sinon il faudrait qu'il y en ait sur l'autre carré, on ne peut pas dire les voitures jaunes parce qu'on devrait avoir des voitures jaunes de l'autre côté aussi
[E.: My yellow cars or the yellow cars?
C.: You must say my yellow cars, if not then there would have to be some on the other parking, you can't say the yellow cars, because you'd have to have yellow cars also on the other side]
10,2 years
E.: L'avion?
C.: Oui, parce qu'il n'y avait qu'un dans le jeu et on savait que c'était à moi
[E.: The aeroplane?
C.: Yes, because there was only one in the game and we knew it was mine]

The same children were quite capable of giving an explicit response on other items:

6,5 years
E.: Pourquoi pas les voitures jaunes fermées?
C.: Parce qu'y en a pas de jaunes qui restent qui sont aussi ouvertes
[E.: Why not the closed yellow cars?
C.: Because there are no yellow ones left that are also open]
6,7 years
E.: Pourquoi les camions/les camions bleus?
C.: Parce qu'il y a le rouge qui reste
E.: Alors pourquoi les voitures rouges et bleues?
C.: Parce qu'ici y a encore d'autres voitures
[E.: Why the lorries/the blue lorries?
C.: Because the red one is left behind
E.: Then why the red and blue cars?
C.: Because here (on the parking lots) there are still some other cars]
6,9 years
E.: Pourquoi les camions/les camions bleus?
C.: Parce que tout d'abord c'est tous les camions qui partent et il ne reste que des voitures, mais ici on risquerait de se tromper si on dit pas bleu parce qu'il reste un camion rouge
[E.: Why the lorries/the blue lorries?

C.: Because first it's all the lorries that go and there are only cars left, but here (my blue lorries) you'd risk making a mistake if you didn't say blue, because there's a red lorry left]

7,11 years

E.: Pourquoi les camions *bleus*?

C.: Puisqu'il en reste un on est obligé de dire bleu

[E.: Why the *blue* lorries?

C.: Since there's one left you are obliged to say blue]

8,3 years

E.: Pourquoi pas avion vert?

C.: On n'a pas besoin de dire vert parce qu'il y a pas chez moi d'avion rouge

[E.: Why not green aeroplane?

C.: You don't need to say green because there's no red aeroplane on my parking lot]

8,11 years

E.: A-t-on besoin de dire mes *deux* camions bleus?

C.: Oui . . . ah non, pas si je dis bleu, ça suffit

[E.: Does one need to say my *two* blue lorries?

C.: Yes . . . oh no, if I say blue that's enough]

10,3 years

E.: Pourquoi pour l'item 'mes voitures' tu n'ajoutes pas les couleurs?

C.: Parce que si on dit bleu et rouge, ça veut toujours dire qu'il reste une autre couleur, mais ici vous les avez mises toutes, alors on peut dire seulement mes voitures

[E.: Why for my cars no colours?

C.: If you say blue and red that always means there's another colour left, but here you put them all, so you can just say my cars]

From 7 years, those children who used 'my aeroplane' or 'my yellow cars' all accepted that it could also be called 'the aeroplane', 'the yellow cars', invoking non-duplicate subclass or singularity. Only from 8 years and in relatively few cases in older children could an explanation be given regarding the appropriateness of 'les' or 'mes', as it pertains to the question of overdetermination:

8,0 years

E.: Qu'est-ce qui est mieux, les ou mes?

C.: Les, parce que c'est plus vite, il y a moins de lettres . . . ah non, trois, trois, ben, les c'est quand même mieux, c'est parce que l se dit plus vite que m!

[E.: Which is better, 'les' or 'mes'?

C.: 'Les', because it's faster, there are less letters . . . oh no, three, and three, well, 'les' is still better, it's because you can say 'l' quicker than 'm'!]

9,1 years
C.: Mon avion . . . non, *l'*avion parce qu'y en a pas d'autres, vous m'avez dit de le dire le plus court possible
[C.: My aeroplane . . . no, *the* aeroplane (stressed) because there are no others, you said I should say things as shortly as possible]

9,3 years
C.: Mes voitures jaunes . . . euh, les voitures jaunes
E.: Pourquoi changer d'avis?
C.: C'est que les c'est plus court, enfin c'est pas vrai pour les lettres mais c'est comme si . . . j'arrive pas bien à expliquer, on peut dire les deux, les ou mes, mais si là-bas y avait des jaunes alors on serait obligé de dire mes, mais y en a pas, alors c'est mieux de dire les voitures jaunes doivent aller au garage même si elles m'appartiennent
[C.: My yellow cars . . . oh, the yellow cars
E.: Why change your mind?
C.: It's because 'les' is shorter, it's not true for the number of letters, but it's just as if . . . I can't quite explain, but you can say both 'les' or 'mes' but if there (points to other parking lot) there were some yellow ones, then one would be obliged to say 'mes', but there aren't any there, so it's better to say the yellow cars, even if they belong to me]

10,2 years
C.: Les voitures jaunes c'est plus vite que mes voitures jaunes, ça coule
[C.: The yellow cars is quicker than my yellow cars, it's smoother]

'Les' thus seemed to be more neutral as far as presuppositions are concerned for the older child, whereas the younger ones previously quoted felt that 'les' presupposed necessarily both sides. The forms such as 'smoother' and 'quicker' may be due to the fact that 'mes' is really 'les plus possessive'. It is a child of 10,11 years who was the most explicit on this question and on whom I shall conclude:

10,11 years
Ma montre parce que c'est la mienne et *la* montre parce que c'est la seule ici, sinon tu pourrais croire qu'il y en a une autre
[*My* watch because it's mine and *the* watch because it's the only one present, otherwise you'll think there's another one]

Let us now turn to a somewhat more quantitative analysis of the results of this experiment, in respect of adequacy and redundancy of children's utterances.

Adequacy of message. Table 9 gives a breakdown per age group of the proportion of inadequate messages. A message is taken to be 'inadequate' when it is insufficient to enable E.2 to make a correct selection amongst the vehicles. A message is counted as 'adequate' even if it is extremely laborious, the problem of redundancy being dealt with in subsequent tables.

Table 10 gives a breakdown of inadequate messages per item for the total population.

TABLE 9. *Inadequate messages as a function of age*

Age group	Number of subjects	Total number of trials	Number of inadequate messages	(%) of inadequate messages
4,7–5,11	12	156	65	41.0
6,0–6,11	11	133	32	24.1
7,0–7,11	8	103	26	25.2
8,0–8,11	7	80	11	13.7
9,0–9,11	7	74	6	8.1
10,0–11,5	8	84	6	7.1

TABLE 10. *Inadequate messages as a function of item*

Expected response	Total number of trials	Number of inadequate messages	(%) of inadequate messages
1. the lorries	64	13	20.3
2. my cars	61	11	18.0
3. the red cars	57	5	8.8
4. my blue lorries	79	32	40.5
5. the open cars	55	9	16.4
6. my closed cars	68	25	36.8
7. the blue closed cars	65	18	27.7
8. my red open cars	77	33	42.8
9. the/my aeroplane	52	0	0
10. the/my yellow cars	52	0	0

Table 11 gives a breakdown per age group, and table 12 as a function of item type, of the number of items never adequate, i.e. after three trials (or two trials in the case of some small children) the child was unable to correct his message so as to make it possible for E.2 to make a correct selection. It should be stressed that the column 'Number of items' in both tables 11 and 12 does not concern total number of trials, but rather the number of items never adequate, i.e. three trials for one item will count as 'one' unit in the total number of items. It was felt important to make this distinction between tables 9–10 and tables 11–12 in order to show the difference between incapacity to give an adequate message and capacity to correct one's message after noting its inadequacy.

It should be noted that no inadequate message was due to 'incorrect' description of a property, i.e. no child said 'blue' when he should have said 'red'. The errors were of a more subtle nature.

TABLE 11. *Number of items never adequate, as a function of age*

Age group	Number of items (several trials for one item count as one)	Number of items never adequate	(%) of items never adequate
4,7–5,11	114	24	21.1
6,0–6,11	104	5	4.8
7,0–7,11	80	3	3.7
8,0–8,11	69	0	0
9,0–9,11	69	1	1.4
10,0–11,5	78	0	0

TABLE 12. *Number of subjects never adequate, as a function of item*

Expected response	Number of items (several trials for one item count as one per child)	Number of subjects never adequate	(%) of subjects never adequate
1. the lorries	53	2	3.7
2. my cars	51	1	1.9
3. the red cars	53	1	1.8
4. my blue lorries	52	5	9.6
5. the open cars	50	5	10.0
6. my closed cars	49	7	14.2
7. the blue closed cars	50	3	6.0
8. my red open cars	53	9	16.9
9. the/my aeroplane	52	0	0
10. the/my yellow cars	51	0	0

These four tables call for the following comments.

Table 9 shows that whereas the youngest subjects give a relatively high number of inadequate messages (41.0%), figures drop to 24.1% for 6 year olds and 25.2% for 7 year olds. Another decline is to be registered for 8 year olds (13.7%). From 9 years it can be said that almost all inadequate messages disappear (8.1%). Table 11 shows that children of all ages are able to correct their inadequate messages in the light of the consequent action furnished by E.2. For the youngest group, up to 5,11 years, the number of items never adequate represents 21.1% of their total responses. From 6,0 years, the percentage of items never adequate is extremely low, ranging from 4.8% to 0%.

Tables 10 and 12, which break down the data as a function of item type rather than age, are important for the following reasons. Whereas for several items (e.g. 4, 6, 7 and 8) there is a high percentage of inadequate trials (ranging from 27.7% to 42.8%), it will be seen, in the next section on redundant information, that the inadequacy of the message is not due to incapacity to furnish *several* criteria, but to the lack of the ability to express the *relevant* criteria. Whilst inadequate trials were frequent, table 12 shows that the percentage of items never adequate is very small. All items registered under 10% never adequate, except foı items 5, 6 and 8 which ranged between 10% and 16.9%. This again shows that no item represented a special difficulty as far as giving an adequate message is concerned.

Redundant information conveyed. Tables 13 and 14 deal with the question of to what extent the information in the message is redundant. If, for example, all the lorries are in the garage, it is redundant to mention the colours of the lorries. It is also redundant to say 'all' since 'les camions' [the lorries] is a quantified expression covering the whole class of lorries. Likewise, it is redundant to say 'green' aeroplane, since only one aeroplane is present.

The calculation of the actual 'degree of redundancy' may appear arbitrary. For instance, for 'All the lorries from my side and your side', the question arises whether there are seven degrees of redundancy (i.e. the words 'all/from/my/side/and/your/side') or only three, (i.e. 'all/from my side/and from your side'). Either criterion is valid, however, if applied consistently for all subjects and all items. Nevertheless, the former method was chosen since there is less possibility of variation than with the equation of one degree with one 'idea'. The point of the exercise was, of course, not the absolute number of degrees of redundancy but rather the *differences* between age groups and items. Clearly for items 9 and 10, the child's response of 'My yellow cars/The yellow cars' was considered entirely non-redundant and equivalent but 'The two yellow cars, they're mine, they're closed' does contain redundant information. The degrees of redundancy were calculated only for adequate trials in view of the ambiguous status of inadequate trials vis-à-vis redundancy. Degrees of redundancy figures comprise redundancy over and above the words required for the most economical adequate message: e.g. 'My two closed yellow cars' would count as having two degrees of redundancy (the words 'two' and 'closed').

TABLE 13. *Redundancy of message as a function of age*

Age group	Total number of adequate trials	Total degrees of redundancy for adequate trials	Average number of degrees of redundancy per adequate trial
4,7–5,11	91	335	3.67
6,0–6,11	101	327	3.23
7,0–7,11	77	383	4.97
8,0–8,11	69	116	1.68
9,0–9,11	68	129	1.87
10,0–11,5	78	118	1.50

TABLE 14. *Redundancy of message as a function of item*

Expected response (order of presentation in parentheses)	Total number of adequate trials	Total degrees of redundancy for adequate trials	Average number of degrees of redundancy per adequate trial
1. the lorries (1)	51	206	4.01
2. my cars (10)	50	193	3.86
3. the red cars (6)	52	165	3.17
4. my blue lorries (2)	47	71	1.51
5. the open cars (4)	46	266	5.78
6. my closed cars (8)	43	272	6.32
7. the blue closed cars (7)	47	60	1.27
8. my red open cars (3)	44	45	1.02
9. the/my aeroplane (5)	52	40	0.77
10. the/my yellow cars (9)	52	90	1.73

It is clear from table 13 that until 8 years children show a high degree of redundancy per adequate trial. The average number of extra words per item was 3.67 for under 6 year olds and as high as 4.97 for 7 to 8 year olds. A sharp drop occurs in the average rate from 8 years and is maintained at substantially the same level until 11 years. These figures seem striking, since it is often assumed that small children do not give enough information and that older children can add more and more criteria. The problem is obviously not quantitative, since the small children give a great deal of information as compared to the older subjects.

The results show that there does seem to be a tendency with age towards avoiding 'overdetermination'. What is surprising, however, if we compare tables 9 and 13, is that whereas the percentage of inadequate messages drops sharply between 5 and 6 years, and remains substantially the same for 6 and 7 year olds (table 9), the picture is somewhat different as regards redundancy rates (table 13). It thus seems that the drop in inadequacy between 5 and 6 years is not due to the *quantity* of criteria mentioned but rather to the *relevance* of the criteria mentioned for picking out referents. And the increase in redundancy at 7 appears to be the result of children's effort to give as much information as possible, which subsequently becomes more and more economical.

In both tables the drop in inadequacy and redundancy is sizeable from 8 to 9 years and maintained throughout the population up to 11 years.

Comparing tables 10 and 14, it is clear that the inadequacy of the message is not due to the child merely not giving enough information. Items such as 6, 1, 2, 5 are amongst those more frequently inadequate and yet they have high average degrees of redundancy. It should be recalled that table 14 just includes responses which were adequate. Only in items 7 and 8 is the inadequacy rate high and the redundancy rate relatively low. However, since all the items in table 14 show some degree of redundancy, this tends to indicate that relevance of criteria rather than number of criteria is where explanation should be sought. Indeed, the similar comprehension experiment (see experiment 14, p. 192 below) clearly shows that number of descriptive criteria is not the difficult issue for small children but rather the *determinor function* of each criterion.

The figure in parentheses in the first column of table 14 gives the order of presentation of items. Comparing the order of presentation in table 14 with the figures for average degrees of redundancy shows that order of presentation did not affect the results. Indeed, items 6, 2 and 3, for example, came very late in order of presentation yet registered amongst the highest redundancy rates. It should be recalled that children were frequently asked from the outset, in second and third trials for an item, to give a shorter/quicker message. Even so, items coming up late in order of presentation nonetheless registered high redundancy rates.

The following general trend with regard to the redundancy/adequacy problem stems from the results. It is illustrated by item 6 ('my closed cars') which should be responded to simply by 'my closed cars'.

Procedure (*a*) (*inadequate message for E.2's choice*)
Y a des voitures, elles sont rouges, jaunes, bleues, blanches, elles viennent de mon côté
[There are some cars, they are red, yellow, blue, white, they come from my side]

Procedure (*b*) (*adequate, but laborious message*)
Mettez sept de mes voitures à moi, elles sont toutes fermées, y a des rouges fermées, des bleues fermées, des jaunes fermées, puis y a aussi l'ambulance . . . toutes les miennes quoi pas les voitures fermées de l'autre carré
[Put seven of my cars, they are all closed, red closed ones, blue closed ones, yellow closed ones, and also the ambulance . . . all mine, not the closed cars from the other parking lot]
Procedure (*c*) (*adequate and increasingly economical message*)
Mettez toutes mes voitures ferméés . . . mes voitures fermées
[Put all my closed cars . . . my closed cars]

The above procedures represent two trends: first they are valid developmentally in that more of the youngest subjects used procedure (a); procedure (c) was mainly found in the oldest subjects. They are also valid for subjects within a session, in that on second or third trials a child may have passed from (a) to (b) or from (b) to (c). What seems clear is that children using procedure (a) are describing 'what is *in* the garage'. Procedure (b) also describes what is in the garage, but successively takes into account what should remain in the parking lots. Children using procedure (c) reduce the message to the *relationship* between garage and parking lots, and use the possessive adjective in its determinor function.

In summary, the results of this experiment showed that in a situation which called for taking into account the listener's need to have adequate reference, under 8 year olds tend to furnish a lot of redundant information in an attempt to *describe* as fully as possible the referent under focus of attention. These children do not easily relate the referent to the general context from which it is extracted. This clearly seems covered by the concept of 'descriptor function'. The under 8 year olds' use of the determiners studied can be summarized as follows: for the youngest subjects 'les' is used as a pluralizer and at first denotes objects from both parking lots. However, children of all ages used 'mes' easily for reference to belongings taken from their own pockets. Since there were no duplicates of these objects, the noun alone is sufficient referential information. The use of the possessive adjective in only such cases, and its absence elsewhere, shows that it is not being used in its determinor function. Rather it is used as a descriptive statement about the possession property of the child's objects under focus of attention. From roughly 6 years, 'mes' was used to denote the child's parking lot. However, in the case of non-duplicated classes, such children did not use the definite article to cover objects from their parking lot and rejected the experimenter's suggestion to do so. In such a case therefore, 'mes' was used in a limited binary contrastive sense (i.e. 'mes' = those in my lot, 'les' = those in both lots). This can be interpreted as an experiment-generated procedure and not yet the determinor function of the two terms. It is only from 8 or 9 years that children consistently used the determinor function, i.e. 'les' as a totalizer and 'mes' referring to a total subclass. These older children prefered 'les' to 'mes' in the case of non-duplicated classes which came from their parking lot, as if they did not wish to overdetermine.

The results of this experiment also indicate that there is a gradual tendency first to overmark, which leads to adequate but laborious utterances, and then gradually to economy of markers. The latter starts at about 7 or 8 years, and becomes fully operative only from 9 or 10 years. It is hypothesized that overmarking represents a *successive* link between the descriptor function and the determinor function, whereas the real determinor function expresses a *simultaneous* relationship. Inhelder & Piaget (1959) have frequently stressed the younger child's tendency to make successive, juxtaposed relations in cognitive tasks, and they have pinpointed the difficulties faced by the young child with simultaneous relationships.

It would be erroneous to imagine, however, that children under 8 years of age are not endeavouring to convey some aspects of the determinor function. Whilst the addition of 'all' is seen to have a descriptor function at 4 years (i.e. meaning 'a lot' versus the mere plurality of 'les'), as early as 5 years the child's addition of 'all' appears to be an attempt to convey something about the relationship of the referent to the current context. However, at first the child appears to be unsure of what 'all' actually covers, and therefore adds additional markers in postposition, e.g. 'All the cars, even mine'. Postposing is again a sign of successive rather than simultaneous relations. Children of roughly 7 years appear to use 'all' as a totalizer, i.e. in its determinor function. Now, it was stated that over 9 year olds use 'les' to convey class extension and only use 'all' as a special emphasizer to assert a large quantity, i.e. in the case of all the cars going to the garage. Thus, in fact, these older children are expressing the class extension by two markers:

(a) when there are subclass-identifying criteria, e.g. '*Les* voitures *rouges*';
(b) when there is no subclass, e.g. '*Toutes les* voitures'.

Thus, 'les' is rarely used *alone* to convey the class extension function. Recalling the linguistic analysis in chapter 3, it can be argued that the young child's tendency to add special emphasizers, e.g. 'All the cars', 'My cars, not the others', etc., is in fact a natural way of indicating what particular distinction is actually under focus of attention in the current context. The older child, in an experimental setting, and with his seemingly natural tendency and capacity to be linguistically economical, will more readily use the distinction encoded by the article contrasts, but even so, he usually adds other relevant markers.

Finally, other aspects of this experiment also touched on the linguistic hypotheses about the primary and secondary focussing functions of a word. Given that the 6 year old can express totalization by adding 'all', why does he first use the plural definite article to express pluralization rather than totalization? It is suggested that this can be explained intralinguistically. My hypothesis is – and this will be discussed at a more general level in chapter 9 – that children first approach language as if each word were *unifunctional.* Moreover, if they do use one word to express two different functions, they do not do so simultaneously, but in two different utterances, and they seem unaware that the same word is being used. Thus, it is suggested that a plurifunctional word is at first felt to be several homonyms before it can become one word with several functions. The older child can cope with plurifunctionality and only adds extra markers for emphasis purposes. Thus, in a situation where both pluralization and totalization need to be indicated simultaneously, the younger child will call on two different words, e.g. 'tous les X', where 'tous' indicates totalization and 'les' pluralization.

This experiment can of course be criticized for its somewhat unnatural setting. Nonetheless, I feel the analysis has clearly shown that an explanation of the child's use of determiners in terms of class inclusion concepts (Inhelder & Piaget 1959) only partially accounts for the problems involved. There are clearly many intralinguistic issues the child has to come to grips with.

Experiment 4: 'What did I do?'

This experiment touches on both the exophoric and anaphoric functions of determiners in a very simple situation. Four variables, which had been difficult to isolate in the three previous experiments were introduced:

(a) the child neither saw nor heard mention of the object before an action took place;
(b) the experimenter named the object but the child did not see it before action took place;
(c) the child saw the object but did not name it before action took place;
(d) the child saw and named the object before action took place.

The actual technique is described under experimental procedure.

Experimental context. A large opaque bag contained a series of common toy-sized objects such as the following:

shoe	marble
duck	match
camel	cup
dog	watch
horse	bracelet
pig	ball
cow	doll
pencil	hairclip
rubber	etc.

A large tin was placed in the centre of the table between the child and the experimenter. The objects were small enough so that the experimenter could remove them from the bag and they remained, if necessary, completely hidden in his hand.

Experimental procedure. The experimenter explained to the child that his bag was full of tiny toys, and that he would be taking toys from the bag and performing actions, such as putting something into the tin, dropping something, etc. Each time he asked the child 'Qu'est-ce que j'ai fait?' [What did I do?] and avoided 'Que'est-ce que j'ai fait tomber?' [What did I drop?] or 'Qu'est-ce que j'ai mis dans la boîte?' [What did I put in the box?]. In the pilot study for this experiment, most over 5 year olds responded in all situations with an indefinite short NP response for these two latter questions, whereas the question 'What did I do?' implying an NP plus VP gave rise to responses which were differentiated as a function of the item.

There were twelve experimental items, divided into four item types, each of which appeared three times in a varying order dependent on the responses of the child. The actual object which came up in each case was not standardized. Since the game was to appear very natural, the items were run rather rapidly so that the child could give spontaneous rather than 'thought-out' responses. Item types were as follows:

Type 1
E. extracts invisibly an object from the bag and places it quickly in the tin. The child only sees the object when it reaches the tin. E. asks: 'Qu'est-ce que j'ai fait?' [What did I do?]
Type 2
E. extracts an object, says to the child: 'Regarde ça' [Look at this] and then places the object in the tin. E. asks: 'Qu'est-ce que j'ai fait?' [What did I do?]
Type 3
E. extracts an object invisibly, keeps his hand tightly closed and says: 'Dans ma main j'ai caché un tout petit X' [In my hand I am hiding a tiny little X], then he places X in the tin and asks: 'Qu'est-ce que j'ai fait?' [What did I do?]
Type 4
E. extracts an object and asks the child: 'Qu'est-ce que c'est?' [What is this?]; the child names the object, then E. places the object in the tin and asks: 'Qu'est-ce que j'ai fait? [What did I do?].

In some cases, the action of placing the object in the tin was changed to dropping it on the table, rolling it, etc.

As in most experiments, many factors will interrelate to cause choice of one or the other articles. For item types 1 and 2 both the definite and indefinite articles could be used. However, using the indefinite article would imply no presuppositions regarding the total contents of the bag (i.e. whether or not there are two identical objects). Use of the definite article would imply presupposition that it is the only one of its kind in the bag, or simply the only one present in the tin. For item type 3, a definite referring expression would be more appropriate in view of the fact that the experimenter has made a linguistic reference to the object and that it is alone. The modifiers used by the experimenter ('tiny little') could be dropped by the child and, if added, involve overdetermination. An indefinite article is not entirely incorrect. For type 4, however, only a definite article response is correct, implying 'the X to which I (the child) have just referred'.

Population. Sixty-one subjects between 3,4 and 11,5 years participated in the experiment, as follows:

Age	*Subjects*	*Average age*
3,4–3,11	5	3,7
4,0–4,11	8	4,5
5,0–5,11	7	5,6
6,0–6,11	8	6,6
7,0–7,11	9	7,4
8,0–8,11	9	8,6
9,0–9,11	10	9,4
10,0–11,5	5	10,8

Results. Table 15 shows the type of referring expressions used by each age group as a percentage of total trials per item type. The row 'Topicalization' is taken in the sense of one of the forms of the French 'thématisation', i.e. usage of definite article plus pronoun in expressions such as the following:

Tu l'as mis dans la boite, le cheval
[You put it in the box, the horse]
Il est tombé, le crayon
[It fell down, the pencil]
Tu l'as roulée, la voiture
[You rolled it, the car]
La poupée, elle est tombée
[The doll, she fell down]

Such constructions do not seem to be encountered in child language with the indefinite article. In other words, one does not hear:

Il est tombé, un crayon
[It fell down, a pencil]

What is striking in the results of the 3 year olds is the large number of indefinite articles. Despite the small population of 3 year olds, this nonetheless contrasts with the high number of definite referring expressions in other experiments. It is to be particularly noted that prior naming, either by the child or the experimenter, does not give rise to a greater number of anaphoric definite articles. Seeing the object beforehand seems to be an important factor in article usage for small children.

A slight increase in the use of definite articles can be seen for 4 year olds. From 5 years, and more systematically from 6, prior naming is the most important factor for generating definite referring expressions, and prior seeing has very little effect.

TABLE 15. *Type of referring expression used, expressed as a percentage of total trials per item type*

Age group	Total number of trials	Type of referring expression	Seen + prior naming by child ('What's that?/ Do?') (%)	Not seen + prior naming by E. ('In my hand/ Do?') (%)	Seen + no prior naming ('Look at this/ Do?') (%)	Not seen + no prior naming ('Do?) (%)
3,4–3,11	67	Definite article	44	28	31	43
		Indefinite article	56	72	69	57
		Topicalization (pronoun + definite article)	0	0	0	0
		Demonstrative pronoun	0	0	0	0
		Zero article	0	0	0	0
4,0–4,11	109	Definite article	57	38	38	59
		Indefinite article	26	48	62	32
		Topicalization (pronoun + definite article)	2	14	0	0
		Demonstrative pronoun	13	0	0	7
		Zero article	2	0	0	2
5,0–5,11	111	Definite article	49	62	33	29
		Indefinite article	29	17	54	57
		Topicalization (pronoun + definite article)	22	21	18	14
		Demonstrative pronoun	0	0	0	0
		Zero article	0	0	0	0
6,0–6,11	93	Definite article	79	67	40	36
		Indefinite article	10	33	60	64
		Topicalization (pronoun + definite article)	11	0	0	0
		Demonstrative pronoun	0	0	0	0
		Zero article	0	0	0	0

7,0–7,11	106	Definite article	72	44	29	17
		Indefinite article	19	56	71	83
		Topicalization (pronoun + definite article)	9	0	0	0
		Demonstrative pronoun	0	0	0	0
		Zero article	0	0	0	0
8,0–8,11	117	Definite article	76	78	59	28
		Indefinite article	9	14	41	72
		Topicalization (pronoun + definite article)	15	8	0	0
		Demonstrative pronoun	0	0	0	0
		Zero article	0	0	0	0
9,0–9,11	113	Definite article	77	36	24	6
		Indefinite article	9	32	76	94
		Topicalization (pronoun + definite article)	14	32	0	0
		Demonstrative pronoun	0	0	0	0
		Zero article	0	0	0	0
10,0–11,5	58	Definite article	81	74	43	0
		Indefinite article	6	36	57	100
		Topicalization (pronoun + definite article)	13	0	0	0
		Demonstrative pronoun	0	0	0	0
		Zero article	0	0	0	0

It is interesting to note that 'topicalization', whilst registering fairly low figures, does seem to point to some trends. In the 5 year old, 'topicalization' is relatively evenly spread over all types of situation, whereas for older subjects it is only to be found for items where prior naming has taken place. This suggests that its function may change with age (see Karmiloff-Smith in preparation).

This experiment was only followed by an epilinguistic part for a few children, because quite a body of data had already been collected from other experiments on the various problems involved. Since the technique was not standardized as to order, but was already exploratory in nature, test items were not followed by the usual clinical part.

The few children we did question at the end of the session were mainly asked about situation type 1, where the child first names the object. Apart from one advanced 6 year old, under 8 year olds could not explain why they changed from indefinite to definite article. Some of the explanations of the older children are given below:

8,6 years
E.: Pourquoi tu dis d'abord *une* voiture, puis *la* voiture?
C.: Parce que c'est justement celle-là
[E.: Why first *a* car, then *the* car?
C.: Because it's precisely that one]

9,0 years
Parce que c'est celle dont vous parliez déjà, pas une autre
[Because it's the one you were already talking about and not another one]

9,1 years
Si on dit ça c'est un stylo, j'ai fait tomber un stylo, alors il se peut que ça soit pas celui-là, ça pourrait être un autre, quand on dit *le* stylo, on veut dire celui-là, ce stylo-là
[If you say that's a pen, I dropped a pen, it could be not that one, it could mean another one, when you say *the* pen you mean that one, that pen there]

9,5 years
C.: Le, c'est plutôt quand il y en a qu'un seul
E.: Alors pourquoi utiliser une bonteille pour ici?
C.: Parce que j'aurais besoin qu'on dit qu'on a une bouteille, et puis tout d'un coup on la fait rouler, alors on dirait *la* bouteille
[C.: The, it usually means when there is just one
E.: Why use a bottle here then? (item type 4)
C.: Because I'd need someone first to say they'd got a bottle, and then suddenly they roll it, and then one would say *the* bottle]

9,10 years
On dit le stylo parce que c'est le même . . . celui qui s'est fait lâcher
[You say the pen because it's the same one . . . the one that got dropped]
10,1 years
Parce que je l'avais déjà vu et alors je savais quel cheval c'était
[Because I'd already seen it, so I knew which horse it was]
11,1 years
Quand vous l'avez laissé tomber, on savait déjà de quel cheval il s'agissait
[When you dropped it, we knew which horse we were both talking about]

In the situation where the experimenter used modifiers and said, e.g. 'In my hand I've a tiny little church', under 5 year olds tended to repeat the modifiers, e.g. 'You put the/a tiny little church into the tin', whereas some 5 year olds and all 7 year olds and over deleted the modifiers, e.g. 'You put the church into the tin'. Obviously the younger child is overdetermining or, as I shall argue in the synthesis, is actually not using the definite article anaphorically. The older child shows that, since the knowledge about which object is being referred to is shared, it is no longer necessary to add the identifying details: 'tiny little'.

One thing that was rather striking concerned the objects themselves. The observations cannot be systematic because the speed at which the experiment was run made it impossible to select the same object for each different item for all children. However, in many cases it could be noted that extra world knowledge also played a role in article usage. Objects such as a match, a marble, a sheep and a flower, tended to be given the indefinite article irrespective of item type, whereas objects such as a watch, a ball and a church were given definite articles. It is suggested that children are not only concerned with the experimental context, but bring to the situation knowledge about the *usual* setting of objects outside the experimental setting. In other words, matches, marbles, sheep and flowers usually come in groups, whereas one encounters in a given setting only one watch, one ball and one church. Thus, not only the *actual* class extension of objects in the experimental setting but also the *potential* class extension is a factor influencing article usage.

The large number of indefinite articles used by under 4 year olds is one striking result of this experiment. It would seem that theee children decoded the whole task as a naming task. Even where the experimenter or the child named the object prior to the action, i.e. normally calling for anaphoric definite article or pronoun in the second reference, under

4 year olds used predominantly indefinite articles in both references. Slightly older children did use the definite article for the second reference i.e. if the child had done the previous naming and seen the objects. However, if the experimenter named an object hidden in his hand, the 4 year old's second reference was still indefinite. Moreover, as pointed out, under 5 year olds tended to repeat redundant modifiers, e.g. 'tiny little X', in their second reference. Thus, for the under 5 year old, the definite article does not have an anaphoric function.

However, from 5 years and more consistently from 6 years, the child tended to use a definite article in the second reference, whether he or the experimenter did the prior naming. Must one then conclude that in this type of situation the 6 year old can already use the definite article anaphorically? It is argued in the light of data from subsequent experiments, that this is not *intralinguistic* anaphoric reference. Looking at table 15 we see that there is a considerable drop again at 7 years when the experimenter did the naming and not the child. It is really only from 8 years that the difference is very marked between the situations calling for definite reference and those calling for indefinite reference. Thus it is suggested that the under 7 year old's use of the definite article in some 60% of all cases is still partially deictic. However, there is no doubt that some situations will facilitate the child's use of functions that he cannot yet use in all circumstances.

Parts of this experiment touched on the anaphoric function of the definite article. The next chapter covers experiments more specifically designed for this purpose.

5 *Production experiments: anaphoric function of determiners*

The two experiments reported on in this chapter were designed to analyse how children gradually organize the various possibilities language offers for making anaphoric reference, a function which can be indicated by the articles but also by other means.

Experiment 5: girl/boy acting

Naturalistic data on 2 year olds show that once a small child has named an object by using the indefinite article, he will frequently continue his utterance referring to the same object with the definite article (e.g. 'That's a cow, the cow fallen down'). This at first appears to the observer to be a precocious use of the definite article in its anaphoric function. However, one might also argue that in fact the child has two procedures: one for naming, using the indefinite article, and another, quite separate procedure for referring deictically to a referent under focus of attention. It appears anaphoric to the observer who relates the definite referring expression to the previous linguistic mention referring to the same entity. However, it may well be that the child does not initially make such intralinguistic relationships. Experiment 5 was designed in such a way as to leave the child free to express the relationship between two referring expressions in the way he deemed appropriate and did not constrain his responses to the use of articles only.

Experimental context. There were three types of context:

(a) the three objects were all different (e.g. a pig, a box, a dummy, a book, a doll);
(b) the three objects were similar but differed by colour (e.g. three different-coloured whistles, three different-coloured cows); and
(c) the three objects were all identical (e.g. three red cars, three tiny houses, three matchboxes).

A little boy-doll and a little girl-doll were to be the agents of the actions acted out before the child by the experimenter.

Experimental procedure. The experimenter explained to the child that the little boy-doll and girl-doll would perform various actions on objects to be taken from bags. A few simple practice items were carried out. The experimenter stated 'The little girl pushes over the little boy' and asked the child to carry out the corresponding action. The child was then asked to act out: the boy pushes my pencil. Then the experimenter performed an action (e.g. the boy pushes the girl) and asked the child to tell him what had happened. The experimenter then performed a second action (e.g. the girl pushes the experimenter's pencil and then the boy pushes it). The experimenter asked the child to explain what happened.

The experimental items were as follows:

Context	*E.'s action*	*Child's expected response*
Type A bags of three different objects	(1a) boy jumps into X	Le garçon a sauté dans *la* X [The boy jumped into *the* X]
	(1b) girl jumps into X	Et puis la fille a sauté dans *la* X/*y* a sauté [And then the girl jumped into *the* X/*it*]
	(2a) girl pushes Y	La fille a poussé *le* Y [The girl pushed *the* Y]
	(2b) boy pushes Z	Et puis le garçon a poussé *le* Z [And then the boy pushed *the* Z]
Type B bags of three similar but different-coloured objects	(3a) boy acts on X	Le garçon a touché *une* X/*la* X *rouge* [The boy touched *an* X/*the red* X]
	(3b) girl acts on same X	La fille *l'*a touchée/a touché *la* X/*la même* X/aussi *la* X *rouge* [The girl touched *it*/*the* X/*the same* X/*also the red* X]
	(4a) girl acts on Y	La fille a poussé *le* Y *bleu* [The girl pushed *the blue* Y]
	(4b) boy acts on another Y	Le garçon a poussé *le* Y *vert* [The boy pushed *the green* Y]
Type C bags of three identical objects	(5a) boy acts on X	Le garçon a fait tomber *une des* X/*une* X [The boy knocked over *one of the* Xs/*an* X]
	(5b) girl acts on same X	La fille *l'*a fait tomber/a fait tomber *la* X/*la même* X [The girl knocked *it*/*the* X/*the same* X over]
	(6a) girl acts on Y	La fille a poussé *une des*/*une* Y [The girl pushed *one of the*/*a* Y]
	(6b) boy acts on another Y	Le garçon a poussé *une*/*une autre* Y [The boy pushed *a*/*another* Y]

After the experimenter had carried out part (a) of the action, the child was asked: 'Qu'est-ce qui s'est passé?' [What happened?] After the child's utterance, part (b) of the action was performed and again the child was asked to explain what had happened. In this way any problems involved in remembering the two sequences were avoided, since the small child tends to refer to only one of two sequences if the two are presented before he makes his utterance. Actions were varied and involved the child producing such verbs as 'push knock over caress pick up jump into jump out of', All children had at least twelve experimental items, i.e. two responses for each of item types 1–6. These were presented in a clinical fashion, depending on the response of each child. Children who never used colour modifiers for type B objects were asked, when the objects were placed back in the opaque bags, whether the Xs were all the same. This was to verify that they had indeed noticed the different colours but had not judged them relevant for determining which object was referred to.

Population. Sixty-one children between 3,3 and 11,1 years were interviewed (3 year olds have not been included in the results because of the small number of responses). Ages were distributed as follows:

Age	*Subjects*	*Average age*
3,3–3,11	3	3,6
4,0–4,11	8	4,5
5,0–5,11	8	5,9
6,0–6,11	8	6,6
7,0–7,11	8	7,7
8,0–8,11	9	8,5
9,0–9,11	9	9,5
10,0–11,1	8	10,5

Results. This experiment was designed to look at the various procedures language offers for making anaphoric reference. It was therefore decided to make the tables of results as detailed as possible, rather than grouping together several similar types of response. The percentages should therefore be considered with some caution for although total numbers of responses for each age group per context varied between 51 and 78, the percentages can merely indicate general trends.

In order to facilitate the reading of tables 16 to 25, an explanation is given below of the various column headings; where they are self-explanatory (e.g. definite article) no comment is made:

Reference to first actions

deictic pronoun

reference to part (a) of the action is made with a pronoun (e.g. 'The girl pushed it') where there has been no previous linguistic mention made of the referent of the pronoun, although of course context and shared knowledge between speaker and addressee makes the pronoun quite unambiguous

definite article + localization

for identical and similar objects, the child uses the following expressions: 'La fille a poussé la X du milieu/la X près de moi/la X à gauche/la X de ce côté', etc. [The girl pushed the X in the middle/the X closest to me/the X on the left/the X on this side, etc.]

definite article + modifier (*or* idem *with indefinite*)

the child adds a colour modifier

(e.g. 'La fille a poussé la X verte' [The girl pushed the green X])

Reference to second actions on the same class member

pronoun + Re-verb or definite article + Re-verb

the child refers to the object with an anaphoric pronoun, but also adds a repeater operator on the verb

(e.g. 'La fille l'a re-poussé' [The girl re-pushed it]

'Le garçon il l'a re-bougé' [The boy he re-moved it])

definite article + Re-verb

(e.g. 'La fille a re-bougé la X' [The girl re-moved the X])

definite article + 'also/again'

the child uses an anaphoric definite article but adds 'aussi/encore' [also/again] to various parts of his utterance

(e.g. 'La fille aussi a poussé la X' [The girl also pushed the X]

'La fille a poussé encore la X' [The girl pushed again the X]

'La fille a poussé la X aussi' [The girl pushed the X also]

'Aussi la fille a poussé la X' [Also the girl pushed the X])

definite article + 'same'

the child uses an anaphoric definite article but adds the word 'même' [same] as a postdeterminer

(e.g. 'La fille a poussé la même X' [The girl pushed the same X])

deictic definite article

it was of course necessary to make a distinction between those children who first used, say, an indefinite referring expression and then used the definite article in reference to the second action on the same object, and those who used the definite article for both the first action and the second action on the same object. It is these latter responses that were classed as 'deictic definite article', since the definite article for first action is clear from context but has no previous linguistic mention

Reference to second actions on another class member

These have mainly the same column headings as the other tables, except for one difference:

definite article + 'other'

the child uses the definite article plus the postdeterminer 'autre' [other]; this is incorrect because there are more than two objects present
(e.g. 'La fille a poussé l'autre X' [The girl pushed the other X] which should have been:
'La fille a poussé un autre X' [The girl pushed another X])

'*+ modifier*'

means that the modifier did indeed play a determinor function; otherwise the column is headed '*+ redundant modifier*', e.g. in the case of identical objects, colour modifiers cannot act as determiners for picking out the referent

Let us now take a look at the results, first as a function of type of context. Table 16 gives details of the procedures used by different age groups and table 17 groups them according to more general categories, with reference to actions performed on singletons. In the case of singletons, the second action was always necessarily on the same object. Table 17 shows clearly that for all age groups responses with reference to singletons for the first action are definite, figures ranging between 82% and 100%. With respect to the second action performed on the singleton, table 17 again shows very high percentages for definite referring expressions at all ages, ranging between 67% and 92%, the lowest figure being for 10 year olds. However, a closer inspection of the details in table 16 shows that apart from the 7 year olds, some children of all ages attempt to give further precision in their reference to the second action by adding 'also', 'Re-verb' or, in the case of the youngest subjects, some redundant localizers. The use of the anaphoric pronoun is fairly low, 21% at 5 years, down to 4% at 7 years and up gradually to 30% at 10 years. What is interesting about these results in the singleton context is whether or not responses are discriminating, i.e. whether the percentage use of a given expression differs from one context to another. This may help us understand some of the functions a given syntactico-semantic expression has for the child.

Table 18 shows the referring expressions used by children with reference to a first action on one of several entirely identical objects. What is striking is the very high number of definite referring expressions (with or without redundant modifier – this was not broken down because it has been thoroughly studied in other experiments in this study)

TABLE 16. *SINGLETONS: referring expressions used for actions on singletons, expressed as a percentage of total trials for each part of action*

Age group	First action			Second action on the same object							
	Indefinite article (%)	Definite article (%)	Deictic pronoun (%)	Indefinite article (%)	Definite article (%)	Pronoun (+ Re-verb) (%)	Definite article + 'also/again' (%)	Definite article + same (%)	Definite article + redundant localizer (%)	Definite article + Re-verb (%)	Other (%)
4,0–4,11	14	86	0	17	32	0	32	0	12	7	0
5,0–5,11	0	100	0	0	40	21	20	0	7	12	0
6,0–6,11	0	100	0	0	64	8	7	0	14	7	0
7,0–7,11	12	82	6	11	81	4	4	0	0	0	0
8,0–8,11	0	100	0	0	55	11	17	3	6	8	0
9,0–9,11	7	88	5	0	44	20	33	0	0	3	0
10,0–11,1	5	95	0	3	37	30	18	3	0	9	0

TABLE 17. *SINGLETONS: definite and indefinite referring expressions for singletons, expressed as a percentage of total trials for each part of action*

	First action			Second action on same object		
Age group	Indefinite (%)	Definite (%)	Deictic pronoun (%)	Indefinite (%)	Definite (%)	Anaphoric pronoun (%)
4,0–4,11	14	86	0	17	83	0
5,0–5,11	0	100	0	0	79	21
6,0–6,11	0	100	0	0	92	8
7,0–7,11	12	82	6	11	85	4
8,0–8,11	0	100	0	0	89	11
9,0–9,11	7	88	5	0	80	20
10,0–11,1	5	95	0	3	67	30

TABLE 18. *IDENTICAL OBJECTS: referring expressions for first action performed on one of several identical objects, expressed as a percentage of total trials for first action*

	First action performed on one of several identical objects				
	Adequate referring expressions			Inadequate referring expressions	
Age group	Indefinite article (%)	One of the (%)	Definite article + localization (%)	Demonstrative adjective (%)	Definite article (+ redundant modifier) (%)
4,0–4,11	17	0	0	0	83
5,0–5,11	37	0	3	0	60
6,0–6,11	22	7	10	0	61
7,0–7,11	55	4	14	4	23
8,0–8,11	27	3	30	0	40
9,0–9,11	26	5	26	3	40
10,0–11,1	47	20	17	3	13

between the ages of 4 and 6 years, ranging from 83% to 61%. The definite article is of course inadequate reference because of the identity of the objects. Upon hearing the child say 'The girl pushed the X', the experimenter could ask 'Which X?' whereas this question is unnecessary in the case of singletons. However, comparing first action for singletons in table 17 and inadequate definite articles for identical objects in table 18, it can be seen that although not shown among the 4 year old group, the 5 and 6 year olds discriminate fairly clearly between uses of the definite article for the two situations (60% for identicals versus 100% for singletons). From 7 years, the difference in use of the

TABLE 19. *IDENTICAL OBJECTS: referring expressions for second action on same class member of identical objects, expressed as a percentage of total trials for second action*

	Second action on same class member										
	Adequate referring expressions					Inadequate referring expressions					
Age group	Definite article + localizer (%)	Anaphoric definite article (%)	Definite article + Re-verb (%)	Definite article + 'same' (%)	Anaphoric pronoun (%)	Indefinite article (%)	Indefinite article + 'also/again' (%)	Demon-strative (%)	Deictic definite article (%)	Deictic definite article + redundant modifier (%)	Deictic definite article + 'also' (%)
4,0–4,11	5	0	0	0	21	10	10	0	39	5	10
5,0–5,11	0	0	0	17	21	8	4	4	29	4	13
6,0–6,11	8	0	17	12	11	8	0	6	35	0	3
7,0–7,11	12	0	6	34	6	28	0	3	6	3	0
8,0–8,11	14	2	6	31	10	4	2	0	27	2	2
9,0–9,11	18	0	4	43	9	9	0	0	13	4	0
10,0–11,1	37	16	2	17	10	5	0	0	8	0	5

definite article between the two situations is sizeable, although the 40% of definite references in the identical situation for 8 and 9 year olds is rather surprising. The main difference lies in the use of indefinite referring expressions (mainly the indefinite article and in a few rare cases 'one of the') which are appropriate in the identical context. Only 4 year olds seem not to be using the indefinite article as a discriminating response (14% and 17% for the two situations). Whilst the figures remain fairly low, note should also be taken of the preference of a few subjects between 6 and 10 years, particularly 8 and 9 year olds, to seek to use a definite referring expression by adding a localizer.

Table 19 gives details of the referring expressions used in reference to a second action performed on the same object in the identical context. First it should be noted that whilst the anaphoric definite article would be adequate if, for the first action, an indefinite referring expression or a definite article plus localizer had been used, the use of the anaphoric definite article is entirely absent from all age groups except 8 years olds (a mere 2%) and 10 years olds (16%). This fact is striking, particularly when compared to the figures for definite referring expressions in second action on singletons in table 17 (ranging from 67% to 92%). Clearly children do not let the definite article carry alone the burden of indicating anaphoric reference in contexts where a possible confusion might occur in picking out the referent (identical versus the singleton). Use of the anaphoric pronoun was also fairly low for identicals (ranging from 6% to 21%), with the highest figures for the youngest children. This again raises questions as to the *function* of the pronoun for the child, since it is well known that children do make frequent use of pronouns. Spatial localization as a means for determining does increase with age, but it should be pointed out that objects were sometimes placed in a circle, in order to provoke other forms of determination. Thus these figures should be interpreted with caution because the child's natural tendency to use spatial indicators may have been curtailed. There was definitely a tendency to use a spatial reference for identical contexts. Percentages of responses using the word 'same', which one might have expected to be rather high for the identical situation, range between 12% and 43%, with no such responses for the 4 year old group. (As the experiment 16 comprehension task (p. 206 below) shows, this fact is not surprising in view of the child's interpretation of the function of the postdeterminer 'same'.)

As far as the 'inadequate' attempts are concerned for the second action on same object in identical context, it was perhaps somewhat arbitrary to group the first two columns ('indefinite article', 'indefinite article + "also/again"') under the heading 'Inadequate referring expressions'. Of course, whilst use of the indefinite article is not strictly incorrect, the context is potentially ambiguous. It was felt that one should take into account the fact that language has possibilities for more precise reference to a second action on the same object and therefore the indefinite was considered inadequate. In any case, figures remained low at most ages (ranging from 5% to 28%) in respect of indefinite referential expressions. The clearest trends for inadequate reference were found in the use by 4 to 6 years olds of the deictic definite article with or without addition of a redundant modifier or 'also'.

Let us now turn briefly to the expressions used for reference to the second action on another identical object. Table 20 gives details of procedures used. Whilst 4 year olds register very low figures for adequacy of response (only 10%), it should be pointed out that they were never unaware of the fact that the experimenter's action had been sometimes on the same class member and at other times, as in this case, on two different class members. The clinical discussion after the session made this quite clear. The question of course is both whether or not they possess the linguistic capacity to make the necessary distinction and the cognitive capacity to see the need for it to be marked linguistically. Surprisingly enough, use of the indefinite article plus the postdeterminer 'other', which could be considered as the 'most appropriate' response, does not reach the 40% level until 10 years (see table 20). However, again, children increasingly tend to seek to use a definite referring expression by using the definite article plus a localizer. Grouping together the inadequate references using the definite article with reference to another class member (table 20), one discovers high percentages: 81% at 4 years, 56% at 5 years, 44% at 6 years, a drop at 7 years to 19%, and again an increase to 38% at 8 and 9 years. Such figures covering use of definite articles for reference to action on *another* class member (where both speaker and addressee share the same referential information) raise rather serious questions about the contention of some authors that the indefinite/definite contrast is achieved by 3 or 4 years of age. This will be fully discussed later. It can also be noted from table 20 that there are no occurrences of 'Re-verb' for reference to action on another class member, which tends to indicate that 'Re-verb' has a real psychological function when used. There are also no occurrences of 'indefinite article + "also"'

TABLE 20. *IDENTICAL OBJECTS: referring expressions for second action on another class member of identical objects, expressed as a percentage of total trials for second action*

	Second action on another class member											
	Adequate referring expressions					Inadequate referring expressions						
Age group	Indefinite article (%)	'One of the' (%)	Indefinite article + 'other' (%)	Indefinite article + 'also' (%)	Definite article + localizer (%)	Demon-strative/ definite article + pointing (%)	Definite article + 'also' (%)	Definite article + Re-verb (%)	Definite article (%)	Definite article + 'other' (%)	Definite article + redundant modifier (%)	Pronoun (%)
4,0–4,11	5	0	5	0	0	15	5	0	51	5	5	9
5,0–5,11	11	0	25	0	4	0	17	0	35	4	0	4
6,0–6,11	15	2	29	0	10	5	0	0	26	0	13	0
7,0–7,11	39	0	30	0	12	0	0	0	14	5	0	0
8,0–8,11	7	2	18	0	35	2	0	0	23	10	3	0
9,0–9,11	11	2	23	0	26	2	0	0	28	6	2	0
10,0–11,1	7	16	40	0	20	2	0	0	7	4	0	0

whereas this would be quite an appropriate response. Again this shows that 'also' has a specific psychological function, because it is used for reference to second action on the *same* object.

Table 21 briefly summarizes percentages of adequate referring expressions for the identical context with regard to first action, second action on same class member, and second action on different class member. Percentages of adequate responses for all three columns do not reach over 50% levels until 7 years. Figures for 4 year olds are particularly low. A slightly more rapid increase is registered for references to a second action on a different class member, as compared to second actions on the same class member.

TABLE 21. *IDENTICAL OBJECTS: percentage of adequate referring expressions for identical objects*

Age group	First action (%)	Second action on same class member (%)	Second action on different class member (%)
4,0–4,11	17	26	10
5,0–5,11	40	38	40
6,0–6,11	39	48	56
7,0–7,11	73	58	81
8,0–8,11	60	63	62
9,0–9,11	57	74	62
10,0–11,1	84	82	83

We shall now consider the results obtained in the context where objects were similar but could be identified by their colour, i.e. the addition of a modifier with reference to first action has a determinor function. If the colour is mentioned for the first action, then for the second action on the same object, mention of colour is redundant. If the second action is on a different class member, then the colour modifier is essential for picking out the referent.

Table 22 shows the procedures used for referring to the first action performed on one of several different-coloured objects. Clearly the predominant procedure at all ages except 5 is to use the definite article plus the appropriate modifier. Here, determination by localizing spatially is almost entirely absent for all age groups. Thus spatial determiners, i.e. the temporary relation between an object and its position, are only used when the object's own properties (e.g. colour) cannot be used to pick out the referent. Use of the indefinite article, whilst roughly the same

TABLE 22. *SIMILAR OBJECTS: referring expressions for first action performed on one of several similar but different-coloured objects, expressed as a percentage of total trials for first action*

	First action performed on one of several different-coloured objects								
	Adequate referring expressions						Inadequate referring expressions		
Age group	Definite article + modifier (%)	Definite article + localizer (%)	ø article + modifier (%)	Indefinite article (%)	'One of the' (%)	Indefinite article + modifier (%)	Demon-strative (%)	Deictic definite article (%)	Deictic pronoun (%)
4,0–4,11	50	0	0	11	0	0	0	33	6
5,0–5,11	18	0	5	22	0	0	0	55	0
6,0–6,11	45	0	0	18	0	0	0	37	0
7,0–7,11	55	0	0	24	0	14	0	7	0
8,0–8,11	85	5	0	0	0	0	0	10	0
9,0–9,11	52	5	0	5	0	11	5	16	5
10,0–11,1	59	0	0	11	15	11	0	4	0

for all contexts for 4 year olds, was lower for other ages with respect to the similar context as compared to the identical context. A comparison between singleton context and similar context, with respect to use of the indefinite article, shows considerably higher percentages for similar context. Indefinite article plus modifier, an adequate response in the similar context, was very low compared to the use of definite article plus modifier. Children thus seek to use a definite referring expression at all ages. Still striking are the relatively high percentages for the definite article alone (which is inadequate) for 4, 5 and 6 year olds (33%, 55%, and 37% respectively). However, the figures are substantially lower than those registered for inadequate usage of the definite article in the identical situation. This comparison is slightly misleading, however, since we did not break down the corresponding figure in table 18 between definite article and definite article plus redundant modifier. In table 22, of course, this breakdown was essential in view of the function of the colour modifier.

Table 23 gives the details of responses to the second action performed on the same class member in the similar context. Again there is a total absence of the anaphoric definite article alone, whereas in fact this would be a very appropriate response. 'Re-verb' and localizers are also almost entirely absent. The postdeterminer 'same' is seldom used and the anaphoric pronoun only registers figures reaching 21%. Clearly, apart from 5 year olds (13%) and 6 year olds (45%), the majority of the responses in this context are definite article plus the colour modifier which, as pointed out, is redundant. One would not say: 'This morning I saw a little boy with red hair and blue eyes and the little boy with red hair and blue eyes . . .' but rather 'He' or just 'The boy'. Since the figures registered for the definite article are slightly lower for reference to the second action than to the first action, this means that a few of the subjects who incorrectly used the deictic definite article for reference to the first action did endeavour to give more precise information for the second action.

Table 24 gives details of the referring expressions used for reference to a second action on another object (different colour). From 6 years, clearly the most predominant response is a definite referring expression with the addition of the appropriate colour modifier. The use of indefinite referring expressions, which would be an adequate response, is rare, only appearing at 5 and 10 years. This again shows that, whenever they can, children prefer to use definite referring expressions.

TABLE 23. *SIMILAR OBJECTS: referring expressions for second action performed on same class member of similar objects, expressed as a percentage of total trials for second action*

	Second action on same class member											
	Adequate referring expressions						Inadequate referring expressions					
Age group	Definite article + modifier (%)	Definite article + localizer (%)	Definite article + 'same' (%)	Anaphoric pronoun (%)	Anaphoric definite article (%)	Anaphoric definite article + Re-verb (%)	Indefinite article + modifier (%)	Indefinite article + 'also' (%)	Indefinite article (%)	Deictic definite article + 'also' (%)	Deictic definite article (%)	Demon-strative (%)
4,0–4,11	75	0	0	0	0	0	0	25	0	0	0	0
5,0–5,11	13	0	13	21	0	13	0	0	0	0	40	0
6,0–6,11	45	0	0	5	0	5	0	0	10	0	30	5
7,0–7,11	60	0	5	5	0	0	10	0	14	0	0	0
8,0–8,11	92	0	4	0	0	0	0	0	0	0	4	0
9,0–9,11	61	7	7	13	0	0	5	0	0	0	7	0
10,0–11,1	64	9	9	18	0	0	0	0	0	0	0	0

TABLE 24. *SIMILAR OBJECTS: referring expressions for second action on another class member of similar but different coloured objects, expressed as a percentage of total trials for second action*

	Second action on another class member											
	Adequate referring expressions							Inadequate referring expressions				
Age group	Indefinite article (%)	Indefinite article + modifier (%)	'One of the' (%)	Indefinite article + 'other' (%)	Indefinite article + 'also' (%)	Definite article + modifier (%)	Definite article + localizer (%)	Definite article (%)	Definite article + 'also' (%)	Definite article + 'other' (%)	Demon-strative (%)	Pronoun (%)
4,0–4,11	0	0	0	0	11	33	0	33	6	17	0	0
5,0–5,11	10	10	0	29	4	10	0	29	4	4	0	0
6,0–6,11	7	0	0	15	0	63	0	15	0	0	0	0
7,0–7,11	10	26	0	0	0	52	0	6	0	6	0	0
8,0–8,11	0	0	0	0	0	100	0	0	0	0	0	0
9,0–9,11	0	5	0	0	0	74	16	5	0	0	0	0
10,0–11,1	0	10	0	0	45	45	0	0	0	0	0	0

A comparison between table 25, for adequate responses to the similar context, and table 21, for comparable data for the identical context, shows that when the child can use a colour modifier to pick out a referent, success rates are very high, particularly in the case of 4 year olds. This would point to the fact that children do want to determine as precisely as possible, but cannot always find the adequate linguistic means to do so. However, we should be cautious about drawing such a conclusion in view of the results of some of my other experiments, which show either the redundant use of modifiers or, for the youngest subjects, a lack of essential colour modifiers despite having noticed the different colours (see for example the results of experiment 2).

Finally, table 26 singles out the use of the postdeterminers 'same' and 'other' when adequately used for reference to the second action, on same class member or different class member respectively. This table was drawn up mainly for comparison purposes with the experiment 16 comprehension task involving postdeterminers (see p. 206 below), but it is intrinsically interesting in that it shows postdeterminers are predominantly used for reference to objects in the identical context.

In general, experiment 5 was particularly rewarding with respect to several of the hypotheses discussed in chapter 3. It should be borne in mind that both the child and experimenter shared the same information about the current context and events happening therein. Despite this, and despite the inadequacy of the small child's referential expressions, the results of this experiment indicate that small children nonetheless do attempt to give some precision to avoid indeterminacy of reference. In order to overcome potential indeterminacy of reference, children intially rely on properties inherent in the object under focus of attention, e.g. colour, shape, etc., then on its temporary spatial location, e.g. 'The X in the middle', 'Close to me', etc. Only at a later phase of development did children identify the object by situating its relationship to other objects in the current context.

One important fact stemming from the results of this experiment is that rarely, if ever, do children let the definite article *alone* carry the burden of anaphoric reference, where possible indeterminacy of reference could exist due to contextual factors. Thus, even when a correct initial indefinite reference was made, this was not followed by the definite article alone, as would be perfectly adequate, but children added additional markers such as 'Re-verb', 'also', etc, Some subjects even used multiple marking, e.g. 'Et la fille *aussi re*-bouge *encore le même* X' [And the girl *also*

TABLE 25. *SIMILAR OBJECTS: percentage of adequate referring expressions for similar objects of different colours*

Age group	First action (%)	Second action on same class member (%)	Second action on different class member (%)
4,0–4,11	61	75	44
5,0–5,11	45	60	63
6,0–6,11	63	55	85
7,0–7,11	93	70	88
8,0–8,11	90	96	100
9,0–9,11	73	88	95
10,0–11,1	96	100	100

TABLE 26. *Addition of postdeterminers 'same' and 'other' as determiners referring to second action*

	'Same' Second action on same class member			'Other' Second action on different class member	
Age group	Singletons (%)	Identical objects (%)	Similar objects (%)	Identical objects (%)	Similar objects (%)
4,0–4,11	0	0	0	5	0
5,0–5,11	0	17	13	25	29
6,0–6,11	0	12	0	29	15
7,0–7,11	0	34	5	30	0
8,0–8,11	3	31	4	18	0
9,0–9,11	0	43	7	23	0
10,0–11,1	3	17	9	40	0

re-moves *the same* X *again*]. 4 year olds even added markers in the case of singletons where obviously no ambiguity could exist. This seems to support the idea that linking intralinguistically is a difficult problem for the small child, which he is only able to attempt by multiple marking. The additional markers were far less frequent in the case of the similar situation where an extralinguistic property of the object (e.g. its colour) made reference clear. However, in these cases younger subjects all repeated the colour modifier in their second reference, whereas it is then redundant if the definite article were really functioning anaphorically.

The results of this experiment lend support to the explanatory hypothesis that the definite article functions first as a deictic, supporting the analysis made by Lyons (1975). Under 7 year olds even used the definite article to refer to the experimenter's actions on *another* class member in the identical situation. Thus the definite article clearly points to the referent under focus of attention, irrespective of the fact that it is different to the one just mentioned. In other words, the definite article is not used to link referents intralinguistically. Similarly, in the identical situation, between 83% and 61% of responses of under 7 year olds used the definite article to refer to one of several identical objects in the *first* action. The evidence adduced from this experiment is perhaps the clearest support of the hypothesis concerning the deictic nature of the definite article, and it is also backed from the results of other experiments.

Experiment 6: story completion

This story completion task used a very simple design, based on a test series of Maratsos (1976). Maratsos told his 3 and 4 year old subjects a series of stories involving either one X and one Y, or several Xs and several Ys. At the end of the story, the child had to answer a question concerning either X or Y. In the case of a story involving one X/Y, the child's response should be '... *the* X/*the* Y', whereas when several Xs and Ys were involved, the child's response should be '... *an* X/*a* Y'. According to Maratsos, this distinction between the definite and indefinite reference is achieved as early as 3 years, as long as speaker and listener share the same information. Only one of his stories, the so-called 'Cave story' involving lots of boys and girls, seemed to cause any problems for indefinite reference; children's responses for that story were mainly definite. For all those concerning animals, a significant indefinite/definite contrast was made, according to Maratsos, by both 3 and 4 year olds. Since other authors, e.g. Warden (1973) in a broad study for English, and Bresson *et al.* (1970) on 4 and 5 year olds for French, found, on the contrary, that young children's referring expressions were predominantly definite when the test involved visible objects rather than a verbal story with no tangible support, it was decided to take the story completion task with a much broader population than the two age groups studied by Maratsos.

Experimental context. There were no tangible objects, the story being entirely verbal.

Experimental procedure. The child was informed that the experimenter would tell him short stories which he should listen to very carefully since there would be a question afterwards to which he must guess the answer. The stories ran as follows:

Definite referring type

(a) E.: Dans le préau, il y avait un petit garçon et une petite fille. Un seul garçon et une seule fille. Ils s'amusaient ensemble et couraient tous les deux très vite. Puis tout d'un coup un des enfants est tombé et s'est mis à pleurer. Devine qui c'était

C.: *La* fille/*le* garçon (expected response)

E.: C'est qui qui jouait dans le préau?

C.: Une (la) fille et un (le) garçon

[E.: In the playground there was a little boy and a little girl. Just one boy and one girl. They were having fun running about together very fast. Then suddenly one of the children fell down and started to cry. Guess who it was

C.: *The* girl/*The* boy (expected response)

E.: Who was playing in the playground?

C.: A boy and a girl (or the)]

(b) E.: Dans la forêt il y avait un écureuil et un chat qui jouaient ensemble. Un seul écureuil et un seul chat. Ils se chassaient, puis tout d'un coup un des animaux est monté dans un arbre. Devine qui c'etait

C.: *L'*écureuil/*le* chat (expected response)

E.: C'est qui qui jouait dans la forêt?

C.: Un (l') écureuil et un (le) chat

[E.: In the forest there was one squirrel and one cat playing together. Just one squirrel and one cat. They chased one another, then suddenly one of the animals climbed a tree. Guess who it was

C.: *The* squirrel/*The* cat (expected response)

E.: Who was playing in the forest?

C.: A squirrel and a cat (or the)]

Other similar stories were used for definite referring expressions.

Indefinite referring type

(c) E.: Dans le préau il y avait beaucoup de garçons et beaucoup de filles. Ils couraient dans tous les sens. Puis un des enfants est tombé et s'est mis à pleurer. Devine qui c'était

C.: Un(e) garçon/fille, un des . . .

E.: C'est qui qui se trouvait dans le préau?

C.: Beaucoup de garçons et de filles

[E.: In the playground there were many many boys and many many girls, all playing together. They were running all over the place. Then one of the children fell and stated to cry. Guess who it was

C.: *A*/*one of the* girls/boys (expected response)

E.: Who was in the playground?

C.: Lots of boys and girls]

(d) E.: Dans la forêt il y avait beaucoup d'écureuils et de chats qui se chassaient. Il y en avait vraiment beaucoup. Tout d'un coup un des animaux est monté dans un arbre. Devine qui c'était

C.: *Un/un des* écureuils/chats

E.: Qui c'est qui chassait dans la forêt?

C.: Beaucoup d'écureuils et de chats

[E.: In the forest lots of squirrels and cats were chasing each other. There were lots and lots of them. Suddenly one of the animals ran up a tree. Guess who it was

C.: *A/one of the* squirrels/cats (expected response)

E.: Who was chasing in the forest?

C.: Lots of squirrels and cats]

Several reserve stories of this type were used for indefinite referring expressions. Of course, the question 'Guess *who* it was' tends to induce a definite referring expression, as pointed out in chapter 2, but I wished to remain close to Maratsos' design, for comparison purposes.

The reason why, after the child's response, the experimenter asked a question about who was in the story was to ascertain whether the child remembered that there were many or only one X involved. This was an important check that the child had actually understood the story when giving his response.

Each child received at least four stories; two definites and two indefinites. One story was kept as a special check for indefinite reference. It was a story about many mothers and fathers. Since children normally use definite referring expressions for mother or father, it was thought that if they were capable of using an indefinite referring expression for this story (i.e. '*a* papa/*a* mama'), this would be a strong argument that they could use the non-specific reference function of the indefinite article.

At the end of the interview, the child was asked questions about why he had said 'the' versus 'a', etc.

Population. A total of sixty-eight subjects between the ages of 3,3 and 11,1 years participated in this experiment, as follows:

Age	*Subjects*	*Average age*
3,3–3,11	6	3,5
4,0–4,11	11	4,6
5,0–5,11	8	5,5
6,0–6,11	9	6,5
7,0–7,11	12	7,6
8,0–8,11	8	8,7
9,0–9,11	8	9,5
10,0–11,1	6	10,6

Results. It should be recalled that this experiment was designed for comparison purposes with the results found by Maratsos on very young children.

Table 27 gives a breakdown of the type of referring expressions encountered for the two types of story. The column 'other' contains responses which mention none of the persons or animals involved in the story, but some new element, e.g. a third animal not mentioned in the experimenter's story. For example, to a story about boys and girls who fell over, some children gave a proper name (their own name or the name of one of their school mates, e.g. Juliette), or replied something along the lines: 'I knew a girl who fell over and her mummy was angry because she got her dress dirty', or responded 'All of the girls fell down'. This was frequently the case amongst 3 to 5 year olds, as can be seen from the percentages on the table. Maratsos, however, does not mention having encountered this type of response, although he does mention having averaged scores for 'non-responses'. The few percentages of 'other' amongst the older children mainly involved responses of the type: 'Someone else', 'Maybe a bird came by just as they were playing', etc., i.e. never proper names, but extraneous elements.

TABLE 27. *Definite and indefinite referring responses for story completion, expressed as a percentage of total trials*

		Expected response = definite			Expected response = indefinite		
Age group	Total number of trials	Definite article (%)	Indefinite article (%)	Other (%)	Definite article (%)	Indefinite article (%)	Other (%)
3,3–3,11	24	40	20	40	62	11	27
4,0–4,11	47	63	11	26	48	40	12
5,0–5,11	33	90	10	0	59	24	17
6,0–6,11	36	83	9	8	63	37	0
7,0–7,11	58	100	0	0	48	44	8
8,0–8,11	40	91	9	0	21	64	15
9,0–9,11	41	90	10	0	14	86	0
10,0–11,1	30	100	0	0	0	89	11

It can be seen from the table that for 3 year olds the expected definite response was not particularly high (40%). When the expected response was indefinite, figures were very low (11%). With respect to 4 year olds, 5 year olds and 6 year olds, responses were predominantly definite, even in the case of an expected indefinite response. Even at 7 years, there were still 48% of definite responses in the indefinite situation. Only from

8 years are the figures for the indefinite responses over the 50% mark and only markedly so for 9 and 10 year olds. This is obviously very different from Maratsos' findings on 3 and 4 year olds. It would seem unlikely that this is solely due to the fact that he was experimenting in English, whereas the subjects of this study were French-speaking.

Nor does it seem to be the case that it was due to the children forgetting the details of the story (singularity of protagonists or several of them). Only 7% of the errors for the expected indefinite response can be accounted for by the child having responded afterwards that only one X was involved. One of such erroneous responses gave rise to a spontaneous correction but this was in an older child:

8,9 years (indefinite story)
C.: Le chien
E.: Combien d'X y avait-il?
C.: Un . . . non plusieurs . . . alors excusez-moi, j'aurais dû dire *un* chien
[C.: The dog
E.: How many Xs were there?
C.: One . . . no several . . . then I'm sorry I should have said *a* dog (stressed)]

In all other cases, and at all ages including the small subjects, children always remembered that there were 'Many many Xs' but still gave a second definite response 'the X'.

Amongst the indefinite responses for the indefinite situation, it was only from 8,2 years that any children used 'One of the Xs' instead of 'An X'. The responses of some 6 year olds, seen in the following examples, provide insight into the dual problem involved for the child.

6,3 years (indefinite story)
C.: Le X
E.: Combien d'X y avait-il?
C.: Beaucoup . . . mais un seul qui est monté dans l'arbre dans l'histoire
[C.: The X
E.: How many Xs were there?
C.: Many . . . but only one which climbed the tree in the story]
6,11 years (indefinite story)
C.: La X
E.: Combien?
C.: Plusieurs, mais qu'une fille qui est tombée
[C.: The X
E.: How many?
C.: Many, but just one girl who fell down]

Clearly there is a problem of distinguishing between reference to an X under focus of attention, and situating that X within the general context of the story. This problem is clearly overcome when the child can use: 'One of the Xs', 'The Xs' referring to the general context and 'one' picking out the particular X under focus from the general context. It is interesting that small children made definite reference to one of several Xs, even in a verbal story with no visible objects which could be pointed at. 'One of the' only occurred after 8,2 years. Furthermore, it was only these older subjects who could furnish indefinite reference to the word 'mama' or 'papa', i.e. 'A papa/One of the papas', whereas some of the younger children who had been successful in giving indefinite reference to other stories gave definite reference for the fathers/mothers story.

Two 6 year olds at the end of the session gave the following explanations for their use of an indefinite expression:

6,9 years
Parce qu'il y en avait plusieurs dans l'histoire
[Because there were several in the story]
6,10 years
(child gave two erroneous definite responses and then an indefinite response)
E.: Pourquoi une X cette fois?
C.: Parce qu'il y en avait plusieurs, pas qu'une seule
[E.: Why an X this time?
C.: Because there were several of them, not just one (although he had remembered that there were several for both of the other trials)]

Most of the over 8 year olds responded: 'Because there were several in the story'. The use of the definite article was almost always explained by the fact that there was only one X in the story. However, there were two interesting responses with regard to the use of the definite article, as follows:

7,11 years (advanced)
Le, parce que vous aviez déjà parlé du garçon
[The, because you had already spoken of the boy (i.e. clearly an anaphoric reference)]
9,10 years
Si on avait dit un, alors ça aurait pu être un autre chat
[If one had said a, then it could have been another cat]

The fact that children between 3 and 5 very often gave proper names for stories involving boys and girls may explain why Maratsos had significantly more definite responses for his 'Cave story'. However, I found predominantly definite responses also for stories involving animals, and this up to roughly 8 years (between 48% and 62% were definite in the indefinite situation between 3 and 7 years inclusive). There seems to be no satisfactory explanation for the striking difference between my results on a wide age span and those of Maratsos on 3 and 4 year olds. I knew my subjects personally very well and the experimental setting was extremely relaxed for the child.

The major difference resides in the language, in that in French the definite article is also marked for number. However, in view of the overall results of experiments 1–6, and considering the results of Warden (1973) for English, it seems unlikely that the linguistic variations are alone sufficient to explain the difference in results. Distinguishing between making reference to an object under focus of attention and situating that object within the general context of the setting, appears to be a problem, until roughly 7 years, in both situations where objects are visible and in story-telling tasks.

Thus, it can be said that in many instances under 8 year olds use definite referring expressions when they should be using indefinite referring expressions. Since there were no concrete objects either to point at or for the experimenter to touch, these predominantly definite responses show that the results of experiment 1 were not atypical of the general problems involved. Focus of attention, be it in temporary discourse contexts or by the experimenter touching a particular object in a concrete situation, elicits deictic definite reference on the part of young children, whereas indirect reference (see experiment 2) tends to elicit more indefinite referring expressions. A task analysis of both contexts and the way in which the child decodes the task is thus an essential facet of experimentation in the field of referring expressions.

Up to now, the experiments have dealt with aspects of French determiners which are relevant to English determiners also, even if there are differences between the languages as explained in chapter 3. In the next chapter, however, we shall be concerned with a phenomenon peculiar to some but not all languages, that is the indication of grammatical gender distinctions.

6 *Production experiments: gender-indicating function of determiners*[1]

Experiments 7–11 covered the gender-indicating function of determiners. In part, these experiments fall outside the central theme of this study and will therefore be reported on fully elsewhere. However, since surface markers used for referential expressions simultaneously indicate gender distinctions in French, and since languages with grammatical gender offer possibilities of making more specific pronoun reference than do languages without, it was felt useful to cover the gender-marking function in a chapter here.

There are, in brief, two theoretical approaches to the diachronic evolution of the gender category and its function in specific language families. One rests on semantic theories, e.g. the 'sexus theory' and implicit versions thereof, in which the origins of gender are posited to lie essentially in extralinguistic reality. Grammatical gender is held to be an extension of natural classificatory criteria. The distinctive phonological features are thus taken to stem from the need to indicate such natural distinctions. This was the position of the early Semitic philologists (see Wensinck 1927 for discussion) and can also be found amongst certain Indo-European philologists (see Fodor 1959 for discussion).

The second embraces various theories concerned with the internal laws of language. Many linguists (e.g. Brugmann 1889; Meillet 1952; Martinet 1956) have sought an explanation of the origins of gender in its syntactic function of indicating the relations between sentence segments. Natural gender is thus seen to have stemmed from grammatical gender and not vice versa.

The definition of the category of gender has not been clearly agreed upon. Do we consider that English, for instance, manifests a gender category (albeit semantic) in its distinction of lexical items such as 'actor/actress', 'shepherd/shepherdess', 'who/what', 'someone/something', 'he/she/it', etc.? Or do we confine the gender category to those

[1] A few paragraphs of this chapter are taken from Karmiloff-Smith (1978a).

languages in which gender has syntactic implications of concord, i.e. non-variable noun genders give rise to morphological changes in other variable sentence elements (e.g. article, adjective, pronoun and, in some languages, verb)?

If we opt for the latter definition, what is the function of gender in such languages? For some authors gender is considered to be a practically redundant phenomenon from a semantic and a syntactical point of view. Although reference is made to the rare cases where gender is indeed used to disambiguate homonyms, it is justifiably argued that even in such cases context is usually more than adequate to clarify any ambiguity (e.g. '*le* mousse' in French means 'cabin boy', whereas '*la* mousse' means 'moss'). And just where gender distinctions would be particularly informative semantically (e.g. 'un enfant/une enfant', 'le concierge/la concierge', etc.), the distinction is far more frequently already apparent in lexical terms, e.g. 'fille/garcon', 'oncle/tante', where the gender of the article is redundant (see Lyons 1968 for discussion).

Some authors, such as Durand (1938), Dubois (1965) and Mok (1968), have endeavoured to demonstrate that the category of gender has important syntactic, semantic and classificatory functions both in written and spoken language. Together with, say, word order and the category of number, gender is seen as a powerful device for marking syntagmatic cohesion, i.e. for linking various entities across noun and verb phrases. There are, for instance, gender markers both for animate and inanimate nouns on the verb in the past tense in Russian, on the participle with copula in French, as well as in certain verb phrases in the Semitic language family.

One area of agreement amongst the majority of authors seems to be that, at least as far as the Indo-European language family is concerned, there are no entirely uniform semantic classificatory criteria which would make it possible to predict the gender of more than a handful of lexical groups (see Lyons 1968 for discussion). In French, for instance, the words for 'victim' and 'recruit' are feminine even if they are used to refer to males; the words for female 'doctor/professor' are masculine. 'Armchair' and 'sun' are masculine whereas 'chair' and 'moon' are feminine. The two synonyms for bicycle differ in gender. Cross-linguistic comparisons are particularly informative in this respect: the word for 'soap', for example, is masculine in French, feminine in German and neuter in Russian. It would be difficult to explain this series of facts semantically. It is possible, however, that the greater the number of genders a language has (e.g. Swahili, which has six), the more likely one may be to find semantic classificatory criteria.

All nouns in French take either masculine or feminine gender, whether they be animates or inanimates; adjectives, pronouns, etc., must show concord of gender with the noun to which they are linked. Prediction of gender is frequently possible in French from noun suffixes but these latter rarely carry semantic information. Given that there are no consistent semantic criteria, how does the young French-speaking child learn which form of the articles to use, for instance, for each noun?

Perhaps the most obvious hypothesis is that gender is initially closely linked to semantic distinctions, along the lines of the historical 'sexus theory' mentioned above. Children do indeed make a distinction between the two sexes very early; they often have the somewhat embarrassing habit of calling all males 'Papa', but they rarely make the mistake of using this term for females. Having made this distinction cognitively, the child might then notice the consistent patterns in language dealing with the very same distinction. On this basis, the child might progressively form equivalence classes for masculine ('un, le, il, petit, bon', etc.) and for their feminine counterparts ('une, la, elle, petite, bonne', etc.) where each applies to words covering the two sexes (e.g. 'père, frère, garçon/mère, soeur, fille', etc.). Natural gender markers would then gradually be generalized to nouns covering inanimates where no semantic link exists with grammatical gender. Finally, the gender function of the articles would be used syntactically. This hypothesis relates to recent explanations of early child language in terms of initially expressing semantic intentions (e.g. Brown 1973), and also to the view that initial conceptual distinctions are subsequently reflected in language usage.

However, a second hypothesis could be formulated, i.e. that the child is sensitive to phonological oppositions and pays less attention to the gender of articles than to noun suffixes. Furthermore, whereas the semantic hypothesis would explain pronoun gender concord semantically, this hypothesis would predict that the gender of anaphoric pronouns is affected by phonological rules.

Gender not only has a local lexical concord function but also has a reference function (e.g. pronouns). When children are involved in acquiring the various deictic, exophoric, anaphoric and quantifier functions of determiners, how is this affected by their acquisition of the gender-indicating function?

Based on interesting suggestions sent to us by Braine (1970), a large-scale pilot study was made on the gender acquisition problem. On the basis of these results, five experiments were devised to test the various implications of the alternative hypotheses.

The full analysis of the results (i.e. on adjective concord) will not be given here, but rather those aspects which are more particularly relevant to the problem of article usage.

Experiments 7–11: grammatical, natural and phonological clues

Experimental context for experiments 7–11. A series of thirty nonsense words, obeying the rules of phonemic combinations in French, were assigned to pairs of identical but different-coloured pictures of imaginary objects, imaginary animals and Martian-like female and male persons. Figs. 3, 4 and 5 are typical examples of the drawings used. The

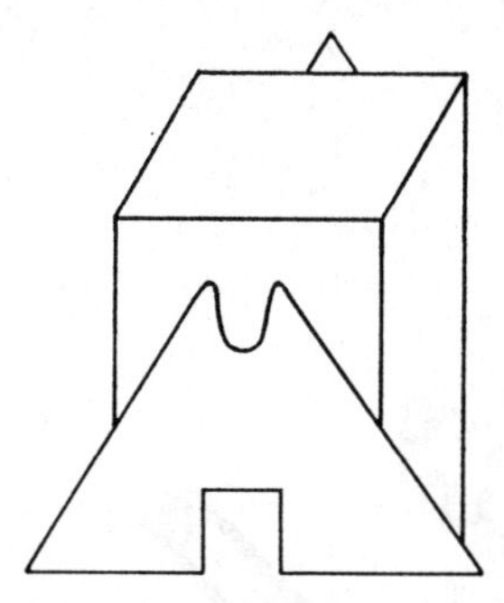

Fig. 3. Example of a typical drawing of imaginary object, used for experiments 7–11

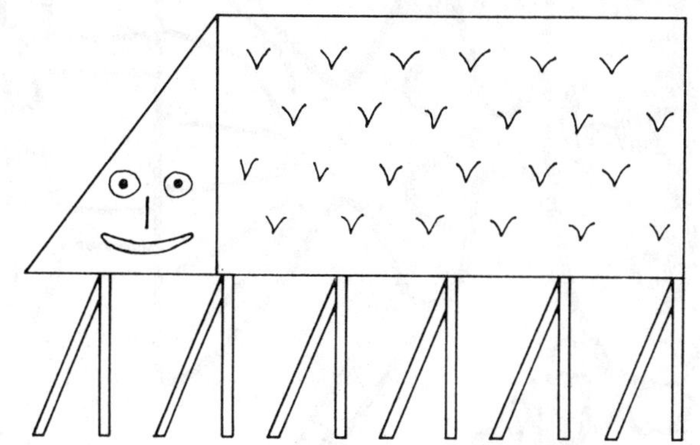

Fig. 4. Example of a typical drawing of imaginary animal, used for experiments 7–11

Figs. 5a and 5b. Examples of typical drawings of imaginary female and male Martian-like persons, used for experiments 7–11

colours chosen for the pairs of pictures were those involving phonological distinctions for French gender (e.g. 'vert/verte', 'gris/grise', 'blanc/blanche', 'brun/brune'). The nonsense word endings were either typically masculine, typically feminine, or had a suffix which gave no indication of gender (see below). The actual spelling of the words in the nonsense list is of course irrelevant, in that all words were presented to the children orally; a word like 'taninque' could of course be marked for gender in written language (e.g. '*le* tan*inc*/*la* tan*inque*'). In spoken language, however, the pronunciation of 'taninc/taninque' is identical. Thus, it could be of either gender. Prior to each experiment, and in order to introduce the technique, some existing nouns with their correponding pictures were used. These nouns either obeyed gender/noun suffix rules or were exceptions to such rules. The words used for the introductory technique are listed overleaf.

The three gender/suffix categories were evenly distributed amongst the three classes of drawings: objects, animals, persons. In the five experiments, the experimenter was particularly careful to avoid providing any additional gender information and confined his questions or comments to expressions which carry no gender clues in spoken language (e.g. 'ça', 'quel/quelle X?', 'ça c'est quoi?', 'bicron jaune?', etc., and not 'lequel/laquelle?', 'celui-là/celle-là' or 'le vert/la verte').

List of experimental nonsense words

Masculine suffix	*Feminine suffix*	*Arbitrary suffix*
bicron	podelle	fodire
plichon	forsienne	dilare
golcheau	bicrienne	rile
coumeau	barienne	coumile
fasien	goltine	taninque
maudrien	fasine	broucha
forsien	plichette	chalique
maudrier	coumette	fadiste
bravais	bravaise	
brouguin	spodine	
chalois		
goltois		

List of experimental existing words

Concord between suffix/gender	*Discord between suffix/gender*
un tap*is*	*une* fourm*i*
un coch*on*	*une* mais*on*
une cour*onne*	*un* téléph*one*
une fl*ute*	*un* parach*ute*

Experimental procedures for experiments 7–11. Five different approaches were used:

Experiment 7: article gender and noun suffix were consistent (e.g. '*un* bicr*on*/*une* brav*aise*');

8: no article gender was provided for objects, animals and persons (e.g. 'deux bicrons/deux bravaises');

9: for objects and animals, article gender and noun suffix were inconsistent (e.g. '*une* bicr*on*/*un* brav*aise*');

10: sex of the person depicted in the picture and noun suffix were inconsistent, with no marked article (e.g. *females* called 'deux bicr*ons*', *males* called 'deux brav*aises*');

11: given the name of a male picture (e.g. 'un bicron'), children were asked to create a name for the equivalent female picture, and vice versa.

The basic technique for experiments 7–11 was as follows:

Experimenter	*Child's expected response*
E. shows child picture of a grey pig.	
Qu'est-ce que c'est? [What's this?]	Un cochon gris [A grey pig]
Idem with a green pig	Un cochon vert [A green pig]
E. then hides one of the two pictures, or places an object on one of them, or performs another appropriate action.	
Qu'est-ce que j'ai fait? [What did I do?]	Vous avez mis un crayon sur *le* cochon vert [You put a pencil on the green pig]
Idem with two pictures of houses	Vous avez caché *la* maison ver*te* [You hid the green house]
Idem with other known objects taken from list above	

The introductory part preceded all the experiments. Once the child had clearly understood the experimental task with known words, the experimental items were introduced:

Experimenter	*Child's expected response*
Experiment 7	
Voici l'image d'une plichette. Qu'est-ce que c'est?	Une plichette
[Here's a picture of a plichette. What is it?]	[A plichette]
Voici une autre image. Qu'est-ce que tu penses que cela représente?	Une autre plichette, mais grise
[Here's another picture. What do you think it is?]	[Another plichette, but a grey one]
E.'s action . . .	Vous avez mis un jouet sur *la* plichette br*une* [You put a toy on the brown plichette]
Idem with 'un bicron'	Vous avez caché *le* bicron ver*t* [You hid the green bicron]
Etc.	
Experiment 8	
Voici deux fasines. Qu'est-ce que c'est?	Deux fasines
[Here are two fasines. What is here?]	
E.'s action . . .	Vous avez caché *la* fasine blan*che*/ *une* des fasines [You hid the white fasine/one of the fasines]
Quelle fasine? (quel/quelle gives no audible clue)	*La* fasine blan*che*
[Which fasine?]	[The white fasine]
Voici deux maudriers	Deux maudriers
[Here are two maudriers]	
E.'s action . . .	Vous avez retourné *le* maudrier gri*s* [You turned over the grey maudrier]
Etc.	
Experiment 9	
Voici l'image d'une bicron. Qu'est-ce que c'est?	Une bicron

Experimenter	*Child's expected response*
[This is a picture of a bicron. What is it?]	
Et ça? [And this?]	Aussi une bicron [Also a bicron]
E.'s action . . .	Vous avez caché *la* bicron ver*te* [You hid the green bicron]
Idem with '*un* forsi*enne*'	Vous avez mis un jouet sur *le* forsienne bru*n* [You put a toy on the brown forsienne]
Etc.	

Experiment 10

Voici deux images. Ce sont des filles ou des garçons? [Here are two pictures. Are they girls or boys?]	Des filles [Girls]
C'est juste, des filles. Ce sont deux plichons. [That's right, girls. They are called two plichons]	Deux plichons
E.'s action . . .	Vous avez caché *la* plichon gri*se* [You hid the grey plichon]
Filles ou garçons? [Girls or boys?]	Filles [Girls]
Voici deux images . . .? [Here are two pictures . . .?]	Des garçons [Boys]
C'est juste, des garçons. Ça s'appelle deux forsiennes [That's right, boys. They are called two forsiennes]	Deux forsiennes
E.'s action . . .	Vous avez mis un jouet sur *le* forsienne ver*t* [You put a toy on the green forsienne]
Des filles ou des garçons? [Girls or boys?]	Des garçons [Boys]
Etc.	

Experiment 11 was run somewhat differently to the others. The child was first introduced to the problem with known words as in the preceding experiments. Then the technique was as follows:

Experimenter	*Child's expected response*
Experiment 11	
Voici deux garçons, ce sont deux bicrons	Deux bicrons
[Here are two boys, they are called two bicrons]	
E.'s action . . .	Vous avez caché *le* bicron ver*t* [You hid the green bicron]
Voici une autre image. Ce personnage vient du même pays que les bicrons. Essaie d'inventer un nom pour ça, comment pourrait-on l'appeler?	Une bicronne (une bicron, une bicrotte, etc.)
[Here's another picture (female). The person comes from the same country as the bicrons. Invent a name, how could you call this? (avoiding any gender marks, of course)]	
Est-ce un garçon ou une fille? [Is it a boy or a girl?]	Une fille [A girl]
E.'s action . . .	Vous avez caché *la* bicronne blan*che* [You hid the white bicronne]
Voici deux filles, ce sont deux forsiennes [Here are two girls, called two forsiennes]	Deux forsiennes
E.'s action . . .	Vous avez caché *la* forsienne gri*se* [You hid the grey forsienne]
Invente un nom pour ça, même pays, etc. [Invent a name for this, same country, etc.]	*Un* for*sien* (un forsier, un forsienne, etc.)
Une fille ou un garçon? [Girl or boy?]	Un garçon [Boy]
E.'s action . . .	Vous avez caché *le* forsien ver*t* [You hid the green forsien]
Etc.	

In all of these experiments, a series of items was presented in a standardized order, after which a more exploratory approach was taken, asking children to explain if possible the implicit rules they had used spontaneously.

Population: experiments 7–11. A total of 341 monolingual French speaking children between the ages of 3,2 and 12,5 years were interviewed in the five experiments. In general the subjects participated in only one gender experiment, although many had been subjects for other experiments. Those few subjects who had participated in more than one experiment concerning gender were interviewed again, after an interval of several months, when different nonsense words were used. The population was distributed as follows for the five experiments:

Age	*Subjects*	*Average age*
3,2–3,11	24	3,5
4,0–4,11	43	4,6
5,0–5,11	45	5,6
6,0–6,11	47	6,5
7,0–7,11	47	7,5
8,0–8,11	38	8,6
9,0–9,11	27	9,5
10,0–10,11	14	10,6
11,0–11,11	7	11,6

Forty-nine additional subjects received half the experimental items, so they are therefore not included in the quantitative analyses, although occasional reference is made to them in the more qualitative discussion and regarding epilinguistic data.

Results. We shall be concerned here only with some aspects of the results of the overall gender study. No reference will be made to adjective concord, although it could be argued that such a linguistic phenomenon also has a determinor function in that it serves as an additional clue to determining to which word the attributive or predicative adjective is attached. For the sake of brevity, however, data from the five gender experiments are analysed here as they pertain to the gender-marking function of the French articles.

Tables 28 and 29, giving some data from experiment 7, where the experimenter provided a gender clue with the indefinite article, show that if the child can find a phonological clue, he will use that for determining the gender of the definite article. When no such clue is available, i.e. in the case of the 'arbitrary suffixes', figures for successful gender attribution are somewhat lower at all ages before 7 years. However, it

TABLE 28. *Masculine indefinite article furnished: percentage of successful use of maculine definite article in the case of concord (data from experiment 7)*

Age group	Natural gender clue + phonological clue, e.g. '*un* brav*ais*' for male picture (%)	No natural gender clue but phonological clue, e.g. '*un* bicr*on*' (%)	No natural gender clue and no phonological clue, e.g. '*un* coum*ile*' (%)
3,2–3,11	90	100	80
4,0–4,11	89	100	64
5,0–5,11	100	100	78
6,0–6,11	100	100	91
7,0–7,10	90	90	90
Average errors (%)	6.2	2.0	19.4

TABLE 29. *Feminine indefinite article furnished: percentage of successful use of feminine definite article in the case of concord (data from experiment* 8)

Age group	Natural gender clue + phonological clue, e.g. '*une* fors*ienne*' for female picture (%)	No natural gender clue but phonological clue, e.g. '*une* plich*ette*' (%)	No natural gender clue and no phonological clue, e.g. '*une* dil*are*' (%)
3,2–3,11	78	78	64
4,0–4,11	100	100	78
5,0–5,11	100	100	95
6,0–6,11	100	91	94
7,0–7,10	100	100	90
Average errors (%)	4.4	6.2	15.8

should be noted that children of all ages, from 3 years, *can* use the gender of the indefinite article to decide upon the gender of the definite article if there is no phonological clue on the suffix. Percentages are somewhat lower for the feminine article, particularly for 3 year olds, but still well above 50% levels. It can thus be assumed that where no stronger clues exist, children from 3 years are implicitly aware of the articles' function of indicating gender distinctions.

Table 30 gives some results from experiment 8, which analysed children's capacity to provide the gender of either article on the basis of phonological clues alone. Clearly, children are able to do so from 3 years, with again very slightly lower figures for the feminine gender. The results of the over 9 year olds, however, show a tendency at that age to attribute masculine gender to all unknown words, despite the potential feminine phonological clue on the suffix. Such a tendency was borne out by the comments of older children in the epilinguistic part at the end of sessions; masculine seems to be used as a sort of 'neuter' (i.e. unmarked) when there is no clue from an article.

TABLE 30. *No marked article furnished: percentage of responses according to phonological clue from suffix (data from experiment* 8)

Age group	Masculine article for masculine suffix (%)		Feminine article for feminine suffix (%)	
	'Deux bic*rons*'	'Deux maudr*iers*'	'Deux plich*ettes*'	'Deux fas*ines*'
3,4–3,11	100	100	100	67
4,0–4,11	100	71	71	72
5,0–5,11	93	79	91	100
6,0–6,11	100	85	94	57
7,0–7,11	100	100	69	75
8,0–8,11	100	93	86	70
9,0–10,3	100	84	38	50

Experiment 9 looked at the conflict between grammatical gender and phonological clue from the suffix, i.e. the child was given, for instance, 'une bicron' which should become '*la* bicron' or 'un forsienne' which should become '*le* forsienne'. Table 31, which compares discord with cases of no discord (e.g. 'un chalois'), shows that correct responses are very high at all ages for cases of no discord. This could be due to the phonological clue from the suffix and not necessarily to the article furnished. Looking at the results for cases of discord, the former explanation seems very plausible. Under 6 year olds, when given 'un goltine', responded more often with the femine definite article than the masculine. When given 'une plichon', under 5 year olds tended to give the masculine definite article more often instead of the feminine. Under 5 year olds thus seem to be using the suffix furnished, rather than the gender of the indefinite article as a clue to gender.

A change begins from 5 years, but first mainly for the feminine article. It would seem that for 5 year olds the feminine indefinite article is more marked than the equivalent masculine one. From 6 years, children are able to use the clue from grammatical gender based on each of the articles, but the results are never as clearcut as for cases of no discord. Thus at all ages, the phonological clue is effective. (This neglects of course a qualitative analysis which clearly shows the spontaneous corrections and hesitations that the phonological strategy in fact remains very strong in the older child also.)

TABLE 31. *Discord between grammatical gender and phonological clue from suffix, expressed as a percentage of correct responses according to grammatical gender (data from experiment 9)*

	Discord		No discord	
Age group	Masc. grammatical gender + fem. suffix, e.g. '*un* golt*ine*' (% of masc. definite article)	Fem. grammatical gender + masc. suffix, e.g. '*une* plich*on*' (% of fem. definite article)	Masc. grammatical gender + masc. suffix, e.g. '*un* chal*ois*' (% of masc. definite article)	Fem. grammatical gender + fem. suffix, e.g. '*une* brav*aise*' (% of fem. definite article)
3,4–3,11	44	46	100	78
4,0–4,11	43	37	89	100
5,0–5,11	19	93	100	100
6,0–6,11	74	78	100	100
7,0–7,11	79	68	100	89
8,0–8,11	72	71	100	84
9,0–9,11	82	79	100	94
10,0–10,11	96	75	95	85
11,0–11,10	95	83	100	100

Table 32 gives a selection of the data obtained from experiment 10 designed to study conflict between a natural gender clue (sex of person in picture) and a phonological clue from the suffix. A comparison is made in this table of the differences in responses to the cases of discord between the two clues and those of concord (i.e. no discord between natural gender and arbitrary suffix). Does the child base himself on the natural gender clue in order to provide the gender of the article or on the phonological clue? The results clearly show that until 10 years children use the phonological clue for article gender, irrespective of whether the picture is of a girl or a boy. (As pointed out, there were absolutely no problems of recognizing female/male distinctions in the pictures.) And even if the figures for 10 year olds increase with respect to furnishing the masculine article for the masculine picture despite feminine suffix, it should be recalled that there is a tendency from 9 years to 'masculinize' unknown terms. Furthermore, the very low percentages of feminine articles for the female picture (20% at 10 years and 40% at 11 years) clearly suggest that at all ages in the case of discord, the tendency is to use the phonological clue for providing the gender of the article accompanying a noun and not the natural gender clue. In the case of the arbitrary suffixes, there was potentially nothing to stop the child using the natural gender clue. It can be seen from table 32 that whilst the natural gender is taken into account more frequently than in the case of the marked suffixes, there is nonetheless a tendency to give only masculine articles, even with respect to a picture of a female. This was particularly the case between 5 and 8 years, but again strikingly so at 10 years. No 10 year old referred to the female picture with the feminine article. Thus whilst children can take natural gender into account in cases of no discord, they actually tend to base themselves almost entirely on phonological procedures.

TABLE 32. *Discord between natural gender and phonological clue from suffix, expressed as a percentage of correct responses according to natural gender (data from experiment* 10)

Age group	Discord: Female pictures + masc. suffix, e.g. 'deux bicr*ons*' (% of fem. article)	Discord: Male pictures + fem. suffix, e.g. 'deux forsi*ennes*' (% of masc. article)	No discord: Female pictures + arbitrary suffix, e.g. 'deux coum*iles*' (% of fem. article)	No discord: Male pictures + arbitrary suffix, e.g. 'deux fad*istes*' (% of masc. article)
3,4–3,11	20	28	50	80
4,0–4,11	34	29	42	75
5,0–5,11	16	20	24	83
6,0–6,11	18	20	34	100
7,0–7,11	25	34	34	100
8,0–8,11	29	13	25	71
9,0–9,11	46	48	80	87
10,0–10,11	20	80	0	100
11,0–11,11	40	64	44	100

Tables 33 and 34 give the results of experiment 11 regarding the ways in which children exploit the various possibilities of the gender system in French. Table 33 gives details according to suffixes, whereas table 34 groups the data under the general procedures used, irrespective of suffix. What is of interest to us here is when the articles are used by the child to indicate change in natural gender, i.e. when can the child manipulate rather explicitly the gender-indicating function of the articles. A consideration of the final two columns of table 34 shows, without recourse to further detail, that compared to their other procedures children of any age rarely place the burden of natural gender *solely* on article gender. The penultimate column in table 34 'Article changed to match natural gender', barely goes beyond 30% at any age. From 6 years and more particularly from 8 years, children do tend to change *both* article and suffix to match natural gender. However, the data from the previous column suggest that they are probably matching the suffix

TABLE 33. *Procedures used for creation of name for male and female Martian-like persons, expressed as a percentage of total responses per age group (data from experiment 11)*

Age group	Neutral suffixes					Masc. article and suffix given: name for female to be created					Fem. article and suffix given: name for male to be created				
	No change (%)	Lexical compound (%)	Article changed suffix unchanged (%)	Article and suffix changed (%)	Other + refusals (%)	No change (%)	Lexical compound (%)	Article changed suffix unchanged (%)	Article and suffix changed (%)	Other + refusals (%)	No change (%)	Lexical compound (%)	Article changed suffix unchanged (%)	Article and suffix changed (%)	Other + refusals (%)
3,3–3,11	38	8	0	0	54	37	0	13	0	50	46	0	0	9	45
4,0–4,11	64	10	10	3	13	50	4	9	14	23	34	9	25	14	18
5,0–5,11	42	8	38	8	4	12	4	36	32	16	9	0	25	43	23
6,0–6,11	8	15	42	27	4	0	11	57	32	0	4	0	4	92	0
7,0–7,11	19	0	52	29	0	9	0	42	49	0	0	0	22	78	0
8,0–8,11	0	0	67	33	0	0	0	17	83	0	0	0	8	92	0
9,0–9,10	0	15	46	39	0	0	0	0	100	0	0	0	25	75	0

TABLE 34. *General strategies, as a function of age, for creating new words for persons of opposite sex, expressed as a percentage of total responses (data from experiment* 11)

Age group	Refusal (%)	Existing word, e.g. 'a girl' (%)	No change in article nor suffix, from name of opposite sex (%)	Lexical compound, e.g. 'une bicron-fille' (%)	Article changed to match natural gender (%)	Article and suffix changed to match natural gender (%)
3,3–3,11	16	34	41	3	3	3
4,0–4,11	2	15	51	8	14	10
5,0–5,11	9	6	21	4	33	27
6,0–6,11	1	1	4	9	32	53
7,0–7,11	0	0	9	0	39	52
8,0–8,11	0	0	0	0	31	69
9,0–9,10	0	0	0	5	24	71

to natural gender and then matching the article to that suffix. The results of experiments 9 and 10 reinforce this interpretation that the gender of the articles *alone* does not carry sufficient semantic information.

Looking again at table 33, it can be seen that between 5 and 8 years there is a slight tendency to allow the feminine article to carry a more communicative burden regarding natural gender, than is the case for the masculine article. This obviously coincides with the idea that the feminine is the 'marked' term. (Likewise in English, 'dog' can be male or female, whereas bitch is the marked feminine term.) The full discussion of the gender results is of course not made in this book.

Finally, whilst it can be shown that both younger and older children use predominantly phonological procedures in French gender problems, one essential difference should be stressed. The older child uses these phonological rules for extended syntagmatic cohesion, i.e. to govern anaphora as well as lexical concord. For example, in the clinical discussion after experiment 10, children were asked to make up a story about the persons in the pictures. Rather consistently, children under 6 years tended to base the gender of the noun on the phonological clue but the gender of subsequent pronoun on extralinguistic factors, as can be seen from the following extracts from a story about the female 'bicron':

5,7 years

Bon, y avait une fois *un* bicron ver*t* et *un* bicron br*un*. *Elles* étaient très amies (...) alors *le* bicron ver*t* est sorti (...) et ensuite *elle* est allée (...) et puis c'est *elle* qui a (...)

[Well, once there was a green bicron and a brown bicron. They were close friends (...) and the green bicron went out (...) and then she went (...) and afterwards it was she who (...)]

(E. intervenes: Elle, c'est qui?
[She, that's who?])

Celle-là, *le* bicron ver*t*
[That one, the green bicron]

Since the relevant gender markers do not appear in the English translation, they have been italicized in French, but this of course does not imply that the child accentuated them. Below are some further examples which also point to the fact that for small children local lexical concord is phonologically based, whereas the choice of pronouns and demonstratives is semantically based:

3,4 years (female picture)
Sur *le* goltois, *la* vert*e*
[On the goltois, the green one]
3,9 years (male picture)
Sur *la* bravaise, *celui*-là (points)
[On the bravaise, that one]
4,6 years (female picture)
Le goltois, y en a qu'*une*
[The goltois, there is only one]
6,5 years (male picture)
La forsienne, *il* a la tête ovale
[The forsienne, he has an oval-shaped head]

Small children thus juxtapose a number of different procedures within the same situation; the gender of nouns is based on phonological clues from the word endings whereas the gender of pronouns is clearly semantic, based on the sex of the extralinguistic referent.

Most over 6 year olds, and all children over 8 years, also used the phonological procedure for lexical concord, but extended the same procedure to pronoun reference, which thus appears to be intralinguistic, based on the gender of the previous linguistic mention of the referent. The following extract from the story-telling situation about the *female* 'bicron' is particularly illustrative in this respect:

9,0 years
C'est *le* bicron ver*t* qui est parti (...) ensuite *il* est allé chez (...) c'est *lui* qui a trouvé (...)

[It was the green bicron who left (...) then he went to X's house (...) it was he who found (...)]
(E. intervenes: Lui, c'est qui?
[He, that's who?])
(child points to picture): Ben, c'est *lui* . . . non, non, *elle*, je veux dire *la* bicr*onne* . . . *celle* qui est ver*te*
[Well, it's he . . . no, no, she, I mean the bicronne . . . the one that is green]

Below are some further examples of the older child's tendency to use gender for syntagmatic cohesion, thus making intralinguistic reference to the noun previously mentioned. It is important to note that when faced with the conflict between grammatical gender and natural gender, these children make revealing modifications to noun suffixes, which thus leaves the phonological procedure intact. Here are examples from over 8 year olds:

8,3 years (female picture)
Un bicron . . . *elle*, *elle* . . . *le* bicron . . . *elle* . . . *la* bicr*onne elle* est partie (series of hesitations and spontaneous corrections of article gender, pronoun gender and word ending)
9,0 years (female picture)
Un goltois . . . *elle* est tombée *la* golt*oise*
[A goltois . . . she fell down the goltoise]
9,6 years (male picture of a bravaise)
(after numerous spontaneous corrections of the gender of the pronoun, the child declares): Il faut répéter bravaise chaque fois parce que il et bravaise ça va pas ensemble
[One has to repeat bravaise each time, because he and bravaise just don't go together]
10,6 years (female picture)
Un golt*ois* qui (...) *il* ne pouvait pas faire (...) alors *il* (...) ben, *le* golt*ois il* s'est décidé . . . c'est bête, je dis tout le temps il, et je devais raconter l'histoire de ces filles . . . des golt*oises*, quoi
[A goltois who (...) he didn't manage to (...) so he (...) well, the goltois he decided to . . . it's stupid, I keep saying he, and I had to tell a story about these girls, goltoises in other words]

The fact that small children base the gender of their pronoun reference on the extralinguistic referent, whereas older children refer intralinguistically, clearly points in the same direction as the hypothesis developed elsewhere in the text, that so-called anaphoric reference may be a rather late achievement. Small children's referential expressions appear to be essentially deictic in nature.

It is also noteworthy that whilst the phonological procedure is predominant, it is the last to be rendered explicit in the epilinguistic part of the session. Thus, when asked at the end of sessions to explain why they had attributed one gender to an item in preference to the other, younger children never referred to word endings, but invoked the semantic (natural gender) or syntactic (grammatical gender) clues although they had only rarely used these latter during the experimental items. Since the epilinguistic awareness of gender problems falls somewhat outside the general issues of concern to us here, a discussion of children's awareness of the differences between phonological, semantic and syntactic clues will be reported on elsewhere.

Whilst the gender-indicating function of determiners may seem somewhat marginal to the central problem here, it did seem important to give some thought to the gender function, in that this again adds to the plurifunctionality of French determiners. Now the results of the five experiments seem abundantly to point to the predominance of phonological procedures in the child up to roughly the age of 9 years. Whereever a phonological clue is available, it tends to override both natural gender clues and clues from the gender of the indefinite article. Hesitations and spontaneous corrections were particularly informative in this respect.

As early as 3 to 4 years, i.e. as soon as articles were used consistently, the child constructed a very powerful, implicit system of phonological rules, based on the consistency, but not necessarily on the frequency, of phonological changes in word endings. Classification by gender was clearly based on suffixes. This phonological procedure was so strong that neither syntactic clues (i.e. gender of the indefinite article furnished) nor semantic clues (i.e. sex of persons depicted in the drawings) were determinant in eliciting gender agreement. Most behaviour was dominated by the phonological procedure. For the very small children, this led to suprising errors in adjective gender concord even in the case of very familiar terms, such as 'maison', whose masculine suffix but feminine article is inconsistent with phonological rules (e.g. they responded 'la maison vert' instead of 'verte').

From the quantitative analysis of the results, it would appear that the phonological procedures are gradually (in some cases from 6 years, but more frequently at roughly 9 years) replaced by the natural gender clues and by the more foolproof syntactic ones, since consideration of the articles in conflictual situations does indeed increase with age. However, two facts emerge from a close examination of the errors and, particularly, of the spontaneous corrections. First, although the phonological procedure is already strong in the 4 year old, these young children were also quite capable of making use of syntactic and semantic clues when noun suffix information was *not* available, i.e. in the case of arbitrary word endings not providing potential phonological clues. Second, although older children take the semantic and syntactic clues more frequently into consideration, they also consistently made revealing changes in the suffixes so that the latter agreed with the article or the sex of the person (e.g. for '*un* fors*ienne*' they responded '*le* fors*ien*'; for '*une* bicr*on*' they responded '*la* bicr*onne*') or they avoided pronouncing the suffix by using the definite article and agreed adjective (i.e. 'la grise' [the grey one] instead of 'la bicron grise'). In both these cases, they avoided the conflict between two competing procedures, leaving the phonological one intact. Furthermore, there were frequent spontaneous corrections denoting the strength of the phonological procedure and the conflict between competing procedures (e.g. for '*un* fors*ienne*' the children responded for instance 'la for . . . le forsien . . . forsienne . . . le forsienne verte . . . non, vert'.)

It should be recalled that our results showed that younger children use the gender markers on pronouns extralinguistically, i.e. to point to the sex of the person in a picture, whereas older children use pronouns anaphorically, i.e. gender of pronoun coincides with gender of antecedent noun, irrespective of the sex of the referent. It should also be recalled that the phonological procedure is the *last* to be rendered explicit epilinguistically and the *last* to be exploited when children are requested to create words. When creating words for persons, the youngest children invented lexical compounds (e.g. 'la fille-goltois'), from 6 years and more consistently from 8 years the children changed both article and word ending, and less frequently just the article alone. This points to the fact that like anaphoric reference in experiment 5, children do not place on the article *alone* a heavy semantic burden, in this particular case that of indicating natural gender. They prefer to add additional markers, e.g. suffix changes. However, a slightly more frequent tendency was noted to let the marked term, i.e. the feminine article, carry the semantic burden alone.

With these gender results in mind, we must ask ourselves three questions. First, if the phonological procedure works so well in most cases for predicting French gender, why do children gradually make

use of the semantic and syntactic clues? The following interacting factors are probably involved:
(a) the child is already building syntactic and semantic procedures for language phenomena apart from gender, and language is a system rather than a mere juxtaposition of isolated microsystems;
(b) the linguistic environment does offer frequent exceptions to the phonological rules and there are patterns in the exceptions since they co-occur with other gender marked words;
(c) the child is already using determiners such as the articles for many different functions, thus becoming more aware of the articles in general and of *their* phonological changes.

This reasoning leads to our second and third questions. Once the child comes to use the syntactic clues for gender, why does the less foolproof phonological procedure continue to be the most dominant one? And why is the phonological procedure the last to become explicit? It should be mentioned that although singular articles are marked for gender, they are unstressed morphemes. Furthermore, plural inflections on the articles, demonstratives, etc., erase gender marks in French (see Mok 1968 for discussion of linguistic relations between gender and number). Finally, quantifiers and many adjectives have two homophones for gender in the spoken language.

However, the fact that gender is not always clearly marked on articles does not seem a sufficient explanation of the predominance of the phonological procedure in French gender-acquisition processes. It is suggested that the phonological procedure remains predominant in French because it is through phonology that gender presents the most consistent patterns. These patterns, although they are applied locally by the small child, can serve later as an ever-extending discourse strategy for syntagmatic cohesion. In the older child, the phonological procedure thus remains powerful because of its morphological function.

7 *Comprehension experiments: deictic, exophoric and quantifier functions of determiners*

Whilst several authors have studied article contrasts (see chapter 2), the majority of the experiments have concerned production tasks. Comprehension experiments, when they have been used, have either given rise to somewhat unsatisfactory results or have been based on experimental designs which, as Brown (1973) put it, placed a very 'unusual communication burden' on the articles, particularly on the indefinite article. This same criticism can be levelled at some, but perhaps not all, of the comprehension tasks reported on in this chapter and the following one. The difficulty of conceiving natural designs for comprehension tasks in the study of determiners seems to point to an underlying theoretical problem.

The three comprehension experiments reported on in this chapter covered the deictic, exophoric and quantifier functions of the singular and plural indefinite and definite articles, the singular and plural possessive adjectives and the quantifier 'all'.

Experiment 12: the playrooms

This experiment concerned comprehension of the singular definite and indefinite articles used exophorically or deictically. In all comprehension tasks, responses to NPs containing the indefinite article were never 'incorrect', since one can use 'un X' [a/one X] to refer to an object alone in its context as well as to one of several objects. The singular definite article, however, can only be used to refer to an object alone in its context, as far as the deictic or exophoric functions are concerned. It is only in its anaphoric function, i.e. only once an object has been singled out linguistically, that the definite article can refer to one of several identical objects present. This latter use will be analysed in experiments 15 and 16.

Experimental context. The context of this experiment is similar to that of one of the production tasks (experiment 1), and although the procedure was somewhat different, the layout was identical (see fig. 1, p.65). A girl-doll and boy-doll are each placed in their playroom. For half the subjects the girl's playroom was on the left; for the other half it was on the right. There were four basic contexts:

Context	*Boy's playroom*	*Girl's playroom*
A	three different-coloured brushes	one brush
	one watch	four different-coloured watches
	one whistle	one spoon
B	four different-coloured rubbers	one rubber
	one box	three identical boxes
	one balloon	one car
C	four different cows	one cow
	one car	four identical cars
	one doll	one dummy
D	three different-coloured books	one book
	one ball	one green ball, two identical balls
	one pencil	one babybottle

Experimental procedure. The child is told that the dolls will be given groups of toys to play with and that after a few games, the toys will be changed. The game is to guess each time to whom the experimenter is talking, in whose playroom the experimenter is standing, when he says: 'Prête-moi un/le X' [Lend me a/the X]. The child must guess if the experimenter is speaking to the boy or the girl. There were sixteen experimental items, and objects were changed for each set of four items except in context A, where the first two items were practice ones. The items, spoken with normal intonation, were as follows (asterisked questions were asked during the second run):

Context	*E.'s utterance*	*Child's expected response*
A.1	A qui je parle: prête-moi le sifflet?	Au garçon
	[To whom am I saying: lend me the whistle?]	[To the boy]

Context	*E.'s utterance*	*Child's expected response*
A.2	A qui je parle: prête-moi la cuillère?	A la fille
	[To whom am I saying: lend me the spoon?]	[To the girl]
A.3	A qui ... prête-moi une brosse?	Au garçon
	[To whom ... lend me a brush?]	[To the boy]
	*Comment le sais-tu?	Parce qu'il en a plusieurs
	*[How do you know?]	[Because he's got several]
A.4	A qui ... prête-moi la montre?	Au garçon
	[To whom ... lend me the watch?]	[To the boy]
	*Comment le sais-tu?	Parce qu'il n'a qu'une montre
	*[How do you know?]	[Because he's only got one watch]
A.5	A qui ... prête-moi la brosse?	A la fille
	[To whom ... lend me the brush?]	[To the girl]
A.6	A qui ... prête-moi une montre?	A la fille
	[To whom ... lend me a watch?]	[To the girl]
B.7	A qui ... prête-moi une gomme?	Au garçon
	[To whom ... lend me a rubber?]	[To the boy]
B.8	A qui ... prête-moi la boîte?	Au garçon
	[To whom ... lend me the box?]	[To the boy]
B.9	A qui ... prête-moi la gomme?	A la fille
	[To whom ... lend me the rubber?]	[To the girl]
B.10	A qui ... prête-moi une boîte?	A la fille
	[To whom ... lend me a box?]	[To the girl]
C.11	A qui ... prête-moi la vache?	A la fille
	[To whom ... lend me the cow?]	[To the girl]
C.12	A qui ... prête-moi une voiture?	A la fille
	[To whom ... lend me a car?]	[To the girl]
C.13	A qui ... prête-moi une vache?	Au garçon
	[To whom ... lend me a cow?]	[To the boy]
C.14	A qui ... prête-moi la voiture?	Au garçon
	[To whom ... lend me the car?]	[To the boy]
D.15	A qui ... prête-moi un livre, je veux lire?	Au garçon
	[To whom ... lend me a book, I want to read?]	[To the boy]
D.16	A qui ... prête-moi une balle, je veux jouer?	A la fille
	[To whom ... lend me a ball, I want to play?]	[To the girl]

Items A.3–6 and B.7–10 were first run one after the other, and then rerun in a more exploratory fashion at the end of the session. After each of the second runs, the experimenter asked the child: 'How do you know (it's the boy/the girl)?'. If for, say, B.9 ('Lend me the rubber') the child chose the girl, the experimenter asked: 'Could I have said B.9 to the boy? Why/Why not?' etc.

Items D.15 and D.16 were introduced as a further attempt to test the child's understanding of the use of the indefinite article as a non-specific reference. For these two items, it would seem really incorrect to choose the playroom containing only one book or one ball. At all times the experimenter stressed to the child that he could see exactly what was in the room of the doll to whom he was talking. Needless to say, in this experiment, as in all other experiments, the experimenter did not overstress the words 'the' and 'a' but spoke with normal intonation as if he were really asking to borrow a toy. At the end of the session, however, with children who had failed to understand the definite/indefinite contrast, the experimenter tried a few extra items with unnatural stress on the articles.

It should be mentioned that the use of the verb 'lend' was psychologically preferable to the verb 'give' because some children would not allow the doll with only one X to 'give' a toy to the experimenter, 'because she'll have no Xs left', etc. Furthermore, the more natural 'one of the . . .' ('un des X . . .') had to be avoided because the plural is marked on the vowel of the definite article in French and this might have sparked off correct responses due to singular/plural contrasts and not to the article contrast which I wished to analyse. Indefinite and definite singular articles both imply that the experimenter wants to borrow *one* object. However, the definite article presupposes that the object the experimenter wants is a singleton in this particular context, whereas the indefinite article presupposes that several are present and the experimenter wants any one of them.

If in response to an item the child said that the experimenter was talking to *both* dolls because both had the particular item requested, the experimenter responded: 'Yes, maybe, but actually I'm only in one of the playrooms and talking to one of the dolls, which one do you think it is likely to be?', and the experimenter repeated the item.

Population. Fifty-six children between 3,2 and 10,8 years participated in this experiment. Of these, 84% were also interviewed in experiment 1, the comprehension task always preceding the production task. The population distribution was as follows:

Age	*Subjects*	*Average age*
3,2–3,11	7	3,6
4,0–4,11	9	4,5
5,0–5,11	8	5,6
6,0–6,11	7	6,7
7,0–7,11	7	7,5
8,0–8,11	7	8,5
9,0–9,11	6	9,6
10,0–10,8	5	10,5

It was decided only to analyse the responses of those children who looked at *both* of the playrooms before answering, to ensure that in their responses they were implicitly attending to the task problem. One 3 year old and two 4 year olds looked at one of the dolls' rooms only and gave all their responses for that room. Their responses have therefore been removed from the analysis which covers a total of fifty-three subjects.

Results. Table 35 gives the results in the form of percentages of total responses per utterance type. As can be seen, at all ages between 3 and 10 years, children registered very high success rates (between 85% and 98%) in choosing the context containing a singleton, when the experimenter's utterance contained the definite article.

The picture is markedly different with respect to the indefinite article. The youngest subjects (3 year olds) were correct in 90% of trials in choosing the room with several Xs. This figure drops to 68% for four year olds, and down to 29% for five year olds. Between 6,0 and 7,11, children's responses still only reach 48% and 59% for choosing the more adequate context. This is clearly different from their high success rates with the definite article (between 87% and 96%). It is only from 8 years that gradually the choice for the indefinite article falls on the room with several Xs (67%), reaching the high success level of the 3 year olds only from 9 and 10 years (82% and 91%).

Though these results seem at first rather suprising, the details emanating from the more clinical part will confirm the hypothesis that 5 to 7 year olds are interpreting the indefinite article in its *numeral* function (see pp. 181–3). (It should of course be recalled that responses to the indefinite article are never entirely 'incorrect'. However, the choice

TABLE 35. *Choice of context as a function of definite and indefinite articles*

		Definite article		Indefinite article		Indefinite article + 'I want to' (items D.15 and D.16)	
Age group	Total number of trials	Reference to singleton (%)	Reference to one of several (%)	Reference to singleton (%)	Reference to one of several (%)	Reference to singleton (%)	Reference to one of several (%)
3,2–3,11	112	85	15	10	90	0	100
4,0–4,11	144	86	14	32	68	0	100
5,0–5,11	128	98	2	71	29	13	87
6,0–6,11	112	96	4	52	48	0	100
7,0–7,11	112	87	13	41	59	0	100
8,0–8,11	112	86	14	33	67	6	94
9,0–9,11	96	93	7	18	82	0	100
10,0–10,8	80	93	7	9	91	0	100

of the room containing several Xs is the more appropriate response, in view of the presupposition that if the X is alone, one would have used a definite referring expression. Thus it is the fact that the definite article is *not* used that is a clue to the more appropriate response.)

The striking difference between the columns covering the indefinite article alone and those covering the indefinite article plus 'I want to plus verb' is not without significance. Clearly the high success rates at all ages (between 87% and 100%) shows that this addition of 'I want to plus verb' confers on the indefinite article its non-specific function in contrast to its numeral function. It is the latter function which probably explains the responses of the 5, 6 and 7 year olds when 'I want to plus verb' is not added.

Let us now take a look at the more interesting aspects of the results of this experiment, which concerns the justification given by children for their choice. These data have been divided into the responses concerning each utterance type. Translation of the indefinite article 'une' into either 'a' or 'one' is usually clear from each child's utterance.

Justification given for (correctly) choosing singleton context for definite article. Whilst children under the age of 4,8 made correct responses, no child under this age was able to furnish a justification for his choice. Between 4,9 and 4,11, whilst the choice was correct, the children gave justifications which showed that they were not aware of the implicit rule they had used, as can be seen from the following examples of children who chose the singleton for the experimenter's 'Lend me the X':

4,9 years
Au garçon, parce que les garçons ils aiment les voitures
[To the boy, because boys like cars]
A la fille, parce qu'elle veut plus sa vache
[To the girl, because she doesn't want her cow any more]
4,11 years
A la fille, parce qu'elle a une vache
[To the girl, because she has a cow (indefinite article not stressed)]

Whilst the last example would seem to be referring to the singleton, we shall see from the next set of examples that this is probably not the case. The next examples, also of children choosing the singleton, cover the rest of the age span and are not strictly divisible into subgroups:

5,5 years
Lui, parce que lui, il a *une* X et elle, elle en a trois
[He, because he has *one* X and she has three (stressed)]
5,7 years
Au garçon, parce qu'il a qu'une X, lui
[To the boy, because *he* has just one X]
5,10 years
Au garçon, parce qu'elle a plusieurs X et lui *seulement une*
[To the boy, because she has several Xs and he just one]
5,11 years
Au garçon, parce qu'il a *une de* X
[To the boy, because he has one X]
6,5 years
A la fille, parce qu'elle, elle a un seul X
[To the girl, because she has only one X]
7,4 years
Au garçon, parce qu'il n'a pas des X, il en a une
[To the boy, because he hasn't got some Xs, he has one]
8,0 years
Lui, parce qu'il en a qu'une de X
[He, because he's got only one X]
8,3 years
A la fille, parce qu'elle a une de X, pas plusieurs
[To the girl, because she has one X, not several]
8,8 years
Lui, parce qu'il n'en a qu'une seule
[He, because he only has one]
8,10 years
Elle, parce qu'elle a juste une de X
[She, because she has just one X]

Whilst all the above subjects clearly mark what they have understood by stressing the context – 'only one', 'one only', and various slightly ungrammatical forms such as 'un de X', 'qu'une de X', 'juste une de X'– none of those children actually refers to the *linguistic* clue from the definite article used in the experimenter's utterance. This was only to be found in more advanced subjects:

7,7 years
Quand on dit une, il y en a plusieurs, autrement on dit la balle ou ta balle, ça doit être la fille alors, elle elle en a une et lui quatre
[Because when you say 'une' [a/one] there are several, otherwise you say the X or your X, it must be the girl then, she's got one and he's got four]

9,2 years
A la fille, parce que pour le garçon vous auriez dit une des X
[To the girl, because for the boy you would have said one of the Xs]
10,8 years
Au garçon, on dit le pour le garçon et un pour la fille, parce qu'elle en a pas seulement un
[To the boy, you say the (singular) for the boy and (?)a/one for the girl, because she has more than one]

Can one use the definite article to refer to one of several? After the children had given their spontaneous responses and explanations for their choice of a singleton for the definite article, the alternative response was proposed to them: can I say 'Lend me *the* X to the doll which has several Xs'? The question of course is not very clear because one can say anything (practically) to anyone. Nonetheless the results were not without interest. The general trend of most 3 and 4 year olds, as well as some 5 year olds, was to agree that the definite article could be used to refer to one of several:

3,4 years
(agreed, but handed several Xs to E. in response to 'Lend me the X')
4,3 years
Oui, parce que le garçon il a aussi une X
[Yes, because the boy also has an X]
4,11 years
Oui, parce que le garçon aussi il a une X . . . des X
[Yes, because the boy also has an X . . . someXs]
5,6 years
Oui, parce que lui, il a une X . . . aussi des X
[Yes, because he has an X . . . also some Xs]

It was not until 6 years that children responded with an empathic 'no', i.e. that the definite article could not be used to refer to one of several, as can be seen from the following examples:

6,4 years
Non, parce qu'il n'a pas qu'une seule, il en a trois
[No, because he hasn't got only one, he has three]
6,7 years
Non, on peut pas, il en a plusieurs
[No, you can't, he has several]
7,2 years
Non, parce qu'il n'a pas une X . . . il en a, mais pas *une*

[No, because he hasn't got an X . . . he has some but not *one* (second indefinite article stressed)]
7,6 years
Non, parce qu'il a pas seulement une, il en a plusieurs
[No, because he doesn't have just one only, he's got several]

From roughly 8 years, children were more explicit about the presuppositions contained in the use of the definite article, when asked if the latter could be used to refer to one of several:

8,4 years
Non, parce qu'il ne saurait pas laquelle c'est
[No, because he wouldn't know which one it is]
9,8 years
Non . . . enfin oui . . . mais il devrait dire choisis-la, il ne pourrait pas dire prends-la
[No . . . well yes . . . but he'd have to answer choose it, he couldn't say take it]
9,10 years
Non, parce que lui il en a plusieurs, il faudrait préciser, il faudrait dire la X rouge; pour la fille, eh bien ça va de dire la X parce qu'elle n'en a qu'une
[No, because he has several, you'd have to give more details, you'd have to say the red X; for the girl it's okay to say the X, because she's only got one]
10,4 years
Non, il devrait vous demander lequel
[No, he would have to ask which one]
10,7 years
Non, il faut dire une de tes trois X
[No, you must say one of your three Xs]

Those children who in the task items had mistakenly chosen for the definite article the playroom with several Xs, all agreed without exception that the definite article could be used to refer to the singleton.

Justification given for the choice of playroom for indefinite article. No response is essentially wrong for the items containing the indefinite article, as was pointed out earlier. Nonetheless, one might argue that the fact that the definite article is *not* used implies that reference is being made to one object amongst several rather than to a singleton.

No justifications were given before the age of 4,9 years. Responses after that age are divided into the two choices available. The first examples are taken from the childeren who thought the utterance with the indefinite article made reference to the room containing one of several Xs:

5,5 years
A elle, parce qu'elle a plus de X que le garçon
[To her, because she has more Xs than the boy]
6,4 years
Au garçon, parce qu'il en a plus et elle seulement une
[To the boy, because he has more and she only one]
6,7 years
Au garçon, parce qu'ils ont tous les deux des X mais le garçon il en a trois
[To the boy, because they both have Xs but the boy he has three of them]
7,4 years
A la fille, parce qu'elle a des X
[To the girl, because she has some Xs (no stress on plural indefinite article)]

The following examples, also from children who chose the room with several Xs for the indefinite article, show a greater awareness again in older children of the presuppositions conveyed by article usage:

7,0 years
Au garçon, parce que si on dit une X, ça veut dire qu'y en a plusieurs
[To the boy, because if you say an X, it means that there are several of them]
7,8 years
Au garçon, parce qu'il en a plusieurs, si c'était la fille, alors on dirait: prête-moi ta X, parce qu'elle en a seulement une
[To the boy, because he has several, if it were the girl one should say: lend me your X, because she only has one]
8,0 years
A la fille, parce qu'elle peut en donner une, parce qu'il faudrait qu'on dise au garçon: prête-moi la X; quand c'est une, il s'agit de la fille; au garçon on doit dire la X
[To the girl, because she can give one of them, because we'd have to say to the boy: lend me the X; when it's (?)a/one it's the girl; to the boy you must say the X]
8,3 years
A la fille, parce qu'elle en a plusieurs, elle peut vous donner n'importe laquelle
[To the girl, because she has several of them, she can give you any one of them]

All older children gave responses like the two 7 year olds above. The last example is particularly interesting because it bears witness to the non-specific reference function ('n'importe laquelle') of the indefinite article in this particular context.

Let us now briefly look at the responses of children having chosen the singleton for utterances with the indefinite article:

4,9 years
Au garçon, parce que lui il a qu'une seule X
[To the boy, because he has only one X]
4,11 years
A la fille, parce qu'elle en a seulement une
[To the girl, because she only has one]
5,4 years
A la fille, parce qu'elle a une X, une seule
[To the girl, because she has (?)an/one X, only one]
6,4 years
Une X, ça veut dire qu'il en a qu'une
[An X, that means he has only one]
6,10 years
Au garçon, parce qu'il n'a qu'une de X et elle, elle en a deux, c'est pluriel
[The boy, because he's only got one X and she, she has two of them, it's plural]
7,8 years
Au garçon, il en a *une*, mais elle en a plusieurs
[The boy, he's got *one* but she has several (indefinite article stressed)]

The correction, 'elle a une X, une seule', of the 5 year old cited above is interesting, in that it shows an implicit awareness of the ambiguity of the indefinite article in French, its use for both non-specific reference and as a numeral.

No child over 7,8 gave this sort of response. The above examples tend to confirm the hypothesis that at some point in development, children interpret the use of the indefinite article in such contexts in its numeral function rather than in its non-specific reference function. The following example from an 8 year old clearly illustrates the conflict between the two functions:

8,0 years
(long hesitation) Prête-moi une brosse ↗ . . . c'est le garçon, parce qu'il a une brosse . . . non, c'est la fille, parce qu'elle a une de brosse et le garçon en a trois . . . non, le garçon, parce qu'il peut vous donner n'importe laquelle de ses brosses
[Lend me a brush . . . it's the boy because he's got a brush . . . no, its the girl, because she's got one brush and the boy three . . . no, the boy, because he can give you any one of his brushes]

Can one use the indefinite article to refer to a singleton? This question was asked of those children who had correctly chosen the context with several Xs. Only one child of 5,1 years agreed that this was possible, adding 'Because he has an X too'. All the other subjects disagreed. The youngest ones, up to 7,6 years, justified the disagreement by invoking 'He only has one'. It was from 7,7 years that children added that the definite article must be used for singletons. Their responses were almost identical and are not quoted. A response from a 9 year old, however, is worth quoting *in extenso*:

9,2 years
E.: Est-ce que je peux dire: prête-moi une X au garçon?
C.: Non, parce qu'il n'en a qu'une et si vous lui dites: prête-moi une X, il pourrait en donner une autre, s'il en avait une autre, et vous vous voulez celle qu'il a là, alors il faut dire: prête-moi *la* X
[E.: Can I say: lend me an X to the boy?
C.: No, because he has one only and if you say to him: lend me an X, he could give you another one, if he had another, and you want the one he's got there, so you must say: lend me *the* X (stressed)]

The following example also illustrates the problem of shared knowledge between speaker and addressee in the use of articles:

10,3 years
E.: Est-ce que je peux dire: prête-moi une X à la fille?
C.: Non . . . ben oui, si vous n'aviez pas vu sa chambre, alors vous ne saviez pas qu'elle n'avait qu'une seule
[E.: Can I say: lend me an X to the girl?
C.: No . . . well yes, if you hadn't seen her room, so you didn't know she just had one]

Can one use the indefinite article to refer to one of several? This question was asked of those subjects who had resolutely chosen the singleton for the indefinite article. Between 4,11 and 6,6 years, children did not allow the use of the indefinite for reference to one of several and justify this by adding 'No, because he has three'. As of 6,6 the responses became more explicit, again demonstrating that they interpreted the indefinite article in its numeral function:

6,7 years
E.: Est-ce qu'on peut dire: prête-moi une X à la fille?
C.: Non, parce que la fille elle a plusieurs et vous avez dit une
[E.: Can I say: lend me an X to the girl?
C.: No, because the girl has several and you said (?)a/one]

6,10 years
C.: Non, parce que vous avez dit *une*, pas plusieurs
[No, because you said *one*, not many]
6,11 years
C.: Non, parce que tu as dit une vache, alors ça doit être la fille, elle a une seule et lui il en a quatre . . . (murmurs) prête-moi une vache . . . eh bien, peut-être tu parles aux deux
E.: Et si je parlais seulement à l'un des deux?
C.: Alors ça doit être la fille, tu as dit une, et elle en a une
[C.: No, because you said (?)a/one cow, so it must be the girl, she has one only and he has four . . . (murmurs) lend me a cow . . . oh well, maybe you're talking to both of them
E.: And if I were just talking to one of them?
C.: Then it must be the girl, you said (?)a/one and she's got one]

From 7,0 years this question gives rise to conflict with earlier responses according to the numeral function, as can be seen from the following examples:

7,0 years
E.: Peut-on dire: prête-moi une X au garçon?
C.: Non . . . ah oui, bien sûr on peut, tout à l'heure je me suis trompé, c'est pas la fille, c'est le garçon parce qu'il en a plusieurs
[E.: Can I say: lend me an X to the boy?
C.: No . . . oh yes, of course you can, just now I was wrong, it's not the girl, it's the boy because he's got several]
7,2 years
Non . . . oui . . . non . . . attends une minute, la fille elle en a une de gomme et le garçon trois, mais tu peux aussi dire une gomme au garçon
[No . . . yes . . . no . . . wait a minute, the girl has got one rubber and the boy three, but you can also say: (?)a/one rubber to the boy]
7,8 years
Non, c'est une, vous n'avez pas plusieurs . . . euh . . . mais oui on peut, puisque lui il vous en donne une
[No, it's (?)a/one, you didn't say several . . . oh, yes you can, because he can give you one of them]

Any children over 7,6 who had chosen the singleton initially agreed that one could also use the indefinite article to refer to the context containing several Xs.

In summary, the results of this experiment reveal that whilst all subjects interpreted the definite article as referring to a singleton, the indefinite article caused problems. 3 year olds were correct in

room containing several Xs when interpreting the indefinite
ıey were too young to undergo epilinguistic testing. The
ı to drop at 4 years, and between 5 and 7 most children
ıe indefinite article, the room containing a singleton. All
lid extremely well, however, with the definite article. It is
.at the results from other experiments indicate that the
›rrect interpretation of the definite article has a different
ling to the age of the children. The youngest subjects
ked the room containing a singleton because the definite
ıctioning deictically for them, and older subjects made a
ce but based on exophoric reference. That the definite
ıg understood deictically by the under 6 year old was also
he clinical part of the session. Suprisingly, small children
he definite article could be used to refer to one of several
ıugh their initial interpretation was correct. From 6 years
enter's suggestion that the definite article be used for re-
.e of several Xs was emphatically rejected, i.e. it therefore
oric reference to a singleton.
rd to the indefinite article, it is suggested that the youngest
rpret it correctly because of the absence of focus of attention
.efinite article implies for them). The interpretation of the
olds seems to stem from concentrating on a new function
the indefinite article: that of being a numeral. Moreover, as
ther experiments, I often encountered spontaneous ut-
ı slightly ungrammatical type, that showed the children
7 years wished to draw a distinction between two functions
y had now become sensitive. They would use 'une de X'
', and 'une X' to mean 'a'. This shows that they are implicitly
› meanings. From 7 years, conflicts between the numeral
. the non-specific function of the indefinite article became
he epilinguistic part of the session also showed similar
dren added markers such as 'qu'une'/'seulement une'/
., which again bears witness to the numeral interpretation.
olds interpreted the indefinite article as a non-specific
d in the epilinguistic part of the session talked of 'n'importe
y one] and 'Il devrait dire choisis-la, il ne pourrait pas dire
He would have to say choose it, he couldn't say take it],
vitness to an understanding of non-specific reference.
n 8 years that children could render explicit the pre-

suppositions contained in the use of the definite article and explain the inadequacy of its use in non-specific reference. It is mainly from 8 and 9 years that children made reference to the *linguistic* clues they had used, whereas the majority of younger subjects referred to aspects of the current extralinguistic context.

What is striking is that for items where 'Lend me an X, I want to play', etc., was added, children of *all* ages were successful in interpreting the utterance as a non-specific reference. The explanation may lie in the lilt or intonation which such an expression gives rise to. The items were spoken as naturally as possible, with no special emphases, but nor were normal intonational patterns avoided. Another explanation could be that, if specific reference had been meant, 'I want to play with *it*' would have been more normal. As pointed out in a discussion by Tanz (1977), children's interpretation of the pronoun 'it' is deeply interwoven with definite reference. Thus the early non-specific interpretation when we added 'I want to play' may be due to the *absence* of specific reference markers.

This experiment appears to show that the definite article is interpreted very early as referring to a singleton. However the experimental procedure was limited to a single sentence with a concrete extralinguistic referent. Experiment 13, which follows, was designed to show whether the function of the definite article remains as clear when used in discourse.

Experiment 13: story comprehension

Stories are usually very predictable. Much of the semantic and syntactic information contained in them is not carefully attended to because of this predictability. It would therefore be difficult to test a childs understanding of indefinite/definite articles in stories which stick to habitual settings. It was thus decided to use counterpragmatic stories; the definite article alone would carry the semantic burden of informing the addressee that only one X was involved in the story, the setting of which normally would involve several Xs (e.g. usually there is more than one flower in a garden, more than one apple in a fruit basket, etc.). It should be recalled that young children very frequently produce definite referring expressions to denote singularity, and it was therefore of interest to observe their behaviour in comprehension.

Experimental context. There were no experimental objects, the stories being entirely verbal with no concrete support.

Experimental procedure. Each child was told at least two stories containing definite articles at key points. The child was informed that he must listen very carefully to the story since the experimenter would ask him a question about it afterwards. The stories were as follows.:

Story 1
Un jour les maîtresses se trouvaient toutes dans la salle des maîtres. Il y avait un grand panier de fruits[1] sur la table, plein de toutes sortes de fruits. Tout d'un coup, un petit garçon est entré à toute allure dans la salle, il a pris la pomme et il s'est vite enfui. Les maîtresses, elles étaient très fâchées
[One day the teachers were all in their common room. There was a big basket of fruit on the table, full of different fruit. Suddenly a little boy ran in, took the apple and rushed out again. The teachers were very angry]
Questions:
How many apples are there left now?
(expected response: None)
How many apples were there before the boy rushed in?
(expected response: One apple)
How do you know?
(expected response: You said he took *the* apple, so that means there was only one, etc.)
E. repeats story:
What did I say the boy did?
(repetition: The boy ran in and took *the* apple)

Story 2
Le petit chien d'Anne-Marie courait autour de son jardin. Il courait, il courait. Bientôt le chien il s'est senti très fatigué. Alors il s'est aplati par terre pour dormir et il a écrasé la fleur qui poussait dans le jardin. Anne-Marie était trés fâchée
[Mary's little dog was running about in her garden. He ran and ran. Soon the dog got very tired. He flopped down to sleep and crushed the flower growing in the garden. Mary was very angry]
Questions:
How many flowers were growing in Mary's garden?
(expected response: One)
How do you know?
(expected response: You said he crushed *the* flower, etc.)
E. repeats story:
What did I say the dog did?
(repetition: He flopped to sleep and crushed *the* flower)

[1] 'Fruit' is a count noun in French; one can say 'un fruit' or 'des fruits'.

In each case, the definite article was pronounced normally with no special stress. At the end of the session, however, one of the stories, or a new one made up on the spot, was told a second time and the definite article was then heavily stressed. 'La pomme', la fleur', were purposely chosen because of the feminine gender of these words; the definite/indefinite contrast being far clearer in the feminine ('une/la') than in the masculine ('un/le'). It should be added that in the second story, the verb 'was growing' does not in spoken language give a clue to singularity although it is marked for plural in written French, e.g. 'la fleur qui pouss*ait*' versus the written plural 'les fleurs qui pouss*aient*'. Moreover, had it been the indefinite article, the verb would have been the same (i.e. 'une fleur qui poussait') but the indefinite article could have implied several flowers present and one of them got crushed.

It is of course realized that the definite article would only in exceptional cases carry such a heavy semantic burden. If the content of a story is counter pragmatic, there will normally be other linguistic clues marking the unusualness, e.g. 'the *only* apple/flower'. However, I was interested in seeing how, and when, children pick up the semantic information carried by an expression which they use in production tasks at an early age to express unity.

Population. Forty-seven subjects between 4,1 and 11,1 participated in this experiment, as follows:

Age	*Subjects*	*Average age*
4,1–4,11	5	4,6
5,0–5,11	5	5,5
6,0–6,11	7	6,5
7,0–7,11	7	7,8
8,0–8,11	9	8,7
9,0–9,11	7	9,4
10,0–11,1	7	10,5

Results. Table 36 gives the percentages of total responses where children interpreted the story as referring to one apple or one flower, or to several. The results show very clearly that in the vast majority of cases until 8 years, children do not use the clue from the definite article. Rather they use their world knowledge of normal situations where there are several apples in fruit baskets and several flowers in gardens. It should be recalled that they had no difficulties in interpreting the definite article correctly in isolated sentences (see results of

TABLE 36. *Counterpragmatic stories containing definite article, interpreted as implying one alone or one of several, expressed as percentage of total responses*

	Answer to question		Repetition of E.'s statement			
Age group	'One' (%)	'Several' (%)	Definite article (%)	Definite article + 'only' (%)	Indefinite article + 'only' (%)	Indefinite article (%)
4,1–4,11	25	75	100	0	0	0
5,0–5,11	14	86	100	0	0	0
6,0–6,11	29	71	91	0	0	9
7,0–7,11	30	70	95	0	0	5
8,0–8,11	61	39	23	15	25	37
			(38 definite)		(62 indefinite)	
9,0–9,11	78	22	12	29	14	45
			(41 definite)		(59 indefinite)	
10,0–11,1	67	33	71	5	0	24
			(76 definite)		(24 indefinite)	

experiment 12). In this experiment, for children between 4,1 and 7,11, the majority of responses, i.e. between 70% and 86% were based on 'pragmatic procedures', i.e. world knowledge of such situations. From 8,0 years and up to 11 years the picture changes, but not strikingly so; between only 61% and 78% of responses of these older children shows that the semantic information conveyed by the definite article has been noted. Still a certain number of responses are obviously based on 'pragmatic procedures'.

What is interesting is the way in which children repeated the experimenter's utterance (also shown on table 36). Those children between 4 and 8 years who interpreted the story to mean that several Xs were involved, nonetheless could repeat the experimenter's utterance correctly with the definite article. 8 and 9 year olds, however, were able to pick up the information conveyed by the definite article, but they surprisingly repeated the experimenter's utterance quite incorrectly and gave the form (indefinite) which would have been pragmatically more likely. Although in a few cases they did repeat the definite article alone (23% and 12% of responses), for quite a few responses children added the word only ('la seule X') and swore that that was exactly what the experimenter had said. What these children seem to be doing is conferring on the terms their *normal functions*, i.e. the definite article would not carry the semantic burden alone. It is only the 10 year olds who were able both to interpret the definite article in 67% of responses and to give a correct repetition with the definite articles alone (71% of responses).

This small, and not entirely satisfactory experiment (because open to the criticisms mentioned in chapter 3), nonetheless points to some interesting trends. Accentuating the definite article in the third trial made no difference to the youngest subjects. It did however affect the responses of 6 and 7 year olds in many cases. They were obviously expecting the definite article to have its normal function and for an extra indication to be present, in this case intonation, or the addition of 'only' as the children spontaneously did when some counterpragmatic information was to be conveyed. One or two 7 and 8 year olds interrupted the experimenter and asked '*La* pomme?' (stressing the article), as if their anticipation of hearing 'une pomme' had been contradicted.

Just as children's repetitions gave the clues to the procedures they used to interpret the story, so their responses to the experimenter's questions were revealing. Here are a few examples from children who did *not* pick up the clue from the definite article:

6,5 years
E.: Combien . . .?
C.: Beaucoup . . . enfin au moins deux, parce que dans les jardins il y a toujours beaucoup de fleurs . . . ou pas du tout
[E.: How many . . .?
C.: Lots . . . at least two, because in gardens there are always lots of flowers . . . or none at all]
8,9 years
C.: Il y avait tout un tas de pommes . . . enfin trois ou quatre, normalement il y a pas mal de pommes et d'oranges
[C.: There were a whole lot of apples . . . well three or four, usually there are quite a few apples and oranges]

The fact that these children added 'There are *always* . . .' or '*Usually* there are . . .' indicates that, as they were listening to the story, they were anticipating its details by fitting it into their world knowledge of similar situations rather than picking up specific syntactic clues. It is this approach that I call 'pragmatic procedure'.

The next two examples from slightly older children show a somewhat different approach. The 8 year old's use of the modal 'must' tends to indicate that he heard the syntactic clue from the definite article but that it conflicted with his pragmatic procedure. The 9 year old did not appear to rely on the pragmatic procedure:

8,10 years
Il devait y avoir pas mal de pommes, y en a toujours, ça coûte moins cher que les mandarines
[There must have been quite a lot of apples, there always are, they're cheaper than mandarines]
9,5 years
On peut pas savoir combien, parce que vous n'avez pas précisé dans l'histoire
[No-one can know how many there were, because you did not give details in the story]

The following examples are from children who did pick up the clue from the definite article, but were not consciously aware of the clue they had used:

8,6 years
E.: Combien . . .?
C.: Une seule
E.: Comment le sais-tu?
C.: Parce que vous avez dit qu'il s'est endormi et qu'il a écrasé une fleur
[E.: How many . . . ?
C.: Only one
E.: How do you know?
C.: Because you said he fell asleep and crushed a flower (no stress on indefinite article)]
9,1 years
E.: Combien . . .?
C.: Une pomme
E.: Comment le sais-tu?
E.: Parce que vous avez dit une pomme seulement
[E.: How many . . .?
C.: One apple
E.: . . . know?
C.: Because you said one apple only]
9,8 years
E.: . . . sais-tu?
C.: Parce que vous avez dit la seule fleur du jardin
[E.: . . . know?
C.: Because you said the only flower in the garden]

Finally, there are examples from children who both picked up the clue and were able to tell the experimenter precisely how they knew:

8,9 years
Vous avez dit *la* pomme alors il n'y avait qu'une seule
[You said *the* apple, (stressed) so there must have been just one]
9,8 years
Tu avais dit *la* fleur, la seule alors
[You said *the* flower, (stressed) the only one therefore]
10,2 years
Quand vous dites la, ça veut dire une seule
[When you say the, then it means one only]

A few children were also capable, as in other experiments, of invoking the presuppositions that can be inferred from *not* using the other article:

9,10 years
Une seule, sinon vous auriez dû dire il a écrasé des . . . une des fleurs
[Just one, otherwise you would have had to say he crushed some . . . one of the flowers]
10,8 years
Dans l'histoire, il y en avait qu'une, voux avez précisé, vous avez dit *la* pomme. Si y en avait eu plusieurs, alors on aurait pu dire *une des pommes* et il en restait d'autres pour les maîtresses
[In the story there was only one, you were precise, you said *the* apple. (stressed) If there had been several, then one could have said *one of the* apples, and there were others left for the teachers]

It is interesting to note that older children can make inferences based on the *absence* of a marker and not just from clues actually present in an utterance.

In summary, the results of this small experiment are considered important for two reasons. The use of the definite article alone for conveying counterpragmatic information is of course open to the criticisms discussed under 'The experimental dilemma'. However, given that children decode and use the definite article deictically from 3 years and exophorically from roughly 6 years, it was important to ascertain whether they could pick up a similar clue from the definite article in connected discourse and without the extralinguistic support used in other experiments. The results clearly show that it is not until 8 years, and even then not strikingly so, that children pick up the linguistic clue. Before this, children use 'pragmatic procedures', i.e. they anticipate the details of a story from their world knowledge of similar situations. The epilinguistic part clearly showed the nature of this pragmatic procedure; the children explained their responses by using such terms as '*Usually* there are . . . In gardens there are *always* . . .', etc. It is not that the children did not hear the definite article, as can be seen from the repetitions. It is striking that when the older children were successful in interpreting, they then inserted in their repetition the actual linguistic markers normally expected in a counterpragmatic situation (e.g. 'the only X'). It should be recalled that 6 and 7 year olds could pick up the information if the definite article was heavily stressed. Functionally speaking, heavy stress or the addition of emphasizers such as 'only' gives the utterance a normal information burden. In other words, when some counterpragmatic message is to be conveyed, there are linguistic or paralinguistic means for doing so, and under 8 year olds rely on these functional clues. It seems that only from 9 years can children take a more 'abstract' approach to utterances and seek subtle clues, rather than merely relying on world knowledge or obvious functional clues. This holds for an experimental setting. However, it is clear that much of normal discourse understanding for the over 8 year old is also based on a subtle interplay of semantic, syntactic, functional and pragmatic clues.

Experiment 14: the parking lots

The design of this experiment was similar to that of the production task in experiment 3. In the comprehension task, however, no items concerned objects existing only in the child's parking lot, such as the yellow cars, the aeroplane or the child's possessions. The definite referring expression versus the addition of the possessive marker contrast could not be tested in such cases in view of the fact that the nouns themselves would suffice to elicit adequate responses. The contrast therefore had to be tested with objects which were present in both parking lots. All the test items of experiment 14 were devised in such a way that each morpheme of each NP had to be decoded. A correct answer would involve listening to all parts of the item, e.g. 'the red open cars', where 'the' is opposed to 'my', 'red' opposed to 'blue', etc., 'open' opposed to 'closed', and 'cars' opposed to 'lorries'. It should be recalled that in French most adjectives are placed after the noun.

Experimental context. Fig 2. (page 88) illustrates the context of this experiment, which was identical to that of experiment 3, except that here, only one experimenter was required. In other respects the context was similar to experiment 3 (see p. 87 above for details). It should be mentioned that it was because of the comprehension task that green vehicles were not used, to avoid ambiguity between 'ouverte' [open] and 'ou verte' [or green], which had led to problems in a few cases in the pilot study.

Experimental procedure. As in experiment 3, the child was familiarized with the task by using coloured shapes, and it was ensured that distinctions between 'closed/open cars', 'lorries/cars' and the colours were clearly understood. As in experiment 3, the child placed some of his own possessions on his parking lot to mark which was his. The experimenter stressed the difference between the two lots and the fact that both were part of the game. Test items were not given until the experimenter was sure that the child had understood the game.

Unlike experiment 3, in the comprehension task no information was given as to whether the child responded correctly or not. His responses were merely followed by the usual 'aha' grunt. The ten experimental items were as follows:

1. Mets les voitures au garage
   [Put the cars into the garage]
2. Mets tes voitures au garage
   [Put your cars into the garage]
3. Mets les voitures rouges au garage
   [Put the red cars into the garage]
4. Mets tes voitures bleues au garage
   [Put your blue cars into the garage]
5. Mets les voitures ouvertes au garage
   [Put the open cars into the garage]
6. Mets tes voitures fermées au garage
   [Put your closed cars into the garage]
7. Mets les voitures bleues fermées au garage
   [Put the blue closed cars into the garage]
8. Mets tes voitures rouges ouvertes au garage
   [Put your red open cars into the garage]
9. Mets toutes les voitures rouges ouvertes au garage
   [Put all the red open cars into the garage]
10. Mets toutes tes voitures fermées au garage
   [Put all your closed cars into the garage]

Order of presentation for all subjects was: 1, 4, 8, 3, 6, (10), 7, 5, (9), 2. Items 9 and 10 were only given to those subjects who were unsuccessful in interpreting 'the/your' as totalizers in items 6 and 7. For very young subjects failing on most items, these were presented a second time at the end of the experiment, with the words 'toutes/tous' [all] added before each item. If, after the experimenter had given an item, the child asked a question, e.g. 'All of them?', 'The red ones only?', etc., the experimenter replied by saying 'Do what you think is right' and he repeated the item.

Population. Fifty-six subjects between 4,6 and 11,5 years were interviewed, as follows:

Age	*Subjects*	*Average age*
4,6–4,11	5	4,8
5,0–5,11	9	5,3
6,0–6,11	10	6,6
7,0–7,11	8	7,6
8,0–8,11	8	8,5
9,0–9,11	8	9,5
10,0–11,5	8	10,8

89% of the above population were also interviewed in the production task of experiment 3. In such cases, the comprehension task always preceded the production task. This fact makes the very laborious productions encountered amongst a large number of subjects in experiment 3 even more striking.

Results. The plural definite article 'les' has a heavy communicative burden for items without the addition of 'all'. It will be recalled that in the production task (experiment 3), small children used 'les' as a pluralizer for some time before they conferred on 'les' a totalizer function.

Table 37 gives a breakdown of correct comprehension of each item per age group, Table 38 gives the percentage of correct total trials per age group, and Table 39 the percentage of correct total trials per item.

As can be seen, the picture that emerges from the comprehension task is strikingly different from the results of the production task. In comprehension, very high success rates were registered for most items from 5 years, and systematically for all items from 6 years. Indeed, table 38 shows success rates ranging from 80% to 96% between 6 and 11 years.

Whilst success rates are low for 4 year olds in general, the distribution per item of the success rates is particularly interesting for the linguistic

TABLE 37. *Correct comprehension of items, expressed as a percentage of total trials per item*

Age group	Total number of trials	The lorries (%)	Your cars (%)	The red cars (%)	Your blue cars (%)	The open cars (%)	Your closed cars (%)	The blue closed cars (%)	Your red open cars (%)	All the red open cars (%)	All your closed cars (%)
4,6–4,11	50	40	20	0	40	0	20	0	80	20	40
5,0–5,11	90	50	66	34	50	75	66	56	100	78	89
6,0–6,11	100	70	90	80	100	100	100	80	90	90	100
7,0–7,11	80	75	50	75	63	88	88	75	88	100	100
8,0–8,11	80	88	88	88	88	100	100	88	88	100	100
9,0–9,11	80	100	88	100	88	100	88	100	100	100	100
10,0–11,5	80	75	100	75	75	88	88	88	100	100	100

TABLE 38. *Percentage of total trials correct as a function of age*

Age group	Total number of trials	Trials correct (%)
4,6–4,11	50	30
5,0–5,11	90	64
6,0–6,11	100	90
7,0–7,11	80	80
8,0–8,11	80	92
9,0–9,11	80	96
10,0–11,5	80	89

TABLE 39. *Percentage of total trials correct as a function of item*

Item	Total number of trials per item	Trials correct (%)
1. The lorries	56	61
2. Your cars	56	75
3. The red cars	56	68
4. Your blue cars	56	77
5. The open cars	56	84
6. Your closed cars	56	81
7. The blue closed cars	56	73
8. Your red open cars	56	93
9. All the red open cars	56	87
10. All your closed cars	56	93

hypothesis developed in chapter 3, concerning the descriptor versus determinor function of articles, adjectives, etc. As can be noted from table 37, item 8 ('your red open cars') – which seemingly involves attending to a large number of terms – was successfully understood in 80% of trials of 4 year olds, whereas item 2 ('your cars') was only correct in 20% of 4 year olds' trials. It is suggested that this is because item 8 *describes entirely* the objects referred to, thus obviating the necessity to take into account their relationship with the other vehicles present. Item 2, on the contrary, requires an understanding of the totalizer function of the possessive adjective and not merely of its pluralizer function.

Looking now in table 40 at the difference in success rates between items containing the plural possessive 'tes' and those containing the plural definite 'les', it can be seen that for under 6 year olds, far better results were obtained for the possessive adjective. This would again suggest that 'tes' is understood in its descriptor function and not in its function of indicating the subclass relationship with the plural definite 'les'. It will be recalled that in production, children tend to express the pluralizer function of both the definite article and the possessive adjective well before expressing their totalizer functions, the latter being initially expressed by the addition of 'all'.

TABLE 40. *Percentage of correct trials with respect to plural definite/plural possessive contrast as a function of age*

Age group	Plural possessive 'tes' (items 2, 4, 6, 8, 10) (%)	Plural definite article 'les' (items 1, 3, 5, 7, 9) (%)
4,6–4,11	40	12
5,0–5,11	69	55
6,0–6,11	96	84
7,0–7,11	80	82
8,0–8,11	92	92
9,0–9,11	92	100
10,0–11,5	92	85

Table 41 shows that the addition of the quantifier 'tous' [all] gives equal or better results at all ages, both with respect to the possessive adjective and the definite article. Thus, the addition of 'all' implies totalization for those children for whom only the pluralizer function is operative in the definite article or possessive adjective. However, the results for the 4 year olds tend to confirm the hypothesis from experiment 3 that 'all' is first used and, it seems, understood, as meaning 'a lot'. 'All' is not immediately understood as a totalizer. As can be seen from table 41, 4 year olds are only successful in 40% and 20% of trials with the addition of 'all', although of course this is a marked improvement

TABLE 41. *Effect of addition of 'all', expressed as a percentage of total trials correct for each item*

	Possessive		Definite	
Age group	6. Your closed cars (%)	10. *All* your closed cars item (%)	7. The blue closed cars (%)	9. *All* the red open cars (%)
4,6–4,11	20	40	0	20
5,0–5,11	66	89	56	78
6,0–6,11	100	100	80	90
7,0–7,11	88	100	75	100
8,0–8,11	100	100	88	100
9,0–9,11	88	100	100	100
10,0–11,5	88	100	88	100

on the corresponding 20% and 0% without the addition of 'all'. In general, when items for 4 year olds were rerun with the addition of 'all', results were better, but still not at the level of the 6 year old.

If we recall that most items were successfully interpreted by children over 5 years, and all by those over 6 years, does it then follow that children are using class inclusion concepts in comprehension? Hardly. Two important cognitive facts should be recalled. First, as can be seen from fig. 2, subclasses were neatly placed together spatially. Thus the child had a concrete spatial support for grouping subordinate and superordinate classes. Second, upon hearing, say, 'Put the red cars into the garage', the child could make *successive* confirmations (e.g. 'That's red, that's red', etc.) and *successive* negations (e.g. 'That's not red, that's not red', etc.). In this way, younger subjects could deal with the situation *preoperationally*, opposing one subclass to another successively, which is quite distinct from the simultaneous inclusive relationship between a subclass and its superordinate class. In the latter case, the subclass is considered simultaneously from two angles: as a separate subclass, and as part of a superordinate class. Of course, the experiment was purposely designed to make the logical aspects of the context easy, since I was not studying class concepts *per se*, but the plurifunctionality of the linguistic expressions used for them. However, it is clear that the correct interpretation of the oldest subjects compared to the 6 year old subjects does not necessarily have the same cognitive status.

The behaviour of 4 year olds with respect to items 2 and 8 ('your red open cars', 'your cars') supports my hypothesis. Item 8 can be interpreted merely by attributing a descriptor function to the morphemes, whereas item 2 requires aspects of the determinor function. Even though the descriptor function in this case requires the child to take into account several criteria, this is no problem to the 4 year old. Under 6 year olds also understood the plural possessive adjective better than the plural definite article, suggesting that the former is interpreted in its descriptor function and the latter as a pluralizer, i.e. also in its descriptor function. Like the corresponding production task, the addition of the quantifier 'all' improved results at all ages, particularly from 5 years, but far less so for 4 year olds, again suggesting that 'all' first conveys 'a lot', i.e. is first a descriptive statement, and then later becomes a totalizer.

Naturally, the results of this comprehension task are not as rich as those of the corresponding production task. Nonetheless, the general trend of the results of the present experiment confirms many of the hypotheses put forward to explain those of the production experiment. Whilst the explanation in terms of the child's developing concepts of class inclusion clearly furnishes a partial explanation, it is argued that reference to the child's logical operations alone does not suffice to explain the results. Consideration must be given to the child's cognitive activity on the linguistic problem space, e.g. coping with the fact that surface markers are frequently plurifunctional.

8 *Comprehension experiments: anaphoric function of determiners*

It will be recalled that in chapter 5, on production tasks covering the anaphoric function of determiners, children rarely placed the communicative burden on the definite article alone but frequently added such words as 'also/same', used a Re-verb, etc. Although a speaker could use anaphoric 'the' to refer to an entity already introduced linguistically by the indefinite article (example (a) below), it is often more likely that the speaker would use pronominalization (example (b)):

(a) The girl stroked *a* dog and then the boy stroked *the* dog
(b) The girl stroked *a* dog and then the boy stroked *it*

The use of the indefinite article is more complex. Although we can imply two different dogs, as in example (c):

(c) The girl stroked *a* dog and then the boy hit *a* dog

this is not necessarily the case. It could be that we mean the same dog, but in making the statement we wished to focus on the actions. In contrastive situations, it is usually clearer if the speaker adds a post-determiner as in (d):

(d) The girl stroked *a* dog, and then the boy stroked *another* one (dog)

However, since Maratsos (1976) found that very young English-speaking children understood the contrastive meaning 'same one/another one' merely on the basis of the definite and indefinite articles, it was felt useful to use a design similar to his but with a broader population. It should be reiterated, however, that placing such a heavy semantic burden on the articles is unusual in normal language usage.

Experiment 15: girl/boy acting

Experimental context. There were two basic contexts:

Context

A four cows, four bells
B four shoes, four cars

A little girl-doll and a little boy-doll were used to perform the actions on these objects.

Experimental procedure. The child was given the two dolls. He was told that he would be asked to act out the experimenter's utterances with toys. A few practice items (e.g. the boy knocks the girl down) were made to ensure that the child understood what was expected of him. In the experimental design the definite and indefinite articles were placed in the subject or object slots of sentences as follows:

Context	*E.'s utterance*	*Child's expected action*
A.1	Une vache touche la fille Et puis une vache touche le garçon [A cow touches the girl And then *a* cow touches the boy (indefinite in subject slot)]	acts of two different cows
A.2	Le garçon touche une cloche Et puis la fille touche la cloche [The boy touches a bell And then the girl touches *the* bell (definite in object slot)]	acts on same bell
B.3	La fille touche une chaussure Et puis le garçon touche une chaussure [The girl touches *a* shoe And then the boy touches *a* shoe (indefinite in object slot)]	acts on two different shoes
B.4	Une voiture touche le garçon Et puis la voiture touche la fille [A car touches the boy And then *the* car touches the girl (definite in subject slot)]	acts on same car

Several new items were added *ad hoc* for subjects failing the above distinctions; groups of four objects (with names taking feminine gender) were available for this. All subjects were presented with items A.1, A.2,

B.3 and B.4, in that order. At the end of the session, heavy stress was placed on articles to see if that would elicit correct answers for those subjects having failed to make the distinction on earlier items. The interview concluded with some exploratory questions. As far as the verbs are concerned, the pilot study for this experiment showed that if each item had a different verb to avoid monotony, even older children tended to concentrate on acting out the verbs rather than listening to the articles. This is why only one verb was used throughout, but this indicates how important focus is in such circumstances.

Population. Fifty-five subjects between 3,9 and 10,10 were interviewed. Seven 3 and 4 year olds refused to act out the experimenter's utterances although the experimenter knew the children very well from certain of the production experiments, where the child did not refuse. These children are not included in the analysis which covers the following forty-eight subjects:

Age	*Subjects*	*Average age*
3,9–4,11	8	4,5
5,0–5,11	9	5,7
6,0–6,11	7	6,7
7,0–7,11	7	7,5
8,0–8,11	7	8,6
9,0–9,11	5	9,6
10,0–10,10	5	10,5

Results. Table 42 gives the percentage of correct responses, as a function of the syntactic slot the article (and the noun it accompanies) occupied in the sentence, i.e. either in the object slot or the subject slot.

For 4 year olds, although overall success rates are low, it would seem that the syntactic slot does play a role; whereas for the object slot better results are obtained for the indefinite article, it is in the subject slot that the definite article is considerably better understood. Interestingly enough, this coincides with the given/new distinction mentioned earlier: new information is given in the predicate with the indefinite article, whereas given information is placed in the subject slot with the definite article. Though of course this particular experiment can be criticized for its unnatural and afunctional aspects (it was, as explained, taken from Maratsos' study for comparison purposes), it is nonetheless tempting to look upon the small child's different behaviour with respect to the two articles and syntactic slots as somehow related to normal usage. These small children seem to decode the articles better if the definite appears in the more normal subject slot and the indefinite in the more normal object slot.

TABLE 42. *Percentage of correct responses for indefinite/anaphoric definite contrast as a function of sentence position and age group*

	Indefinite ⇒ 2 different Xs		Anaphoric definite ⇒ on same class member	
Age group	Subject slot in sentence (%)	Object slot in sentence (%)	Subject slot in sentence (%)	Object slot in sentence (%)
3,9–4,11	50	81	46	26
5,0–5,11	94	90	41	30
6,0–6,11	86	86	27	72
7,0–7,11	55	58	31	42
8,0–8,11	93	100	58	47
9,0–9,11	57	100	100	81
10,0–10,10	71	83	89	91

Between 5 and 8,11 years, the slot in which the indefinite article was placed seemed to make no difference to the child's success rates; the same applies for 10 year olds. Only the 9 year olds registered far better results for the indefinite article in the object slot, which again confirms the above comments about the given/new distinction.

With regard to the definite article, table 42 shows better results in the subject slot for 4 year olds and 9 year olds and markedly better results in the object slot for 6 year olds. There seems to be no effect of the syntactic slot for the definite article for other age groups, i.e. 5, 7, 8 and 10 year olds. In general, the syntactic slot plays relatively little role in determining successful decoding for the definite article. Table 43 shows that, apart from 6 year olds, syntactic slot as such (irrespective of article used) plays no special role at any age.

Let us now turn to table 44 which gives details of the definite/indefinite contrast, irrespective of syntactic slot. With respect to the indefinite article, which requires that the child act on two different Xs, it can be seen that apart from 7 year olds (57%), all age groups register high success rates, ranging from 71% to 95%.

The picture is strikingly different for the definite article in this experiment. It is not until 8 years that success rates even reach 50%, and essentially not until 9 years that the definite article used anaphorically is really interpreted as meaning the same X as the one referred to

TABLE 43. *Percentage of correct responses as a function of subject slot/object slot in sentence*

Age group	Indefinite and definite in *subject* slot (%)	Indefinite and definite in *object* slot (%)
3,9–4,11	48	48
5,0–5,11	63	46
6,0–6,11	45	79
7,0–7,11	44	49
8,0–8,11	73	58
9,0–9,11	70	89
10,0–10,10	81	88

TABLE 44. *Indefinite/anaphoric definite contrast: percentage of correct responses as a function of age group, irrespective of position in sentence*

Age group	Indefinite article ⇒ 2 different Xs (%)	Anaphoric definite article ⇒ on same class member (%)
3,9–4,11	71	31
5,0–5,11	92	33
6,0–6,11	86	55
7,0–7,11	57	39
8,0–8,11	95	51
9,0–9,11	88	83
10,0–10,10	77	90

in the first part of the utterance. It should be recalled that the definite article in its deictic function is understood very early.

These results differ strikingly from those of Maratsos (1976), who reports significant success rates for *both* articles by 3 and 4 year olds, if speaker and addressee share the same referential information, as is the case in this experiment. Rather the results of this experiment tend to cofirm the general trends of those reported by Warden (1973). Whilst Warden was dealing with somewhat different problems, his overall findings point to 9 years as being the age at which the indefinite/definite contrast has been mastered, the same general picture as emerges from the present experiment.

Let us look briefly at some of the children's spontaneous comments or reactions to the experimenter's questions after the test items:

7,8 years
(gets an indefinite response wrong; this is followed by a definite article item)
Ah oui, pour l'autre là, je comprends maintenant, la fille touche une chaussure et puis le garçon touche une autre de chaussure, je me suis trompé avant

[Ah yes, for the other one I understand now, the girl touches a shoe and then the boy *another* shoe, I got it wrong before]

8,4 years

(many hesitations, after one item asks):

C.: *La* balle?
[*The* ball? (stressed)]

E.: repeats item. Child acts out easily

E.: Tu sembles être plus sûr de ce que tu fais maintenant

C.: Oui, tout d'un coup je me suis rendu compte que c'est la même vache si vous dites *la* vache

[E.: You seem more sure of yourself now

C.: Yes, I suddenly realized that it's the same cow if you say *the* cow (stressed)]

9,3 years

(makes some errors and then suddenly all okay)

E.: Qu'est-ce qui te dérangeait tout à l'heure?

C.: Eh bien je prenais tout le temps la même, pas une autre, quand vous disiez une

[E.: What was your problem before?

C.: Well I kept taking the same one, not another one, when you said (?)a/one]

9,5 years

(makes a few errors with definite article, then suddenly says ah, and laughs)

E.: Pourquoi tu ris?

C.: Parce que, par exemple, vous avez dit que la fille touche une chaussure et le garçon touche une chaussure, ben, ça veut dire deux chaussures différentes, lorsque vous dites *la* chaussure, alors il s'agit de la chaussure que la fille a déjà touchée

[E.: Why laugh?

C.: Because, for example, you said the girl touches a shoe and the boy touches a shoe, well, that means two different shoes, when you say *the* shoe (stressed), well it's the shoe that the girl already touched]

9,10 years

Une, c'est n'importe laquelle, et la, ben ça veut dire que c'est toujours la même
[A, it's any one, and the, that means it's always the same]

10,8 years

C'est facile, il suffit d'écouter, si on dit une ou la. La ça veut dire que les deux ont touché la même, une c'est qu'ils touchent pas la même
[It's easy, you just have to listen, if you say a or the. The, that means the two (dolls) touched the same one, a, it's that they don't touch the same one]

What is interesting in these examples is that the discovery of the experimental problem is not immediate. Many children make a few errors first and then become aware of the importance of the definite article. After noting its function, they then conclude that the indefinite article must imply acting on different Xs. I suggest that part of the child's activity is directed at trying to understand what the *experimenter* is aiming at, when a word carries a heavy communicative burden.

In general, this experiment has borne out the hypothesis that afunctional contexts and unnatural uses tell us relatively little about the way in which children decode the articles. It is not until 8 or 9 years that the child can make a more 'abstract' analysis of the utterance, no longer requiring functional clues. It was nonetheless interesting to note that articles are better decoded by smaller children if they are used for meaningful functions, i.e. new information is given with the indefinite article in the predicate, whereas given information is in the subject slot with the definite article. It was only from 9 years that children could interpret the definite article alone as making anaphoric reference, in sentences which were functionally unusual. This was clear from the fact that it took the older subjects a few items before they were able to see what the experimenter's problem was and then to furnish correct responses. It may therefore be reasonable to hypothesize that something very important takes place in linguistic development from 8 or 9 years, i.e that children are then capable of a more abstract analysis of an utterance and no longer require stress on intralinguistic functional clues or extralinguistic situational clues (Karmiloff-Smith 1979).

Experiment 16: same and another[1]

The previous experiment left us unsatisfied due to the unnatural usage of the indefinite article and to the fact that when such a contrast is to be stressed, one would normally add such terms as 'the same X/ another X' to make the contrast clear.

It is for this reason that experiment 16 was designed. If Maratsos was correct in concluding that 3 and particularly 4 year olds distinguish in comprehension between the two unstressed articles 'the' and 'a', although the results of experiment 15 suggest that this does not occur in French consistently before 9 years, then it should be much easier for the child to make such a distinction if the articles' meanings are emphasized by the addition of the postdeterminers 'same' and 'other'. Although it remains to be seen what their real functions are in early

[1] Some paragraphs of this section are taken from Karmiloff-Smith (1977b).

child language, the words 'same' and 'other', as well as the articles, all appear very early in corpora (Guillaume 1927; Brown 1973; Warden 1973).

Experimental context. There were four basic contexts:

Context

A	completely identical objects (e.g. blue plastic ducks, green toy Volkswagens, etc.)
B	objects of the same class differing only in colour (e.g. blue or pink plastic lambs, red or blue toy Fords, etc.)
C	objects of the same class but differing by several parameters (e.g. brown-wooden-standing cow versus white-plastic-seated cow, small-open-red-sports car versus large-white-saloon car, etc.)
D	objects the only members of their class (e.g. a horse, a truck a toy watch, etc.)

Experimental procedure. There were six basic situation types using very familiar objects such as the above, together with a girl-doll and a boy-doll. The child was asked to act out a series of sentences of the following design, where in sentence type (a) the key word is in the object slot, e.g. 'The girl pushes an X and then the boy pushes (the same/another) X', and in sentence type (b) the key word is in the subject slot, e.g. 'An X pushes the girl and then (the same/another) X pushes the boy'. Examples of task items are as follows:

Context	*E.'s utterance*	*Child's expected response*
A	(a) La fille pousse une X et puis le garçon pousse *la même* X [The girl pushes an X and then the boy pushes *the same* X]	action on one X
	(b) Une X pousse la fille et puis *la même* X pousse le garçon [An X pushes the girl and then *the same* X pushes the boy]	action on one X
	(c) Le garçon pousse une X et puis la fille pousse *une autre* X [The boy pushes an X and then the girl pushes *another* X]	action on two Xs

(d) Une X pousse le garçon et puis *une autre* X pousse la fille — action on two Xs
[An X pushes the boy and then *another* X pushes the girl]

B *idem* for sentences with 'same' and 'other'

C *idem* for sentences with 'same'

D *idem* for sentences with 'same'

Wherever necessary, test sentences were repeated. Certain basic items were presented to all children but the exploratory method was used afterwards: e.g. placing stress on the postdeterminers, reducing or increasing the number and type of objects present at one time, adding such expressions as 'La même X que le garcon vient de pousser' [The same X as the boy just pushed], using somewhat unusual forms such as 'une même X' [a same X], encouraging children to talk about similar objects they possessed, and so forth. Emphasis was not on success or failure to interpret 'the same X' as 'same one' but on the functions such expressions may have at a given level and on how transitions take place.

Population. Forty-seven children between the ages of 2,10 and 7,11 years participated in the experiment. Unlike our other experiments, these children were not selected in more or less random fashion, but from the results of two of the gender experiments where these particular children had proved to be very typical of their age group. No linguistically advanced 3 year olds, for example, were included. However, neither the results here, nor in our other experiments, are intended to stress 'age' but rather order of change from one interpretation to another. The subjects were distributed as follows:

Age	*Subjects*	*Average age*
2,10–3,10	14	3,5
3,11–4,10	14	4,6
4,11–5,10	10	5,5
5,11–7,11	9*	

* 'Average age' is irrelevant because it covers a span of two years of entirely successful subjects. The nine subjects between 5,11 and 7,11 were run merely to check on any problems arising later, since it was clear during experimentation that there were no interpretation problems after 5 years.

Results. Only the basic items were included in the quantitative analysis of the results; the exploratory part of the experiment provided revealing clues for the qualitative analysis.

Table 45 gives a summary of the comprehension task results, expressed as a percentage of the total number of responses to the basic items per situation type for each age group. No distinction has been made between the subject and the object slots for the postdeterminers, the difference in the results being insignificant, although very slightly in favour of correct 'same one' responses first occurring for 'same' in object position.

It should be noted that the columns entitled 'Hesitation' represent the percentage of the 'same one' responses (previous column) which were clearly preceded by lengthy hesitations not apparent elsewhere in the child's behaviour. This table is designed to give a picture of the overall trend. It is in fact the more qualitative analysis of the results, incorporating children's spontaneous utterances, that is more revealing as to the functions 'same' and 'other' have for young children.

The initial comprehension procedure (i.e. until roughly 5 years) is to interpret 'the same X' as meaning another X with the same attributes and not as meaning 'one and the same X'. Only if attributes differ considerably does the young child gradually interpret 'the same X' to mean 'same one'. A different picture emerges from the situations in which sentences contain 'another X', although something of the pattern registered with 'same' is also apparent here. Where class members' attributes differ, all age groups were successful in almost 100% of instances in interpreting 'another X' to mean 'another one'. Over 4 year olds did as well in situations where all Xs were identical. Interestingly enough, where Xs were identical, some 3 year olds tended to interpret 'another X' as meaning 'another kind' rather than 'another one' and thus refused to act out a number of the sentences referring to identical contexts. In contrast, no refusals were registered with these subjects for sentences containing 'another' when objects differed in colour. What was observed with these 3 year olds for 'other' thus seems rather similar to what took place developmentally with 'same'. In an attempt to discover more about 'other' and the two functions it has, a group of 2 year olds was interviewed, but the data are inconclusive in view of the unsuitability of the comprehension task with such small children. It is nonetheless interesting to note that although concerned with somewhat different problems, Donaldson & Wales (1970) showed that small children first interpret the word 'different' to mean 'different kind' rather than 'different one', which tallies with what is suggested by our results on 3 year olds regarding 'other' used anaphorically. As

TABLE 45. *Interpretations of the two postdeterminers by age group and extralinguistic context, expressed as percentage of total responses to basic items per age group*[1]

	2,10–3,10				3,11–4,10				4,11–5,10				5,11–7,11			
The same X	Same one	Hesi-tation	Refusal	Same kind	Same one	Hesi-tation	Refusal	Same kind	Same one	Hesi-tation	Refusal	Same kind	Same one	Hesi-tation	Refusal	Same kind
A Identical objects	5	66	0	95	22	0	0	78	75	52	0	25	96	0	0	4
B Different colours	29	0	41	30	27	0	0	73	94	39	0	6	100	0	0	0
C Different parameters	14	0	59	27	54	85	8	38	97	0	0	3	100	0	0	0
D Singleton	48	0	52	NA	68	0	32	NA	91	0	9	NA	100	0	0	NA
Another X	Another one		Refusal		Another one		Refusal		Another one		Refusal		Another one		Refusal	
A Identical objects	61		39		100		0		100		0		100		0	
B Different colours	100		0		100		0		100		0		100		0	
Total responses	224				207				152				104			

[1] First published in Karmiloff-Smith 1977b, p. 383.

pointed out by Clark (1970), the technique used by the above authors did not allow for verification of the child's possible alternative interpretation of 'same'. However, Donaldson & Wales' results on 'different', used exophorically for direct reference to the extralinguistic situation, point to very similar general developmental trends compared to the present results on 'same' and 'other' used anaphorically.

Let us now take a more qualitative look at the results for each age group. As table 45 shows, 3 year olds interpreted 'same' to mean 'same kind', and acted out test sentences of the type 'The boy pushed a cow and then the girl pushed the same cow' by touching *two identical* cows, when context permitted; they frequently refused to act if objects were not identical. They persisted in this behaviour even if items were repeated and the word 'same' accentuated unnaturally, or if expressions such as '. . . the same cow as the boy just touched' were added. These small children often accompanied their refusals to act with comments such as 'Elle peut pas pousser la même, tu n'as pas mis une autre vache comme celle-là' [She can't push the same, you didn't put out another cow like that one], 'Y a pas le même canard, y a que des bleus' [There's not the same duck, only blue ones], 'Quelle voiture? Celle-là elle est pas la même' [Which car? That one is not the same]. Similar comments were even more numerous when the attributes of class members differed significantly or when there was only one class member. Although the 3 year olds interpreted 'another' correctly provided there was some difference between class members, the 39% of refusals to items containing 'other' if Xs were identical is particularly striking. Here, too, children accompanied their refusals to act out the item '. . . and the boy caressed another dog' by stating: 'Quel chien, celui-là? Mais c'est le même' [Which dog, that one? But it's the same], 'Je peux pas le faire, ils sont tous les mêmes' [I can't do it, they're all the same] 'Y a pas un autre ballon, ils sont tous verts' [There's not another balloon, they're all green].

To summarize for 3 year olds, 'same' is clearly interpreted as meaning 'same kind' and 'other' is often interpreted as meaning 'other kind'. Both of these expressions seem to be interpreted in their descriptor function, i.e. as modifiers telling the child about class attributes, and not in their determinor function.

Let us now turn to the 4 year olds. It is within this age group that the beginnings of transition were to be witnessed. Although there remained a high percentage of incorrect responses to 'same' in the identical situation, in the more exploratory part of the interviews it was often possible to change responses to correct ones by stressing the post-determiner or by adding '. . . same X as the boy just pushed'. It will be recalled that this was not possible with most 3 year olds. Correct interpretations ('same one') could also be provoked for some 4 year olds when recursively singleton X situations were alternated with those containing identical Xs. Comparing 4 year olds to 3 year olds in situations where Xs were similar, it can be seen that the percentage of incorrect responses greatly increased for the older children. This is due to the complete disappearance of refusals to act out. In other words, although 'same' is still interpreted to mean 'same kind', 4 year olds no longer consider it necessary for all attributes to be identical. It was when class members' attributes differed greatly, forming obvious subclasses for the child, that a significant increase was witnessed in correct 'same one' interpretations. These responses were nonetheless preceded by lengthy hesitations, as if there was a conflict for the child between the competing interpretations 'same one' and 'same kind'. Another interesting fact occurred occasionally during the exploratory part of the interview. To a question comparing a red plastic duck to a blue plastic duck, some children replied 'No' when asked 'Est-ce le même?' [Is it the same?] but 'Yes' when asked 'Est-ce le même canard?' [Is it the same duck?]. It may well be that the relations between article, postdeterminer and noun and their respective positions in the NP play an important role in these different interpretations, a point to be expanded later. Items containing 'another' posed no problems whatsoever for 4 year olds.

In summary, 4 year olds clearly interpret 'other' as meaning 'other one', i.e. in its function of postdeterminer, whereas 'same' is still interpreted in its descriptor function meaning 'same kind' and only conflictual situations provoked over 50% successful 'same one' interpretations.

5 year olds registered a very significant change in success rate. They were clearly interpreting 'same' to mean 'same one', although in situations where Xs were identical or similar, many hesitations preceded correct responses, particularly for the first few experimental items. This was not the case with the over 6 year olds. Thus it can be said that from 5, but more systematically from 6 years, children can interpret both 'same' and 'other' as postdeterminers.

Finally, it will be recalled from the results of the previous experiment that it was not until roughly 9 years that anaphoric 'the' was successfully interpreted without the addition of 'same'. It can therefore be assumed that over 5 year olds' interpretation in this experiment is based on the postdeterminers and not on the article distinction alone.

This final experiment furnished important results at two levels. First, it clearly demonstrated that the so-called postdeterminers also have two functions, descriptor and determinor, and that the small child first understands the word 'same' in its descriptor function. Under 5 year olds' preferred interpretation of 'same' was that of 'same kind' rather than the appropriate 'same one' in this situation. It also showed that children are generally using and understanding reference deictically, i.e. pointing to the current context, rather than anaphorically. It will be recalled from production experiment 5, that no 4 year old used the word 'same' to strengthen what should have been anaphoric reference. Thus for small children the word 'same' is clearly a sort of modifier, playing a descriptor function in the sense 'same kind'. From 5 years, and particularly from 6, children interpreted 'same' as referring anaphorically to the same referent as the antecedent refers to. This anaphoric reference seems to occur earlier than in the previous experiments and earlier than in the production tasks. It is suggested that the emphatic marker 'same' helps the child, functionally speaking, gradually to make the anaphoric reference interpretation. However, it may still be pointing deictically at the referent, the correct responses being due to change in the semantics of the word 'same'. The problem of the deictic and textual components of anaphoric reference will be taken up in the concluding chapters.

9 *Synthesis of the child's acquisition of the plurifunctionality of determiners*

> Suit the action to the word, the word to the action; with this special observance, that you o'erstep not the modesty of nature.
>
> (Shakespeare, *Hamlet*)

Even a cursory glance at the overall results of the experimental sections makes it clear that the child's aquisition of referential expressions involves far more than a simple contrastive use of indefinite and definite articles. It would also be an oversimplification to explain the gradual growth in understanding of the functions of determiners solely in terms of the development of non-linguistic cognition. Whilst cognitive development clearly affects linguistic development as far as general mechanisms are concerned, the results of this study demonstrate that many specifically linguistic problems are involved for the child. The general fact that linguistic entities are frequently plurifunctional and that a given function can be handled by more than one form, is perhaps one of the most crucial aspects of the difficulties of language acquisition.

During the presentation of the various experiments, conclusions were drawn as to the implications of the particular results of each task. In this chapter, an endeavour will be made to take a broader look at the overall results with respect (i) to the progressive development of the various functions of determiners and, (ii) to three important phases of language acquisition procedures.

Fig 6 represents a synthesis of the child's gradual aquisition of the various functions conferred upon the definite and indefinite articles. Like any schematic representation, it tends to make development look simpler than it actually is. The diagram merely represents the general trends of levels of acquisition of the different functions; in facilitating circumstances, one or other of the functions may be expressed or understood earlier. The general trend for production tasks was similar to that of comprehension tasks, except that in some cases acquisition

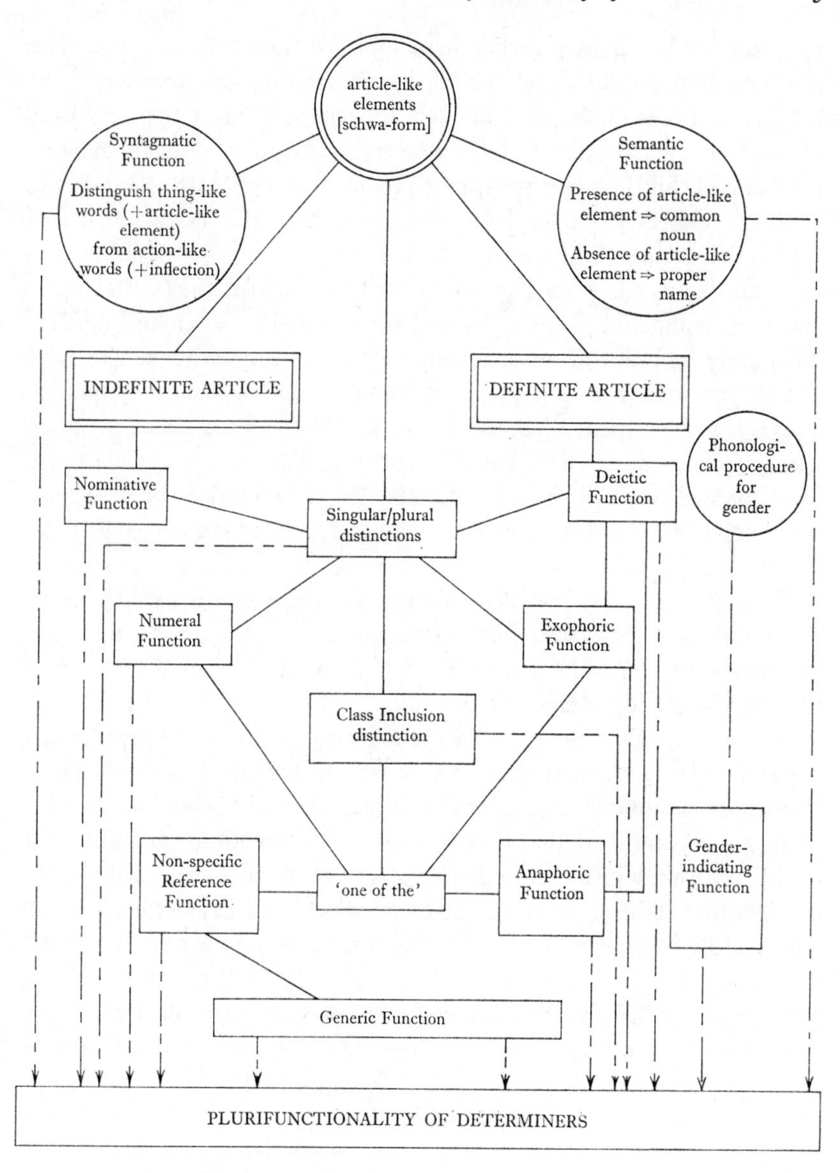

Fig. 6. Synthesis of the child's acquisition of functions conferred on the definite and indefinite articles. (This diagram clearly does not take into account the links each function has with other linguistic categories and with extralinguistic cognitive development)

appeared to be slightly earlier in comprehension. The diagram does not include preverbal development, i.e. the gradual construction of the intricate network of sensorimotor actions schemes (Piaget 1953, etc.) and the complex elaboration of joint attention structures built up between mother and child (Bruner 1975, 1978; Ninio & Bruner 1978; Ryan 1978). Both are clearly the partial foundations of the later linguistic use of referential devices. The diagram begins at the stage when children add to noun-like words what has been called for English the 'schwa-form' and what sounds in French like an 'euh' which is neither 'un' nor 'le'. This early addition of an article-like element is hypothesized to have at least two main functions: (i) it enables the child to make a distinction between proper names (absence of article-like element) and common names (presence of article-like element) (see Katz *et al.* 1974 discussed in chapter 2); and (ii) its addition may be metalinguistic or metacommunicative in nature, as argued in chapter 1, in that it enables the child to separate 'thing-like' words from 'action-like' words. (Adultomorphisms such as noun phrases and verb phrases are purposely avoided.) Thus, the addition of the schwa-form in production, or the child's attention to article-like words in comprehension, may at the initial stage have both semantic and syntagmatic function.

It would appear from naturalistic data (e.g. Guillaume 1927; Brown 1973; Warden 1973) that the two articles usually make their appearance in corpora simultaneously, after the initial use of the schwa-form. This being so, it is unlikely that they have the same function since the child could have used just one of the two forms. My experimental results confirm that children do not initially substitute one article for the other haphazardly in front of nouns as if their meaning were confused. On the contrary, when the two articles are used consistently by small children, they appear to have quite distinct functions and are probably not yet part of a common semantic system for the child. The indefinite article is initially used as part of a procedure for naming, i.e. in its appellative or nominative function. Small children never made the error of using the definite article for this function. My experiments have shown that from the outset the definite article has quite a distinct function. It is used by the child deictically to draw attention to the referent he has under focus of attention. Its use is frequently accompanied by pointing.

The diachronic development of the singular definite article was discussed in chapter 2. Particularly Gough & Chiaraviglio (1970) and Thorne (1972) hypothesized synchronic developments which were similar to the diachronic one. For Gough & Chiaraviglio, the definite article's deep structure is the demonstrative pronoun, whereas for Thorne it is the locative 'there'. Both involve indexical symbols. Lyons (1975) makes a very convincing case not only for the diachronic and synchronic explanation of the definite article, combining the demonstrative pronoun and the locative adverb, but also the ontogenetic evolution. Lyons' argument is essentially that children's understanding of referring expressions is based on a prior understanding of the deictic function of demonstrative pronouns and adverbs. Whilst he had no acquisition data to support his hypothesis, he points out that no data exist which would contradict it. Lyons considers the definite article to be a weak demonstrative pronoun, or an amalgam of a demonstrative pronoun and a demonstrative adverb, and the anaphoric use of the definite article to be a derivative of its deictic use.

There are additional arguments in favour of Lyons' linguistic interpretation. Russian, for instance, which has no definite article, makes frequent use of the demonstrative for marking anaphoric reference. Sign language (Bellugi & Fischer 1972) expresses anaphora by preserving information by *location in space*. French makes frequent use of the demonstrative adjective and pronoun for anaphoric reference (e.g. amalgam of pronoun and adverb in 'celui-là/celui-ci', [the former/the latter], use of demonstrative in 'Il y avait un garçon qui . . . Ce garçon . . .'). Ducrot, on the other hand, (1972) makes a strong case for separating the definite article and the demonstrative, but this does not really contradict Lyons' position since Ducrot is referring to the non-substitutability in cases of anaphoric reference, and Lyons' considers the anaphoric use of pronouns and adverbs to be derivative and secondary to their basic function as deictics. The point to be emphasized here is that what is initially spatial deixis later gets translated into the temporal dimensions of the universe of discourse.

The acquisition data reported on in the preceding chapters are a striking confirmation of the early deictic function of the definite article. Whilst referential devices thus originate in deixis, it could be argued that deixis is not *the* source of reference, as the title of Lyons' paper (1975) suggests, but *a* source of reference. (Note, in passing, the need for the addition of prosodic features such as stress – or underlining – if the articles are to be used constrastively.) There may in fact be two sources of reference: when a small child wants one of two objects, he may point or, if he speaks, he may say either 'that car/that one' or 'big car/red car', etc. One cannot point to the properties of objects unambiguously. These two means of identifying a referent (by deixis or by identifying attributes) appear ontogenetically at approximately the same time (Brown 1973). What is important is that the demonstrative adjective and simple modifiers, such as colour and size adjectives, often appear in corpora prior to the appearance of articles. Thus, there may be two interacting sources of reference. The experiments in this study show that children frequently add modifiers before understanding the determinor function of certain determiners.

With respect to the young child's incorrect use of the definite article, several authors have suggested that the child cannot take into account the listener's lack of shared knowledge with the speaker. This implies that the child knows what the articles' functions are, but that he cannot take into account cognitively the listener's needs. However, several of my experiments have shown that small children do attempt (abortively) to furnish additional referential information by adding (redundant) modifiers, spatial locations, etc. What they do not understand, in my view, is how the articles function as determiners in such circumstances. Thus, it is questionable whether an explanation can be sought solely in the child being 'egocentric' about taking into account the listener's need for referential information. Rather, he is also facing many intralinguistic problems about the functions of different words.

In passing, it might be useful to point out that Piaget's concept of egocentrism has been frequently misinterpreted. It is not merely a negative aspect of child development whereby the child interprets the world solely from his own perspective and not from the listener's. Egocentrism has a positive facet. It is in fact a dynamic concept, in that only by assimilating all new encounters with the environments to his own perspectives, i.e. his current state of world knowledge, can the child (or adult for that matter) cope, even inadequately, with new encounters. If novelties were not assimilated egocentrically, they would go entirely unnoticed or be rejected. Thus egocentrism is a *positive* aspect of child development and of the growth of knowledge generally. It is thus unproductive to look upon egocentrism as characteristic of, say, only the preoperational child and to consider the concrete operational child as freed of egocentric perspectives. Clearly, the young child shows some facets of non-egocentrism, shown in the difference between the experimental results of this study, and even for the older child and adult all *new* problems are first handled egocentrically. When viewed as a functional mechanism, egocentrism is a dynamic and essential part of human growth.

Fig 6 illustrates the fact that when the small child wishes to furnish the name of something, he uses the indefinite article in every case, and that when he wishes to focus attention on an object, he uses the definite article. This indicates that the articles are not initially confused. Each one has a clearly defined, separate function for the small child.

Shortly after the initial nominative and deictic functions are developed, the French-speaking child makes the distinction between singular and plural markers: 'des' [some] covers the nominative function and is used to give the name of a plurality of objects. 'Les' [the] is used deictically to focus attention on a plurality of objects. Thus the plural forms of the two articles initially retain the functions conferred on the singular forms. However, the fact that the indefinite and definite articles now have a common secondary function, that of indicating plurality and singularity, may represent the first trace of what will later become a common system of determiners.

Whilst children of this level interpreted 'les' only as a pluralizer, they understood totalization if 'tous' [all] was added. They also understood the definite referring expression in its anaphoric use if the postdeterminer 'same' was added. In general, the addition of linguistic emphasizers gave rise to earlier success levels. The linguistic analysis in chapter 3 regarding the contrastive uses of determiners shows therefore that the young child's tendency to add special emphasizers is a natural way of expressing the particular distinction which is under focus of attention in the current context. The older child, in an experimental setting, and with his seemingly natural tendency and capacity to be linguistically economical, will more readily use the distinction encoded merely by the article contrasts unless potential ambiguity exists. Fig. 6 is of course an attempt to illustrate the order of the child's developing capacities without the additional emphasizers.

Whilst French-speaking children make an early distinction between the masculine and feminine gender of the singular articles, the experiments testing the gender-indicating function shows clearly that this distinction does not derive initially from the articles, i.e. there is no necessary relation for the small child between 'la' and 'une' or between 'le' and 'un'. Many of the children's hesitations and spontaneous corrections bore witness to this. The experimental results show that the small child bases gender distinctions mainly on word endings. The phonological procedure he uses is so pervasive that it outweighs both natural gender clues (sex of the referents) and any gender clues on the articles furnished by the experimenter. It is only much later in development that the gender-indicating function of the articles themselves plays a substantial role. Prior to that, the articles are 'busy' coping with other functions.

Soon after acquiring the plural/singular distinction encoded by the articles, children tend to become aware of the numeral function of the indefinite article (which is of course acquired earlier when used alone, without a noun), and the exophoric function of the definite article indicating a single entity in the current context. Thus, the definite article is no longer used only deictically to focus on the particular referent under attention by the speaker, but the child also takes into account the extralinguistic setting and the relation of the referent to other objects therein. The distinction between the deictic use of the definite article and its exophoric use was particularly highlighted by children who had difficulties in the story completion task in distinguishing between reference to an X under focus of attention and situating that X within the current discourse context. Once the exophoric function is acquired, children use the definite article when an object is alone and the indefinite article when referring to one of several identical objects. Since it is not until considerably later that children use 'n'importe laquelle' [any one] and other similar expressions, it is argued that the indefinite article means in such contexts 'one' rather than the non-specific 'a'. It occurs at the time that, in comprehension, children's preferred interpretation of 'une X' is 'one X'.

The next function to develop is that of the distinction between 'les' and 'des' as they pertain to class inclusion; 'les' can now be used simultaneously as pluralizer and totalizer, whereas previously it required the addition of 'all' to convey the latter meaning. Whilst this development is of course affected by the ongoing construction of class concepts, a fairly convincing case has, it is hoped, been made that there are also many intralinguistic problems involved. Above all, it is clear that 'les' and 'des' do have specific functions before they can be used to represent class inclusion, and are not merely confused by the child.

The next level is when the indefinite article is clearly used for non-specific reference and the definite article for anaphoric reference. It will be recalled that earlier children could not place the burden of anaphoric reference on the definite article *alone*, but added markers such as 'same/also', used a 'Re-verb', etc., or repeated redundant modifiers. The young child does not conform to Stenning's (1975) principle of 'anaphoric conservatism', since he tends to add multiple markers when ambiguity of reference might occur. It has been argued several times in the preceding chapters that what may appear to the *observer* as an anaphoric reference may in fact be a form of deictic reference, either to the current extralinguistic context, or to a strong mental image of the current discourse context. For the young child, it is not filtered intralinguistically. Piaget (1951) has made a very convincing case for the pervasiveness of mental imagery in early language use, i.e. the small child's utterance is simultaneously supported by vivid mental imagery. It may be that the support of the instantiated mental image is a lasting process and that it is not until much later that the child can cope with exclusively intralinguistic reference.

Further corroboration of the basic difference between deictic and anaphoric reference came from the tasks analysing the gender-indicating function of determiners. It will be recalled that small children when referring to, say, a female 'bicron' used the masculine article to accompany 'bicron' but continued with feminine pronoun; whereas older children continued their discourse with a masculine pronoun despite the fact that the extralinguistic referent was female. This indicates that the small child juxtaposes a phonological procedure for local lexical concord and a semantic procedure for pronominal reference. The latter is clearly deictic. The older child, on the other hand, filters his anaphoric pronoun intralinguistically through the antecedent form by keeping to the same gender in both cases. When he makes his pronoun refer semantically to the extralinguistic reference (e.g. 'elle' for a female 'bicron'), the older child makes corresponding changes to the suffix of the antecedent form (e.g. 'bicron' becomes 'bicronne'), thereby maintaining consistent gender throughout. There is thus both a deictic and textual component. Whereas deictic reference clarifies which X is currently being referred to, truly anaphoric reference seems to be used as a means for holding discourse together, i.e. it has a syntagmatic cohesion function. This leads me to reiterate my contention that very young children do not really use anaphoric reference even though they may follow the use of an indefinite article by a definite one.

The initial deictic function of pronouns was also suggested by my naturalistic data (pointing always accompanied pronouns) and by the results of another experiment in this study but not reported on here (see

Karmiloff-Smith 1976). In a story-telling task based on a series of pictures, younger children tended to use pronouns more rapidly than did older children. The older child seemed to be more aware of the temporary nature of the discourse structure and pronominalized only once the referent was clearly identified linguistically, whereas smaller children's referential expressions (definite articles and pronouns) functioned deictically with pointing gestures.

Whilst this has been a fairly extensive study of the plurifunctionality of determiners, there are of course areas which have not been covered. The generic use of both the singular and plural indefinite and definite articles is one. The problem here resided in finding an experimental procedure; the only ideas involved the child acting out when the determiners were not generic, and making *no* action when they were used generically. Expecting a child to do nothing as proof of a correct response is obviously not a suitable approach when the experimental setting contains many interesting objects. Such a technique would only work with older children, whose capacity for dealing with the generic is already known. Hewsen (1972), when discussing the generic uses of 'the/a', suggests that the indefinite article is never completely free of particular references and so can only be used generically when it could also have been used in the particularizing sense (see also Dahl 1975 for discussion on generics). The acquisition data collected in this study allow us to hypothesize nonetheless that the strength ontogentically of the deictic function of the definite article, as well as the deictic component of the anaphoric function, must make it very difficult for the child to use the definite article generically. Once again, whilst cognitive development obviously affects the child's understanding of the generic concept, there must be intra-linguistic problems involved in the somewhat contradictory plurifunctions of the definite article. From naturalistic data, one longitudinal example of the generic function of the definite article is of interest:

7,9 years

C.: Isabelle a fait une conférence sur son lapin et Alexia elle va faire une conférence sur la tortue

E.: Sur quelle tortue?

C.: . . . la tort . . . ben, la sienne, et puis . . . pas seulement la sienne . . . ben . . . les tortues, sur toutes les tortues

[C.: Isabelle gave a talk about her rabbit and Alexia will give a talk about the tortoise

E.: About which tortoise?

C.: . . . the tort . . . well, hers, and well . . . not only hers . . . well . . . the tortoises, on all the tortoises]

The same child 17 months later:

9,2 years

E.: Tu te souviens qu'Isabelle avait fait une conférence sur son lapin et Alexia en a fait une sur la tortue?

C.: Oui

E.: Sur quelle tortue?

C.: Sur l'animal, la tortue

[E.: You remember that Isabelle gave a talk about her rabbit and Alexia gave one about the tortoise?

C.: Yes

E.: About which tortoise?

C.: About the animal, the tortoise (shrugs shoulders as if it were quite obvious!)]

Understanding this generic use of the definite article involves the child going beyond both deictic reference and anaphoric reference, i.e. abstracting from extralinguistic and intralinguistic reference, and attaining the capacity of giving, linguistically, conceptual existence to what was previously always a particular instantiation. The cognitive process involved may be similar to that of acquiring, say, the abstract concept of the $(+1)$ operator as distinct from instantiations thereof (e.g. $5 + 1 = 6$).

To return to the more general aspects of our results, it should be noted that the distinction drawn between the descriptor and determinor functions of the various words studied seems indeed to have psychological reality. Several experiments demonstrated that children first understand and use words in their descriptor function. Thus, small children will first understand the word 'same' to mean 'same kind' rather than 'same one', will use and understand the plural definite article 'les' to mean plurality of objects before they understand it also to mean totality of objects referred to. One could of course invoke solely non-linguistic cognitive reasons for this. Indeed, it may be cognitively more complex to understand the notion of totality before that of plurality. The cognitive argument is a little more difficult to maintain for 'same kind' versus 'same one', since it would seem cognitively just as difficult, if not more so, to compare two objects and judge their attributes as analogous, than it would be to look upon one object as maintaining its identity, particularly where no spatial or physical changes are involved. Moreover, it should be recalled that whilst 'les' is used as a pluralizer, the same children do express the totalizer function, but by the addition of another word 'all'. Thus, whilst there must indeed exist non-linguistic cognitive mechanisms which could be invoked to explain the development of descriptor to dual descriptor–determinor function, it is argued that *intra-linguistic* reasons must also be invoked. The fact that in dialogic situations with small children referents are usually entirely retrievable from the extralinguistic context could induce the small child to think that it is unnecessary to pick out the referent by special linguistic means. He may thus expect linguistic markers to function as descripters rather than as determiners.

At several points, it has been suggested that children first approach language as if morphemes were unifunctional and that development consists in conferring on a series of unifunctional homonyms the status of a plurifunctional morpheme. Such an argument can be supported by looking at overall trends of the population in this study. In fact, a close analysis of the results as a whole shows that children pass through three phases in their acquisition of the various functions of determiners.

The first phase lasts from roughly 3 to 5 years. During this time, children make use of a wide variety of the forms of determiners. Many of their productions seemed on the surface to be very elaborate. They often appear to use anaphoric referential devices, to understand and use non-specific referential devices and so forth. However, a deeper analysis of the *functions* children actually attribute to the words they are using and a closer look at some of the errors encountered in the experimental tasks suggest two points: (i) children use determiners initially in their descriptor function; and (ii) when they do start to use words in their determinor function also, children are unaware that the same word has a dual function. It is in fact the developments of the second phase, after 5, that makes one raise questions about the actual functions of these words used during the first phase.

The second phase covers the period from roughly 5 to 8 years. During that period several new procedures are encountered. First, there is a tendency to use a separate morpheme for each function the child wishes to convey. This gives rise, from an adult point of view, to redundant marking. The child does not place on one word the burden of conveying more than one meaning. Since in the first phase children do not add these additional markers, it would appear that in the first phase they use a marker to convey one meaning and are not expressing the others.

Another procedure used particularly between 5 and 8 years is the creation of slightly ungrammatical forms to distinguish between the dual functions of a word. Thus, for instance, 'la même X' was used to mean 'the same one' and 'la même de X' was used to mean 'same kind', where normally 'la même X' can have either meaning. Likewise, 'la mienne de voiture' was used to convey the determinor function and 'ma voiture' used for the descriptor function, whereas normally the preposed possessive adjective has a dual function. 'Une X' was used to mean 'an X' and 'une de X' used to mean 'one X'. In each case, these children were attempting to express the determinor function of a word and to mark the distinction between this and its descriptor function. Thus between 5 and 8 years children are aware of the two functions and make a surface distinction between them. Moreover, in their endeavours to make anaphoric reference, they do not merely use a definite referring expression but add other markers, as if they know that the coreference should be marked linguistically but do not yet know on which sentence element to mark it.

These various new manifestations in the second phase, i.e. the addition of redundant markers and the creation of slightly ungrammatical strings for contrastive purposes, suggest that when younger children of the first phase use these morphemes correctly in various situations, they in fact represent for the small child a series of unifunctional homonyms. They may appear to have several functions to the *observer*, but from the *child's* point of view he is using a different word each time. The appearance of redundancy and ungrammatical strings in the second phase thus bears witness to the fact that by then the child is becoming aware of the plurifunctional status of various forms. It should of course be stressed that the 5 to 8 year old does not normally speak ungrammatically or with a lot of redundant markers. Potential ambiguity rarely exists in everyday discourse. However, these additions in experimental tasks do provide clues to the subtle problems with which the intermediate child is grappling, and which are not apparent in the productions of smaller children.

It is towards the end of the second phase that spontaneous corrections serve as a clue to the fact that children are beginning to indicate several functions with one word, i.e. to confer plurifunctional status on determiners, e.g. 'Toutes les voi . . . non, *les* voitures doivent aller au garage' [All the ca . . . no, *the* cars must go to the garage]. Such examples, and the results in general, indicate that the plural definite article covers at this level both pluralization and totalization. Once this is achieved, the older child only adds 'all' for cases of special emphasis. This is also how adults use emphasizers. Costermans (1975), in a cluster analysis of adults' subjective semantic distance judgements with respect to determiners, shows that adults reserve a clear role for emphasizers when special contrasts are to be encoded linguistically.

In the third phase, stretching roughly from 8 to 12 years, almost all redundant marking and ungrammatical forms disappear and it is clear that children now endow morphemes with plurifunctional status. One marker simultaneously carries the burden of indicating several functions and children are thus economical in their utterances. Moreover, the results showed that by this level children seem to have organized determiners into a system of options, i.e. they know when a given determiner has to be used, when it can be replaced by a weaker determiner (e.g. 'the' instead of 'my'), when modifiers are essential referential information and when they can be dropped, etc. In general, the over 8 year old seems concerned to avoid 'overdetermining', i.e. he makes a clear distinction between what must be stated and what can be left unsaid with respect to clarity of referential information, an important Gricean concept.

It is important to recall that small children can use and understand several different functions provided they are expressed through a plurality of unifunctional markers, whereas the older child can cope with plurifunctional markers. However, even the oldest subjects did not place the communicative burden on a single form if ambiguity of reference occurred or if special contrasts were focussed upon. When small children did attempt to give more precise referential information, they did so by identifying permanent properties of the object under focus (e.g. colour, shape, etc.). Failing any inherent identifying characteristics, they made reference to the spatial location. Frequently, utterances were therefore laborious and contained redundant markers used in their descriptor function. Small children thus rely more heavily on *extralinguistic* features to clarify reference. It is not until the second phase that, in cases of ambiguity, children endeavour to make use of *intralinguistic* means, first by overmarking and finally, in the third phase, by using the adult system.

The results of the epilinguistic interview at the end of each experiment show the following general trend. Epilinguistic awareness is generally some one and a half to two years behind spontaneous usage. The same applies in many cases to non-linguistic cognitive tasks (Piaget 1976). Apart from the age gap, trends in epilinguistic awareness are similar to those observed in production and comprehension: first children refer explicitly to the descriptor function of words and only later do they invoke the determinor function. Under 8 year olds tend to mention the clues provided by the *extralinguistic* context although in their spontaneous response they must have used the linguistic clue. Children in the third phase, on the other hand, frequently refer explicitly to the *linguistic* clue upon which they have based their response. Obviously, by then determiners have become detached from the contexts in which they are used and can be reflected upon directly. It may therefore be reasonable to hypothesize that from 8 or 9 years an essential linguistic development takes place, i.e. the child can make a more abstract analysis of an utterance and no longer requires stress on intralinguistic clues nor salience of extralinguistic clues (Karmiloff-Smith 1979). Older children of the third phase can also explicitly invoke the presuppositions implied by the *absence* of the use of another determiner. This, together with spontaneous corrections and the overall experimental results, points to the fact that by 8 or 9 years of age children have established *systems* of mutually exclusive plurifunctional markers, whose primary and secondary focussing functions are clearly interrelated with the use of special emphasizers.

There are of course several other aspects of the use of determiners which have not been covered. Nonetheless, it is hoped that the functional approach on a wide age span has covered a fairly broad part of the problem. Whilst a few aspects of this study only apply to French-speaking subjects, e.g. the gender-indicating function of the articles, most of the theoretical and experimental discussions are, in my view, applicable to English-speaking children. The preliminary results of pilot studies using the basic theoretical and experimental considerations developed here, being conducted with English-speaking children by Alison Garton at Oxford (personal communication) seem to run along very similar lines to the trends observed with French-speaking children. Whilst confirmation is always heartening, it will of course be the controversial data that will provoke new theoretical discussions.

10 *General implications for language acquisition and child development*[1]

Thy words are like a cloud of winged snakes;
And yet I pity those they torture not.
(Shelley, *Prometheus Unbound*)

Underlying much of the research work in child development is an implicit epistemological stand in favour of either innate or learned behavioural patterns. Piaget's genetic epistemology, by contrast, has always posited the constructive interaction of the child and his environment. Whilst Piaget has explicitly stressed the effects of cognition on language growth, he has left implicit the effects the latter might have on cognitive growth. Yet, language acquisition is a dialectical form of problem-solving and the child's constructive interaction with his linguistic environment suggests that language must be a crucial problem area for the child in its own right.

The present study has made it possible to generate a series of working hypotheses about language acquisition for which more theoretical reflection and experimental data on both linguistic and non-linguistic cognition will be required. The important distinction recalled by Cromer (1977) between language *acquisition* models and language *processing* models must be kept in mind. Moreover, there exist the inevitable risks of any theoretical analysis: 'all theories tend to shape the facts they attempt to explain'. (Leontiev, upon receiving Nobel Prize for Economics.) Thus, whilst it is felt that the analysis of this study has demonstrated the plausibility of a functional approach to child language, it should be acknowledged that there are other explanations for the same data. This is surely what science is all about!

It was suggested in the introductory chapter that Piaget had underestimated the importance of language as an experimental variable in

[1] A few of the paragraphs in this chapter have appeared in Karmiloff-Smith 1977b and 1978a.

cognitive tasks, as a problem-space *per se* for children, and as a possible constructive factor in child development generally. Let us therefore now look at some of the general conclusions which might be drawn in these respects from the present study.

We may use as an illustration the results of the final experiment on the changing functions of the word 'same' and examine their implications for a partial reinterpretation of some Piagetian naturalistic and experimental data.

The naturalistic data are taken from one of Piaget's early books and concern the well-known example of 'the slug':

> J. at 2,6: '*that's not a bee, it's bumble bee. Is it an animal*?' But also at about 2,6 she used the term '*the slug*' for the slugs we went to see every morning along a certain road. At 2,7 she cried: '*there it is*!' on seeing one, and when we saw another ten yards further on she cried: '*there's the slug again*'; I answered: 'But isn't it another?' J. went back to see the first one. 'Is it the same?' '*Yes*'. 'Another slug?' '*Yes*'. 'Another or the same?' . . . The question obviously had no meaning for J. (1951, p. 225)

Those conversant with Piaget's deep analyses of child behaviour may have found the last sentence above rather atypical. Did the question really have no meaning for J.? What did J. mean when she exclaimed to Piaget 'encore la limace', and replied affirmatively that it was simultaneously both the same slug and another one?

If interpreted by an adult, 'encore la limace' implies anaphoric reference to a slug already mentioned; otherwise the utterance would have been 'encore une limace'. However, it should be recalled that the indefinite article has as its first function that of naming. Looking at the first part of the above quotation, it is obvious that J. is able to use the nominative function of the indefinite article (e.g. 'That's not *a* bee, it's *a* bumble bee'); there are numerous other examples in Piaget's text of the correct use of the nominative function of the indefinite article. Thus, it would appear that when saying 'Encore la limace', the child's intention was *not* to give the name of the mollusc, which was already shared knowledge between her and her father. Although the English published translation of 'encore la limace' as 'there's the slug again' is of course the more colloquial rendering, let us translate it as 'another the slug', which is closer to the original French. 'Encore' in French can mean 'again' or 'other'. 'Encore un biscuit' means 'another biscuit'. Several of the experiments in this study indicate that for small children the definite article is used deictically; they say 'the X' even when several idential Xs are *visibly* present, and particularly when an X is alone in context. Moreover, Cohen (1952) cites the example of a 23 month old child who, upon seeing a letter in the mailbox, exclaimed: 'Encore la lettre' (instead of 'Encore une lettre'), and at 24 months in a similar situation, stated: 'La lettre . . . l'autre de lettre . . . autre la lettre' [The letter . . . the other letter . . . other the letter]. 'The' is clearly deictic here. In Piaget's example, therefore, J. may have been saying something like 'another the slug', 'encore' implying another *one*, whereas the definite article was deictic and singled out the mollusc's presence in the extralinguistic context. Indeed, with verbs such as 'regarder' (e.g. 'Look at the slug!') the use of the definite article is correct. When J. walked back to look at the first slug before answering Piaget's question, it is conceivable that she was not checking whether it was the same *one* but rather whether it was the same *kind*. Piaget's question may thus have been very meaningful to J. in that the present study shows that for the under 5 year old 'another slug' (another one) can indeed be simultaneously 'the same (kind)'.

The point to be stressed – though it merely touches on one aspect of Piaget's analyses of sensorimotor and preoperational intelligence – is that neither the definite article in 'the slug' nor the pronoun in J.'s exclamation 'There it is!' are necessarily anaphoric or exophoric. The child's intention in using such terms may initially be predominantly deictic. It only seems anaphoric to the *observer* who is connecting the child's discourse and interpreting it intralinguistically.

Piaget makes a very interesting analysis of J.'s use of the term 'the slug'. He suggests that the child is looking upon the two slugs, not as different members of the class of slugs, but as successive reappearances of a single member, a sort of semi-individual, semigeneric prototype (Piaget 1951). Although this interpretation may reflect conceptual development at some early level, basing the particular hypothesis on the child's use of determiners is tenuous, to the extent that the syntactico-semantic *functions* of expressions in child language do not necessarily coincide with those of adults.

Let us now briefly reconsider some experimental data from Piaget *et al.* (1968b) in the light of the results on child language from the present study. Has the verbal component of certain experiments played a somewhat more crucial role than was previously thought? It would, for instance, be very difficult to devise experiments to study identity concepts and yet avoid the use of articles and the words 'same' and 'other'.

Indeed, when Piaget *et al.* (1968b) studied the problems of the epistemology and psychology of identity, they carried out a series of experiments, all of which involved (after spatial rotations, etc., of an object) experimenter questions of the type: 'Is it *the same* drop of water?/Is it *the same* square?' Piaget and his colleagues describe four developmental levels (1968b, pp. 5ff.) in identity concepts: first, a tendency to accept identity, second, a refusal to accept identity, third, acceptance of identity of the object itself but not of its quantitative properties, and finally, a quantitative identity, i.e. conservation.

First, it is noteworthy that although children of the first and third levels accept identity of the object, Piaget suggests that their identical responses have a different cognitive status, based on his overall knowledge of the child's developing concepts. It is, however, the distinction between the first and second levels which I should like briefly to discuss, as they pertain to the *linguistic* component of the tasks. 3 to 4 year olds, when asked 'Is it the same square?' reply in the affirmative. Piaget suggests this is due to their ignoring the transformations involved. 4 to 5 year olds give a negative reply to the same question, because they take the transformations into account. Hence Piaget's two levels. However, if we consider that the expression 'the same X' is interpreted by youngest children in its descriptor function, and not in its determinor function, their affirmative reply could be interpreted to mean 'same kind', i.e. 'it's the same' means to them '*another* square with similar attributes'. For 4 to 5 year olds, already interpreting in privileged contexts 'the same X' in its determinor function, i.e. meaning 'same one', the question will receive a negative reply but also mean 'another square'. Thus, when analysed from the point of view of the functions these expressions have in child language, the opposing replies of the two groups of children cited above may actually have the same cognitive status of non-identity. The two levels distinguished by Piaget may in fact be one level, since children have understood the experimenter's question in two different ways.

We have seen how cautious Piaget is about misinterpreting the similar responses of two different developmental levels as having the same cognitive status. However, the converse also holds true. Children may be giving *different* verbal responses which in fact have the same conceptual status. It seems clear that with development children tend to endow linguistic terms such as 'the same X' with different functions, irrespective of the particular conceptual task about which they are being questioned. It is therefore suggested that language is an important experimental variable, a fact that has hitherto been underestimated in Piagetian research.

The Piagetians have, as pointed out in chapter 1, clearly demonstrated the effects of cognition on language acquisition. There is no doubt that there are many cognitive prerequisites underlying the development of the child's language. However, there is no need to rule out within the Piagetian framework that, just as cognition affects language growth, language may also affect cognitive growth. Does the child, for example, first have a conceptual understanding of, say, past time and then seek the linguistic patterns which express this, or does he first recognize the linguistic patterns of '-ed' suffixation and seek to give them conceptual meaning? Development probably involves an intricate interaction of *both*. However, the characteristics of the input are important.

Some aspects of the present study suggests that children initially expect language to be non-redundant. If the referent is clearly identifiable from the extralinguistic context, the child seeks, for instance, other functions for the determiners which accompany nouns. Thus descriptor functions are acquired earlier than determinor functions. One might make an analogous argument for the results of studies on the functions of verb inflections (e.g. Bronckart & Sinclair 1973; Bronckart 1976). It was shown that small children first use verb inflections to indicate aspect rather than temporal relations. Thus, small children used the distinctions between past tense, present tense and so forth to indicate whether an action had a long or short duration, whether it gave rise to a result or not, etc. They did not use tense inflections initially to express the temporal relation between the event described and the time the utterance about it was made. In Bronckart's study, these results were given an interesting cognitive explanation. However, the child's attention to expressing aspectual features rather than temporal features may also be partially explained by the fact that the input frequently contains redundant markers, whereas small children expect each one to have a separate function. In saying, for example, 'Yesterday I went . . . /Tomorrow I will go . . .', the temporal indication is expressed twice. My naturalistic data show that for some time 'yesterday' means for the child 'any time in the past', and 'tomorrow' means 'any time in the future'. If these words are used to indicate the temporal relations, it is not surprising that children use the verb inflections to indicate something else, i.e. the aspectual features. It is only later in development that children add redundant markers, or indicate dual functions.

Let us return to the examples in experiment 16 (p. 206 above) to continue the discussion of whether language is a problem-space *per se* for children. We have seen that small children express and interpret words initially as if they were unifunctional. What remains to be discussed is why the child first chooses one or other of the dual functions of a word. Why does the small child first opt for the meaning 'same kind' rather than 'same one'? In the tasks performed in experiment 16 there were no spatial rotations, etc., that rendered the situation conceptually difficult in any way. Indeed, the identity concept involved would be of the most primitive type, i.e. object permanency (Piaget 1953), which is acquired before the onset of language and is considered to be, among other things, a prerequisite for it (Sinclair 1971a). It would therefore be difficult to interpret the results of the 3 year olds on the basis of conceptual development in identity. Cognitively, it would seem to be equally difficult, if not more so, to make the comparison between two objects and judge them as 'the same' (kind), as to look upon one object as retaining its identity, particularly when no spatial or other transformations have taken place. Is it that the 3 year old is simply more obsessed at this stage of development with similarities of attributes and thus interprets the linguistic expression as referring to similarities? This may be part of the explanation.

Apart from the fact that children acquire descriptor functions before determinor functions, it may be that they are implicitly basing their interpretation 'same kind' on the position of the word 'same' and particularly its relationship to the other words in the NP. This obviously is not meant to imply that there is any *explicit* metalinguistic activity dividing words into adult classes of articles, adjectives and nouns. But just as the child generalizes patterns in his physical environment, so he does in his linguistic environment (Berko 1958; Brown & Bellugi 1964; Ervin-Tripp 1973; Klima & Bellugi 1973), and this may not be merely aimed at expressing semantic intentions. It has been suggested elsewhere that the child's processing procedures on both linguistic and physical environments are very similar (Karmiloff-Smith & Inhelder 1974/5). Thus there may be implicit classificatory activity going on in the child's cognitive processing of the linguistic input, linking such words as 'big/small/yellow/pretty/*same*' because they occur together in an intonational chunk with article and noun 'the big cow/the same cow'). This is why it was particularly illustrative to note that when asked to compare one of two ducks to the other, the child replied in the affirmative when asked 'Is it the same duck?' but when asked 'Is it the same?' the reply was negative. It could be that when the question involves 'same' only accompanied by an article in French, the word 'same' has a different function than when it is inserted between article and noun and looks more like a modifier.

The following trend is hypothesized. First the child makes an NP chunk based on intonational patterns or on something along the lines of Bever's (1970) 'perceptual segmentation'. Then the child breaks down that global chunk into one, two or three slots based on surface structure input patterns: one slot for something like little words that go with the names of things (determiner); one slot for words which tell us about the thing (modifier); and one slot for the name (noun). The modifier slot would be filled with words like 'big/little/pretty/*same*'. The hypothesis is that the initial choice of interpretation 'same kind' is due to the fact that it matches the classificatory system and the modifier slot position. Simultaneously the child may frequently confirm his 'theory' in that 'same kind' interpretations are more consistent in the linguistic input since 'same one' meanings are often replaced by pronominalization, etc. But gradually the actual semantics of the word 'same' would be more clearly developing into the two functions: 'same kind' and 'same one', particularly from instances where 'same one' meaning is unambiguous. The lengthy hesitations in the transition period and the fact that initial correct responses occur when attributes differ significantly tend to indicate that there may subsequently be a conflict between two competing systems: the two semantic functions of 'same' versus its syntactic relations with the other constituents of the NP. The final understanding in this context of 'same' as meaning 'same one' may be considerably helped by the child's more explicit understanding and use of 'other', whereby 'another X' covers the meaning 'same kind' and thus frees 'same' in such circumstances for the meaning 'same one'. Lastly, another important factor is that small children use determiners deictically in reference to the extralinguistic context, rather than anaphorically, and this probably also affects the younger child's preferred interpretation of 'same kind'. All this points to the fact that children work on linguistic 'objects' in the same way as on physical objects; they need to be sorted, classified, organized into systems.

Very young children are seen to be particularly involved in seeking similarities in the objects in their physical environment and construct 'theories-in-action' based thereupon (Karmiloff-Smith & Inhelder 1974/5). There is every reason to suppose that they are equally involved with similarities in their lingustic environment. Linguistically there is a strong pattern in the treatment of nouns: they take determiners, modifiers, plural inflections, etc. In fact, the pattern of their treatment linguistically is (at least in English and French) far more consistent than their common conceptual attributes. For example, how does the child form a conceptual link between, say, 'a pencil' and 'a cloud', 'a cup' and 'an elephant', let alone between 'a tooth' (object) and 'an arrival' (action), 'a lamp post' and 'a slap', or 'a carpet', 'a noise' and 'the moon'. Since regularity-seeking activities are so pervasive in the small child, it could be that the consistent patterns the child can observe in the linguistic treatment of these words also helps him to form the more general concept of 'things', just as his conceptual progress will enable him to identify and seek such patterns. The presence of articles, for instance, may help the child to recognize that a noun will follow, and that there is a reason for this consistent pattern. He could then seek a conceptual cohesion that is different from his existing conceptual distinction between actions and objects, i.e. the new distinction being intralinguistic, in that actions can be treated linguistically as if they were discrete objects.

The two examples from naturalistic and experimental data, together with the overall experimental results from this study, indicate that many language-specific problems must be solved by the child and that general conceptual development is only a partial explanation for linguistic development. However, it should be stressed that language-specific procedures – be they phonological, syntactic, etc. – are of course rooted in very general cognitive capacities to organize and seek patterns in the environment. Whether a child initially acquires a given category by a phonological, semantic, pragmatic or syntactic procedure will usually depend on the predominant patterns in the input. In French, for instance, most children do seem to acquire the gender distinction by first concentrating on phonological procedures. However, in another linguistic environment (e.g. German, where word endings are not necessarily good clues to formal gender but to semantic cases), different procedures may be used for acquiring gender. It seems clear that children are simultaneously acquiring *many* procedures for coping with their environments. The use of each particular one will depend on aspects of each input. Whilst general trends can be found amongst children of one environment, it should not be overlooked that individual differences do exist, not only in rate of development, but in the procedures used by children of the same level vis-à-vis a particular problem. However, the *form* of the gradual integration of the various procedures into systems is probably universal.

What does appear to be very general is the way in which children first rely heavily on extralinguistic and paralinguistic clues as well as the addition of linguistic emphasizers. There seem to be two complementary processes which probably stretch beyond the sphere of determiners: the child's endeavour to disambiguate by overmarking, use of emphasizers, use of paralinguistic markers, etc., counterbalanced by his progressive endeavour to be economical, as evidenced for instance by the dropping of redundant markers.[1] Can we not consider language itself as a form of 'cognitive economy'? As pointed out in chapter 1, Piaget has frequently stressed that language becomes an increasingly important tool of cognition with age. It can, however, be argued that language is perhaps most important during the early years when action schemes can, through verbal representation, become 'conceptual primitives', i.e. building blocks which are easy to handle. The present study suggests that language is a problem-space *per se* for small children, and that only later in development, around 8 or 9 years, does language become solely a tool of intelligence or something to be explicitly reflected upon metalinguistically. It could be that the cognitive demands which language acquisition places on the small child force him to generate many new procedures earlier and more dynamically than these procedures are generated by his encounters with the physical environment. The fact that the child must, and does, generate multiple representations of the same reality – phonological, semantic, syntactic, pragmatic – surely must affect his capacity for multiple representation in general. Not only language is a problem-space. My initial studies on other modes of representation (to be reported on elsewhere) suggests that in both macro- and microdevelopment, there exists a subtle interplay between using a form of representation as a tool and working on that notational system at a metaprocedural level as a problem-space.

I should like to conclude this study with an attempt to use the results for illustrating a tentative model of acquisition processes which may have some generality and which may suggest an explanation of the results at a procedural level.

[1] 'Overmarking' is also apparent in phonological development (Kornfeld 1971), e.g. when the child has difficulty differentiating a phonological opposition, the natural tendency is to overmark one of them for a certain period, which then allows for the emergence of the other and the subsequent dropping of the redundant emphasis. This is also relevant to the acquisition model proposed in the next paragraphs.

We have seen that at first children endow each new morpheme with one basic function. What makes the child opt for one given function before another? Is it merely that one is more in tune with his current cognitive level than another? It has been argued here that the characteristics of the linguistic input also play an important role. In my view, choice of a given function will depend on the child's capacity to identify the *most consistent* input pattern,[1] e.g. the primary focussing functions of morphemes. Seeking consistent patterns is indeed the most efficient heuristic for coping with any environment, be it physical, conceptual, perceptual, linguistic, or even emotional. It is suggested that the child is not explicitly testing several hypotheses for various different functions and choosing the best one amongst them, but rather that he is recognizing positive examples of the function presenting the most consistent pattern (e.g. the nominative function of the indefinite article) and then seeking to conserve that pattern. In most settings, these pattern-conserving procedures encounter some exceptions. It is suggested that exceptions cannot have the status of counterexamples, i.e. to allow for the general creation of new additional functions, until the basic function is highly compiled and automatic. However, the child may be aware implicitly that he has pushed aside other competing features of the environment. He may keep a 'decision trace' in memory, i.e. the *fact* that a choice was made, but not explicitly *what* the choice was between. Once the child has consolidated the basic function, by keeping it implicitly isolated from other competing ones, he is then in a position to attach to it indicators that there may be exceptions to the implicit rules of the basic or core function. If the exceptions present a pattern, then new additional functions will be created, e.g. exophoric reference for the definite article. If no pattern emerges, then concrete details of the exceptions will have to be stored by a special 'sentry' learned by rote, e.g. for gender 'l*e* squel*ette*'. We have seen, moreover, that the basic phonological procedure for gender in French becomes tabbed with syntactic and semantic standby procedures for dealing with situations where the phonological procedure comes into conflict with other clues. In the case of story comprehension, the results showed that children use a basic pragmatic procedure, which only progressively becomes tabbed with syntactic standby procedures. The fact that the small child can recall the use of the

[1] By 'input pattern', I mean of course to cover not only the observable utterance but also the situational context and the linguistic functions obtaining for the utterance in each particular context.

definite article in repetition shows that a trace remains in memory when the word is not processed because a pragmatic procedure has been used. The older child who processes 'the' as meaning 'only one' repeats the utterance with the addition of the word 'only'. The results of the story comprehension experiment (13) illustrate Minsky & Papert's model (1972) where understanding is seen as using much extraworld default knowledge, e.g. the pragmatic procedure, and then 'debugging' that knowledge in the light of the current information, e.g. the syntactico-semantic clue from the word 'the'.

Only gradually do new functions get added to existing ones. When a morpheme initially has more than one function, it in fact seems to represent for the child a series of isolated homonyms. Procedures also appear to develop isolatedly at first (e.g. the phonological procedure for lexical concord in gender, together with a semantic procedure for pronoun reference). In his comprehensive review of developmental strategies for language, Cromer (1977) placed particular stress on the fact that around the age of 6, children appear to enter an intermediate stage of language development lasting for some three years. During this period, children may use, for example, the rule 'grammatical subject implies agent' in interpreting the 'easy to see' structure, but do not follow the same rule for interpreting the passive. Moreover, Cromer showed that the intermediate child's behaviour was inconsistent from one day to the next, even across a number of items testing the same structure in identical experimental settings.

It can thus be argued that changes in procedure are not only elicited by changes in experimental design, but are actually characteristic of the over 5 year old's behaviour. From roughly 5 years, the child can be said to have built up a series of juxtaposed procedures for language use and understanding, but which now need to be organized into coherent systems of relevant options.

Why do functions and procedures first develop in an isolated fashion? Has this a psychological purpose for the child? It is suggested that the initial isolation of functions enables the child to consolidate each of the functions and render them 'tangible'. If he were simultaneously considering several functions for a morpheme, i.e. slipping to and fro between functions, each function would remain unstable. However, this does not imply that the child is totally unaware of competing procedures nor unaware that there are somehow links between procedures. There must be memory traces of hesitations, i.e. a trace that a decision has been taken without necessarily an explicit awareness of what the decision was.

Once the child becomes aware of one expression fulfilling two different functions, there is a tendency to create temporarily a new form to cover one of the two functions, retaining the original form for the other. It is suggested that this differentiation, by creating slightly ungrammatical forms, helps the child consolidate the two separate meanings normally expressed by a single surface element. Once this consolidation has taken place, the child can then drop the ungrammatical form and use of surface expression for both functions.

Gradually, children introduce relations between functions and thus endow a morpheme with plurifunctional status. Why is this? Are they merely accommodating to the input model? Hardly, for once the various functions are present in the child's utterances, on the surface the child is now using the adult system. There is nothing in the adult model that could inform the child directly that the words he is using as several homonyms actually form one plurifunctional morpheme. It is suggested that the child gradually confers plurifunctional status on words because once procedures are automatized, the child can consider them at a metaprocedural level. He will then notice both their common output (e.g. various procedures all have as their output the definite article) and their common secondary functions, sensing thereby that they are part of a more general *system*. Systemic storate is psychologically 'economical', i.e. the functions no longer need to be 'calculated' but have the status of a primitive and are mutually exclusive.

It should be stressed that the original basic functions do not simply disappear. Children are usually substantially on the right track from the outset; this, in my view, is because they are recognizing positive examples of patterns in the input. The basic functions are maintained throughout development, but their scope and importance may change, e.g. the nominative function to the non-specific reference function of the indefinite article. What we may be interpreting as the disappearance of a procedure (e.g. the phonological procedure in the gender experiment), or interpreting as the integration of a type of behaviour into a broader concept (e.g. in many conceptual spheres such as conservation), may be the reflection of the growing child's capacity to identify the crucial experimental problem which is not typical of his everyday encounters, and to curtail his normally predominant procedure.

This model of acquisition procedures makes the following explanation of epilinguistic awareness seem plausible. It will be recalled that for the gender problem, for instance, epilinguistic awareness was primarily based on syntactic and semantic clues and, surprisingly, not on the predominant phonological ones. It is suggested that this can be explained by the fact that basic procedures and basic functions, because they stem from positive examples, become highly compiled and thus 'automatic', whereas 'sentries' and standby procedures may be more easily retrieved from memory because they are used in special circumstances. They may also be more easily retrievable because they stem from conflict rather than from the highly compiled system based on recognizing positive examples.

How does such a model, inspired by some of the more general aspects of artificial intelligence approaches to thinking, fit within the overall epistemological model of Piaget? Although conceptual progress indeed plays a role in language acquisition, I should like to place stress on the procedural aspect, i.e. the dynamic process of rendering the environment 'tangible'. Only by seeking to conserve patterns and procedures can the child get a 'grip' on the environment and gain what Nelson (1975) has called increasing 'predictive control'. If the child were to take into consideration each new piece of information, constantly remodel his procedures, and slip to and fro between competing theories about the environment, he would not have the opportunity of consolidating the procedures in the first place. This consolidation allows the procedure to become automatic, e.g. a primitive, thus *freeing the representational processing-space* for other developments. Clearly, conserving linguistic patterns (e.g. the syntagmatic metacommunicative function of article-like words) and meanings (e.g. one of the functions of determiners, one of the potentially many meanings of a word, etc.) plays a decisive role in getting a grip on linguistic inputs. All through development, the child tries to conserve, and thus resists new information. Overgeneralization is one way of doing this, and the linguistic environment lends itself to this overgeneralization tendency more than others. Overgeneralization is a powerful device for simultaneously simplifying *and* unifying; this again helps the child to get a grip on the input, but this time, by overgeneralization, the child *imposes* his pattern on it. Thus, there is a constant motion between seeking to recognize positive examples of patterns, on the one hand, and imposing these patterns on the model, on the other hand. Imposing patterns on the environment in turn enables the child gradually to recognize counterexamples and seek new patterns amongst them. The fact that with development there appears to be more interplay between procedures, and that morphemes acquire their plurifunctional status, may be due to the older child's attempt to seek patterns and cohesion, not only in the input, but within his *own* multifaceted approaches to the linguistic input. Thus he uses metaprocedures to organize his own procedures into systems of options.

Every time we take even the smallest step forward in our understanding of child development, it merely serves to highlight how very far we still have to go. Every new answer generates a series of new problems. In this study an endeavour has been made to trace the progressive development of those little words which mean a lot and which acquire their truly plurifunctional status at around 9 years of age. Yet we cannot overlook the fact that the little 3 year old's language is a constant source of astonishment to the observer. New data on very small children's linguistic development may again raise new issues with regard to the language of the older child . . .

And, of course, conveying meaning involves more than words, as Sheridan so amusingly demonstrated:

Sneer: Now, pray, what did he mean by that?

Puff: Why, by that shake of the head, he gave you to understand that even though they had more justice in their cause and wisdom in their measures . . . the country would fall a sacrifice to the hostile ambition of the Spanish monarchy.

Sneer: The devil! Did he mean all that by shaking his head?

(Sheridan, *The Critic*)

Bibliography

Arnauld, A. & Lancelot, C. (1966) *Grammaire générale et raisonnée ou la grammaire du Port-Royal. Ed. critique, H.E. Brekle.* Stuttgart–Bad Carnstatt: F. Frommann

Bates, E. (1976) *Language and context: the acquisition of pragmatics.* New York: Academic Press

Bellugi, U. & Fischer, S. (1972) 'A comparison of sign language and spoken language', *Cognition* 1, no. 213, 173–200

Bellugi, U. & Klima, E. (1975) 'Aspects of sign language and its structure', in J. Kavanagh & J. E. Cutting (eds.) *The role of speech in language.* Cambridge, Mass.: MIT Press

Benedict, H. (1978) 'Language comprehension in 9 to 15 month old children', in R. N. Campbell & P. T. Smith (eds.) *Recent advances in the psychology of language: Language development in mother–child interaction.* New York: Plenum Press

Beneviste, E. (1970) 'L'appareil formel de l'énonciation', *Langages* 17, 12–18

Berko, J. (1958) 'The child's learning of English morphology', *Word* 14, 150–77

Bever, T. G. (1970) 'The cognitive basis for linguistic structures', in J. R. Hayes (ed.) *Cognition and the development of language.* New York: Wiley

Biard, A. (1908) *L'article défini dans les principales langues européennes.* Bordeaux: Publications of the University of Paris

Blanchet, A. (1977) 'La construction et l'équilibre du mobile: problème méthodologique', *Arch. de Psych.* 45, 173

Blanchet, A., Ackerman, E., Kilcher, H. & Robert, M. (1978) 'Une hypothèse sur les connaissances utilisées en situation de resolution de problème', Proceedings of Symposium of the Association of Psych. Scient. de Langue Française , *Cahiers de Psych.* 21, no. 1–2, University of Provence

Bloom, L. (1973) *One word at a time: the use of single word utterances before syntax.* The Hague: Mouton

Bovet, M., Dasen, P. & Inhelder, B. (1972) 'Etapes de l'intélligence sensori-motrice chez l'enfant Baoulé', *Arch. de Psych.* 41, 363–84

Braine, M. D. S. (1963) 'The ontogeny of English phrase structure: the first phase', *Language* 39, 1–14

(1970) 'Gender study: the learning of semi-arbitrary word classes', mimeo
(1976) *Children's first word combinations.* Monograph of SRCD no. 164, vol. 1

Bresson, F., Bouvier, N., Damequin, C., Depreux, J., Hardy, M. & Platone, F. (1970) 'Quelques aspects du système des déterminants chez des enfants de l'école maternelle: utilisation des articles définis et indéfinis', *Cahiers du CRESAS*, Bulletin no. 2

Bronckart, J. P. (1976) *Genèse et organisation des formes verbales chez l'enfant.* Brussels: Dessart & Mardaga
(1977) *Théories du langage: une introduction critique.* Brussels: Mardaga
& Sinclair, H. (1973) 'Tense, time and aspect', *Cognition* 2, 107–30

Brown, R. W. (1973) *A first language: the early stages.* Cambridge, Mass.: Harvard University Press
& Bellugi, U. (1964) 'Three processes in the child's acquisition of syntax', *Harvard Educational Review* 34, 133–51

Brugmann, K. (1889) 'Das Nominalgeschlecht in den indo-germanischen Sprachen', *Zeitschrift für allgem. Sprachwissenschaft* 4, 100

Bruner, J. S. (1975a) 'The ontogenesis of speech acts', *Jl. of Child Language* 2, no. 1, 1–19
(1975b) 'From communication to language: a psychological perspective', *Cognition* 3, no. 3, 255–87
(1978a) 'On prelinguistic prerequisites of speech', in R. N. Campbell & P. T. Smith (eds.) *Recent advances in the psychology of language: Language development and mother-child interaction.* New York: Plenum Press
(1978b) 'Learning how to do things with words', in J. S. Bruner & A. Garton (eds.) *Human growth and development.* Wolfson College lectures (1976), Oxford: Oxford University Press

Cabrejo–Parra, E. (1974) 'Comment les enfants répondent à la question "qu'est-ce que c'est" ', *Cahiers du CRESAS*, Bulletin no. 6

Cambon, J. & Sinclair, H. (1974) 'Relations between syntax and semantics: are they easy to see?' *British Jl. of Psych.* 65, 133–40

Campbell, R. N. & Smith, P. T. (eds.) (1978a) *Recent advances in the psychology of language: Language development and mother-child interaction.* vol. III, 4a. New York: Plenum Press
(1978b) *Recent advances in the psychology of language: Formal and experimental approaches.* vol. III, 4b. New York: Plenum Press

Cazden, C. B. (1972) *Child language and education.* New York: Holt, Rinehart & Winston

Charniak, E. (1972) 'Toward a model of children's story comprehension', MIT Artificial Intelligence Lab. AI-TR-266

Chomsky, N. (1964) 'A review of B. F. Skinner's 'Verbal behaviour', in

J. A. Fodor & J. J. Katz (eds.) *The structure of language: readings in the philosophy of language.* New Jersey: Prentice Hall

(1967) 'Recent contributions to the theory of innate ideas', *Synthèse* 17, 2–11

(1970) 'Remarks on nominalizations', in R. A. Jacobs & P. S. Rosenbaum (eds.) *Readings in English transformational grammar.* Waltham, Mass.: Ginn & Co.

(1975) *Reflections on language.* New York: Pantheon Books

Christophersen, P. (1939) *The articles: a study of their theory and use in English.* Oxford: Oxford University Press

Clark, E. V. & Sengul, C. J. (1974) 'Deictic contrasts in language acquisition', Annual Meeting of the Linguistic Society of America, New York

Clark, H. H. (1970) 'The primitive nature of children's relational concepts', in J. R. Hayes (ed.) *Cognition and the development of language.* New York: Wiley

Cohen, M. (1952) 'Sur l'étude du langage enfantin', *Enfance* 3, no. 4, 203–72

Costermans, J. (1975) 'L'exploration des structures léxicales subjectives et son intérêt en psycholinguistique génétique', mimeo, University of Louvain

Cromer, R. F. (1974) 'The development of language and cognition: the cognition hypothesis', in B. Foss (ed.) *New perspectives in child development.* Harmondsworth, Middx.: Penguin Books

(1977), 'Developmental strategies for language', in V. Hamilton & M. D. Vernon (eds.) *The development of cognitive processes.* London & New York: Academic Press

Culioli, A. (1976), 'Séminaire de D.E.A.'. Unpublished manuscript, Université de Paris VII

Culioli, A., Fuchs, C. & Pecheux, M. (1970) *Considérations théoriques à propos du traitement formel du language.* Paris: Dunod

Dahl, Ö. (1975) 'On generics', in E. Keenan (ed.), *Formal semantics of natural language.* Cambridge: Cambridge University Press

Davey, A. C. (1974) 'A computational model of discourse production', PhD thesis, University of Edinburgh

& Longuet-Higgins, H. C. (1978), 'A computational model of discourse production', in R. N. Campbell & P. T. Smith (eds.) *Recent advances in the psychology of language: Formal and experimental approaches.* New York: Plenum Press

Donaldson, M. & Wales R. (1970) 'On the acquisition of some relational terms', in J. R. Hayes (ed). *Cognition and the development of language.* New York: Wiley

Dore, J. (1975) 'Holophrases, speech acts and language universals', *Jl. of Child Language* 2, 21–40

Dubois, J. (1965) *Grammaire structurale du français: nom et pronom*. Paris: Larousse

& Dubois-Charlier, F. (1970) *Eléments de linguistique française: syntaxe*. Paris: Larousse

Ducrot, O. (1970) 'Les indéfinis et l'énonciation', *Languages* (March), 91–111

(1972) *Dire et ne pas dire: principes de sémantique linguistique*. Paris: Hermann

Durand, M. (1938) *Le genre grammatical en français parlé à Paris et dans la région parisienne*. Paris: Bibliothèque du français moderne

Edwards, D. (1973) 'Sensorimotor intelligence and semantic relations in early child grammar', *Cognition* 2, no. 4, 395–434

Elkind, D. (1968) Editor's introduction to Jean Piaget, *Six psychological studies*. London: University of London Press

Ervin, S. M. (1962) 'The connotations of gender', *Word* 18, 249–61

Ervin-Tripp, S. M. (1973) 'Imitation and structural changes in children's language', in C. Ferguson & D. Slobin (eds.) *Studies of child language development*. New York: Holt, Rinehart & Winston

Ferreiro, E. (1971) *Les relations temporelles dans le langage de l'enfant*. Paris: Droz

& Sinclair, H. (1971) 'Temporal relationships in language', *Jl. Internat. de Psych.* 6, 39–47

Fisher, S. (1975) 'Comparative remarks on different forms of determination', in F. Bresson (ed.) *Problèmes actuels en psycholinguistique*. Paris: Editions of CNRS

Fodor, I. (1959) 'The origin of grammatical gender I', *Lingua* 8, 1–41

Fraser, C., Bellugi, U. & Brown, R. (1963) 'Control of grammar in imitation, comprehension and production', *Jl. of Verbal Learning and Verbal Behaviour* 2, 121–35

Frei, H. (1940) *Intérogatif et indéfini: un problème de grammaire comparée*. Paris: P. Geuthner

Furth, H. (1966) *Thinking without language*. New York: The Free Press

(1970) *Piaget and knowledge: theoretical foundations*. London: Prentice Hall

Gardner, R. A. & Gardner, B. T. (1969) 'Teaching sign language to a chimpanzee', *Science* 165, 664–72

Garman, M. (1977) 'A cross-linguistic study of deixis acquisition', 4th Salzburg International Linguistics Meeting, (August)

Gellrich, P. (1881) *Remarques sur l'emploi de l'article en vieux français*. Leipzig: Langenbielar & Krichlar

Gleason, H. A. Jr. (1961) *An introduction to descriptive linguistics*. rev. ed. New York: Holt, Rinehart & Winston

Goldin-Meadow, S. (1976) 'The representation of semantic relations in a manual language created by deaf children of hearing parents: a language you can't dismiss out of hand', PhD thesis, University of Pennsylvania

Gough, L. & Chiaraviglio J. (1970) 'On the base referential structure of the English noun phrase', *Foundations of Language* 6, 446–62

Grannis, O. C. (1974) 'Notes on "On the notion definite" ', *Foundations of Language* 11, 105–10

Grice, H.P. (1968) 'Utterer's meaning, sentence-meaning, and word-meaning', *Foundations of Language* 4, 225–42

Grize, J. B. (1966) 'Propos pour une méthode', in F. Bresson & M. de Montmollin (eds.) *Thèmes Piagétiens: psychologie et épistémologie génétiques*. Paris: Dunod

Guillaume, G. (1919) *Le problème de l'article et sa solution dans la langue française*. Paris: Nizet (new edition 1975)

Guillaume, P. (1927) 'Les débuts de la phrase dans le langage de l'enfant', and 'Le développement des éléments formels dans le langage de l'enfant', *Jl. de Psych.* 24, 1–25 and 216–29

Halliday, M. A. K. (1975) *Learning how to mean*. London: Arnold

Hewson, J. (1972) 'Article and noun in English', *Janua Linguarum*. The Hague: Mouton

Hill, A. A. (1966) 'A re-examination of the English articles', in F. P. Dinneen (ed.) *Monograph series on language and linguistics*. Washington DC: Georgetown University Press

Hockett, C. F. (1967) *Language, mathematics and linguistics*. The Hague: Mouton

Huppet, M. & Costermans, J. (1974) *Des fonctions sémantiques du passif*. Cahiers de l'Institut de Linguistique, University of Louvain, no. 2, 1–34

Inhelder, B. & Piaget, J. (1959) *La genèse des structures logiques élémentaires*. Neuchatel and Paris: Delachaux & Niestlé

Inhelder, B., Lezine, I., Sinclair, H. & Stamback, M. (1972) 'Les débuts de la fonction sémiotique', *Arch. de Psych.* 41, 187–243

Inhelder, B., Sinclair, H. & Bovet, M. (1974) *Learning and the development of cognition*. Cambridge, Mass.: Harvard University Press

Jespersen, O. (1949) *Modern English grammar*. Copenhagen: Munskaard

Karmiloff-Smith, A. (1974) 'Approche psychogénétique à la fonction déterminative', Project de thèse, unabridged version, 1–39

(1976) 'Little words mean a lot: the plurifunctionality of determiners in child language', PhD thesis, University of Geneva

(1977a) 'Développement cognitif et acquisition de la plurifonctionalité des déterminants', in *Genèse de la parole*. Paris: PUF

(1977b) 'More about the same: children's understanding of postarticles', *Jl. of Child Language* 4, 377–94

(1977c) 'The importance of language as a problem-space per se in child development'. Proceedings of the International Society for the Study of

Behavioural Development Biennial on 'Biosocial aspects of development'. Italian version

(1978a) 'The interplay between syntax, semantics and phonology in language acquisition processes', in R. N. Campbell & P. T. Smith (eds.) *Recent advances in the psychology of language: Language development and mother–child interaction*. New York: Plenum Press

(1978b) 'On stage: the importance of being a non-conserver', *Behavioural and Brain Sciences* 1, 188–90

(1979) 'Language development after five', in P. Fletcher & M. Garman (eds.) *Studies in language acquisition*. Cambridge: Cambridge University Press

(in press a) 'Some aspects of the child's construction of a system of plurifunctional markers', in G. Drachman (ed.) *Salzburger Beiträge zur Linguistik V*. Salzburg: Verglagsbuchhandung Wolfgang Neugebauer

(in press b) 'Adult simultaneous interpretation: a function analysis of linguistic categories and a comparison with child development', in D. Gerver & W. Sinaiko (eds.) *Language, interpretation and communication*. London: Plenum Press

(in preparation) 'The forms and functions of "topicalization": a cross-linguistic study'

& Inhelder, B. (1974/5), 'If you want to get ahead get a theory', *Cognition* 3, no. 3, 195–212

Katz, N. Baker, E. & Macnamara, J. (1974) 'What's in a Name? A study of how children learn common and proper names', *Child Development* no. 45, 469–73

Klima, E. S. & Bellugi, U. (1973), 'Syntactic regularities in the speech of children', in C. Ferguson & D. Slobin (eds.) *Studies of child language development*. New York: Holt, Rinehart & Winston

Kornfeld, J. R. (1971) 'Theoretical issues in child phonology', Proceedings of 7th Annual Meeting of the Chicago Ling. Society 454–68

Kramsky, J. (1972) *The article and the concept of definiteness in language*. The Hague: Mouton

Lenneberg, E. H. (1967) *Biological foundations of language*. New York: Wiley

Levelt, W. J. M. (1974) *Formal grammars in linguistics and psycholinguistics: psycholinguistic applications* vol. III. The Hague: Mouton

Lieven, E. V. M. (1978) 'Turn-taking and pragmatics: two issues in early child language', in R. N. Campbell & P. T. Smith (eds.) *Recent advances in the psychology of language: Language development and mother–child interaction*. New York: Plenum Press

Lyons, J. (1968) *Introduction to theoretical linguistics*. Cambridge: Cambridge University Press

(1970) (ed.) *New horizons in linguistics.* Harmondsworth, Middx.: Penguin Books

(1975) 'Deixis as the source of reference' in E. Keenan (ed.) *Formal semantics of natural language.* Cambridge: Cambridge University Press

(1977a) *Semantics*, vols. I and II, Cambridge: Cambridge University Press

(1977b) 'Deixis and anaphora', in T. Myers (ed.) *The development of conversation and discourse.* Edinburgh: Edinburgh University Press

Maratsos, M. P. (1976) *The use of definite and indefinite reference in young children: an experimental study of semantic acquisition.* Cambridge: Cambridge University Press

Martinet, A. (1956) 'Le genre féminin en indo-européen: examen fonctionnel du problème', *Bulletin de la SLP* 52, 83–95, Paris

Matsubara, H. (1932) *Essai sur la syntaxe de l'article en français moderne.* Paris: Libraire du Rec. Sirey

McNeill, D. (1966) 'Developmental psycholinguistics', in F. Smith & G. A. Miller (eds.) *The genesis of language.* Cambridge, Mass.: MIT Press

Meillet, A. (1952) 'Le genre féminin dans les langues indo-européennes', in *Linguistique Historique et Linguistique Générale.* SLP no. 8, 40. Paris: E. Champion

Mill, J. S. (1949) *A system of logic.* London: Longman

Minsky, M. (1975) 'A framework for representing knowledge', in P. Winston (ed.) *The psychology of computer vision.* New York: McGraw Hill

& Papert, S. (1972) 'Artificial intelligence progress report', AI-MIT, memo no. 252

Mok, Q. I. (1968) *Contribution à l'étude des catégories morphologiques du genre et du nombre dans le français parlé actuel.* The Hague: Mouton

Nelson, K. (1974) 'Concept, word, and sentence: interrelations in acquisition and development', *Psych. Review* 81, no. 4, 267–85

(1975) 'Cognitive development and the acquisition of concepts'. Conference on 'Schooling and the acquisition of knowledge', San Diego

Ninio, A. & Bruner, J. S. (1978) 'The achievement and antecedents of labelling', *Jl. of Child Language* 5, no. 1, 1–15

Perlmutter, D. (1970) 'On the article in English', in M. Bierwisch & K. E. Heidolph (eds.) *Progress in linguistics.* The Hague: Mouton

Piaget, J. (1926) *The language and thought of the child.* London: Kegan Paul, Trench, Truber & Co. (French edition 1923)

(1950) *Introduction à l'epistémologie génétique*, vol. III: *La pensée biologique, la pensée psychologique et la pensée sociologique.* Paris: PUF

(1951) *Play, dreams and imitation in childhood.* London: Heinemann (French edition 1946)

(1953) *The origins of intelligence in children.* London: Routledge & Kegan Paul (French edition 1936)

(1968a) *Six psychological studies.* London: University of London Press (French edition 1964)

(1968b) 'Le point de vue de Piaget', *Jl. Internat. de Psych.* 3

(1970) *Structuralism.* New York: Basic Books (French edition 1968)

(1971) *Biology and knowledge.* Chicago: University of Chicago Press (French edition 1967)

(1975) L'équilibration des structures cognitives: problème central du développement', EEG 33. Paris: PUF

(1976), *The grasp of consciousness: action and concept in the young child.* Cambridge Mass.: Harvard University Press

& Inhelder, B. (1969a) *The psychology of the child.* New York: Basic Books (French edition 1966)

(1969b) 'The gaps in empiricism', in A. Koestler & J. R. Smithies (eds.) *Beyond reductionism.* London: Hutchinson

Piaget, J., Grize, J. B., Szeminska, A. & Vinh Bang (1968a) 'Epistémologie et psychologie de la fonction', EEG 23, Paris: PUF

Piaget, J., Sinclair, H. & Vinh Bang (1968b) 'Epistémologie et psychologie de l'identité', EEG 24. Paris: PUF

Postal, P. M. (1970) 'On so-called pronouns in English', in R. A. Jacobs & P. S. Rosenbaum (eds.) *Readings in English transformational grammar.* Waltham, Mass: Ginn & Co.

Premack, A. J. & Premack, D. (1972) 'Teaching language to an ape', *Scientific American* 227, 92–9

Rappe du Cher, E. (forthcoming) 'Cross-linguistic study of children's production and comprehension of derived sentences', PhD thesis, University of Geneva

Robbins, B. L. (1968) *The definite article in English transformations.* The Hague: Mouton

Russell, B. (1919) *Introduction to mathematical philosophy.* London: Allen & Unwin

Ryan, M. L. (1978) 'Contour in context', in R. N. Campbell & P. T. Smith (eds.) *Recent advances in the psychology of language: Language development and mother–child interaction.* New York: Plenum Press

Saussure, F. de (1916) *Cours de linguistique générale.* Paris: Payot

Schank, R. (1972) 'Conceptual dependency: a theory of natural language understanding', *Cognitive Psych.* 3, no. 4, 552–631

Searle, J. R. (1969) *Speech acts: an essay in the philosophy of language.* Cambridge: Cambridge University Press

(1976) 'Rules of the language game', *Times Literary Supplement* (September)

Sinclair [-de Zwart], H. (1967) *Langage et opérations: sous-systèmes linguistiques et opérations concrètes.* Paris: Dunod

Sinclair, H. (1969) 'Developmental psycholinguistics', in D. Elkind & J. H.

Flavell (eds.) *Studies in cognitive development: essays in honour of Jean Piaget*. Oxford: Oxford University Press

(1971a) 'Sensorimotor action patterns as a condition for the acquisition of syntax', in R. Huxley & E. Ingram (eds.) *Language acquisition: models and methods*. New York: Academic Press

(1971b) 'Piaget's theory on language acquisition', in M. F. Rosskopf et al. (eds.) *Piagetian cognitive development research and mathematical education*. Washington: National Council of Teachers of Mathematics, Inc.

(1973a) 'Some remarks on the Genevan point of view on learning with special reference to language learning', in R. A. Hinde & J. Stevenson-Hinde (eds.) *Constraints on learning*. New York: Academic Press

(1973b) 'Language acquisition and cognitive development', in T. E. Moore (ed.) *Cognitive development and the acquisition of language*. New York: Academic Press

(1974) 'Epistemology and the study of language', in *Problèmes actuels en psycholinguistique*. Paris: Editions of CNRS

(1975) 'The role of cognitive structures in language acquisition', in E. H. Lenneberg & E. Lenneberg (eds.) *Foundations of language: a multi-disciplinary approach*. New York: Academic Press

(1977) 'Représentation, communication et débuts du langage', in 'La Psychologie', *Encyclopédie de la Pléiade*

& Bronckart, J. P. (1972) 'S.V.O. – a linguistic universal? A study in developmental psycholinguistics', *Jl. of Child Exp. Psych.* 14, 329–48

& Ferreiro, E. (1970) 'Production et répétition des phrases au mode passif', *Arch. de Psych.* 40, 1–42

Smith, C. S. (1964) 'Determiners and relative clauses in a generative grammar of English', *Language* 40, 37–52

Snow, C. E. (1972) 'Mothers' speech to children learning language', *Child Development* 43, 549–65

& Ferguson, C. (1977) (eds.) *Talking to children: language input and acquisition*. Cambridge: Cambridge University Press

Spangler, W. E. (1975) 'Rethinking the category "determiner"', *Linguistics* 43, 61–73

Stenning, K. (1975) 'The text life of noun phrases', Working Paper for MIT Workshop on 'New approaches to a realistic model of language'

Strawson, P. F. (1950) 'On referring', *Mind* 59, no. 235, 320–44

Tanz, C. (1977) 'Learning how *it* works', *Jl. of Child Language* 4, no. 2, 225–35

Thorne, J. P. (1972) 'On the notion of "definite"', *Foundations of Language* 8, 562–8

(1974) 'Notes on "Notes on the notion 'definite'"', *Foundations of Language* 11, 111–14

Thomas, O. (1965) *Transformational grammar and the teacher of English.* New York (cited in Spangler 1975)

Vendler, Z. (1967) 'Singular terms', in Z. Vendler, *Linguistics in philosophy.* Ithaca, New York: Cornell University Press

Warden, D. A. (1973) 'An experimental investigation into the child's developing use of definite and indefinite referential speech', Unpublished doctoral dissertation, University of London

(1976) 'The influence of context on children's use of identifying expressions and references', *British Jl. of Psych.* 67, no. 1, 101–12

Webb, P. A. & Abrahamson, A. (1976) 'Stages of egocentrism in children's use of "this" and "that": a different point of view', *Jl. of Child Language* 3, 349–65

Weir, R. (1962) *Language in the crib.* The Hague: Mouton

Wensinck, J. A. (1927) *Some aspects of gender in semitic languages.* Amsterdam: Verhandel der K. nederlandsche Akademie van wetenschappen Nieuwe reeks

Winograd, T. (1972) *Understanding natural language.* New York: Academic Press

(1973) 'A procedural model of language understanding', in R. Schank & K. Colby (eds.) *Computer models of thought and language.* San Francisco: Freeman & Co. 152–86

Yotsukura, S. (1970) 'The articles in English: a structural analysis of usage', *Janua Linguarum.* The Hague: Mouton

Index